THE CLINTON CRACK-UP

the boy president's life after the white house

THE CLINTON CRACK-UP

the boy president's life after the white house

R. EMMETT TYRRELL JR.

THOMAS NELSON
Since 1798
thomasnelson.com

Published in Nashville, Tennessee, by Thomas Nelson, Inc.

Thomas Nelson, Inc. titles may be purchased in bulk for educational, business, fundraising, or sales promotional use. For information, please e-mail SpecialMarkets@thomasnelson.com.

Library of Congress Cataloging-in-Publication data on file with the Library of Congress.

ISBN 10: 1-59555-094-1
ISBN 13: 978-1-59555-094-1

Printed in the United States of America

07 08 09 10 11 QW 5 4 3 2 1

". . . but remember if I live long enough,
I may be one of the historians."

WINSTON CHURCHILL,
TO JOSEF STALIN,
January 31, 1944

CONTENTS

For Paul Johnson, Radical Empiricist
And Charles Brunie,
Classical Liberal and Chairman of the Board

ACKNOWLEDGMENTS

In this chronicle of the Boy President's historically unprecedented retirement, readers will observe him exploiting his former office more exuberantly than any prior president ever has. They will observe him reviving a defunct political career, adapting it to new circumstances, and advancing Hillary toward residency once again at 1600 Pennsylvania Avenue. In fact, it is not a stretch to argue that Hillary's presidential prospects are a consequence of Bill's retirement. Readers will also glimpse the forty-second President of the United States contending with the dark shadows that have always stalked the edges of his mind and never so menacingly as during his restless retirement. For these lurid scenes and for some of the attendant analysis I am grateful to sources who for professional reasons must remain anonymous. All are reliable and trustworthy and have been verified by multiple witnesses and, as often as possible, by documentation, which footnotes will reveal.

I also want to acknowledge my debt to Alexander Hoyt, my agent, who beyond being a wizard in his profession has a fine literary sensibility fortified by vast learning. My long-time colleague John Corry has assisted me with research, as has a new colleague, Dale Van Atta. Both are superb newspapermen and agreeable companions. Alex Donner, a keen student of the Manhattan night, was invaluable. Gil Macklin, a veteran investigator of corruption and of drug trafficking in general, was very helpful. As always I have been assisted by the literary counsel and, especially in the case of this book's subject, by the zoological knowledge of the ageless Miss Myrna Larfnik, who remains unmarried.

My colleagues at the *American Spectator* were tireless and loyal when I found myself distracted by investigations, especially those that took me from Washington to deepest, darkest Manhattan and even to Arkansas and beyond. Suzanne Shaffer, Amy Mitchell, and Katherine Ruddy deserve my thanks as does the Publisher of the *American Spectator*, Al Regnery, whose fertile mind dreamed this project up. As Oliver would say to Stanley, so have I said to Al when my manuscript became a monster: "Well, here's another fine mess you've gotten me into."

For over twenty-five years my colleague at the magazine, Editorial Director Wlady Pleszczynski, has been my friend, advisor, and personal editor. On this manuscript he was more valuable than ever. At an hour of supreme crisis he led the Polish cavalry to my succor. My wife Jeanne, though busy with her own professional life, provided valuable insights into the Clinton mysteries. In running down facts, I have had the assistance of a superb team of young bloods, James Antle, J. P. Freire, Philip Klein, my son, P.D. Tyrrell, and Dave Holman, who before heading off to law school broke some very big stories at the *Spectator*. The law's gain is journalism's loss. Jon Ward, one of the *Washington Times*' ace reporters, helped with a very useful interview, as you will see. Also let me acknowledge the assistance of Ed McFadden and of Roger Kaplan, the latter of whom read the manuscript and provided sound criticism—but Roger, I am publishing it anyway.

Finally I want to acknowledge my debt to Bob Bartley, the late and great editor of the *Wall Street Journal*, who assisted Al Regnery and me in revitalizing *AmSpec* before his death and perhaps even after. Who knows? Working with him if only briefly was enlightening and inspiriting. Seth Lipsky, founder and editor of the *New York Sun*, also deserves my gratitude as do the stupendous members of *AmSpec*'s Board of Directors. The

Hoover Institution has been my resource for much of the intellectual history that has gone into this book. Being a media fellow there has been intellectually rewarding, and it is at Hoover that I deposited *AmSpec*'s papers knowing that this research facility maintains the highest standards of cataloguing, security, and discretion. Its document collection is one of the nation's intellectual treasures, and access to it has enriched my work. I am very grateful.

My colleagues at Thomas Nelson have been first rate, led by my editor there, Joel Miller. A reader of *AmSpec* since his college days, he has displayed an intuitive grasp of the quiddities of the Clinton Saga that I have endeavored to uncover and display.

Once again, my friends, my associates, and with this book in particular, my sources, have made writing a book a pleasure.

RET
Alexandria, Virginia
January 18, 2007

PROLOGUE

O CANADA!

It is September 9, 2006. The fifth anniversary of Osama bin Laden's attack on America is just two days away. In sadness and in anger growing numbers of Americans are focusing their attention on the atrocity: the fiery demolition, the smoldering rubble, the murder of 2,973 unsuspecting civilians. Survivors are being interviewed on American television. Political leaders are recalling that dreadful day. Soon former Mayor Rudy Giuliani, President George W. Bush, and various cabinet officers will be presiding over commemorative services in a Pennsylvania field, at Ground Zero, and in front of the Pentagon's rebuilt wing.

Today, however, Bill Clinton is out of the country. On a friend's private jet he has flown into Toronto where the Toronto Film Festival is being held. Amidst the glitz he will observe another hallowed anniversary, at least for him: his sixtieth birthday. Actually his birthday was August 19. On that day he celebrated with family and friends at what became his favorite summer vacation spot during his presidency, Martha's Vineyard. A day later he observed his birthday again at a rich friend's estate in Nantucket, where Carly Simon sang "Happy Birthday." Then he took the historic event on the road for months of celebration with rich benefactors and "the stars." If this is September 9 he must be in Toronto. On the weekend of October 28–29 he will be in New York City with the Rolling

Stones. Clinton is the first ex-president to treat his nativity thus, but then he is our first boomer president.

Here in Toronto "the stars" are in abundance. They include Kevin Spacey, who will emcee, and Billy Crystal who will deliver a uniquely deferential roast. Singers include Jon Bon Jovi, Tim McGraw, Sarah McLachlan, and James Taylor, among others. The musical director for the evening will be Paul Shaffer from the *Late Show With David Letterman.* The gala is being celebrated at Toronto's venerable Royal York Hotel. I, too, am in attendance. A very nice Friend of Bill (FOB as they say) has invited me as her date. I would be remiss if I did not accept the invitation. The forty-second president of the United States has given me so much amusement for so many years, ever since 1992 when I began covering him in the *American Spectator*, the magazine that I founded and have edited since we were both college students. I owe him.

Here on this gray, damp day in Canada there is added drama of the sort that the world has come to anticipate from the Clintons. Bill is battling the press. ABC is about to broadcast a "miniseries," on the fifth anniversary of 9/11. It is a $40 million dramatization of events preceding the attack, beginning with decisions made during the Clinton years and ending with decisions left unmade in the eight months President Bush had before the twenty-first century's Pearl Harbor. ABC is calling it *The Path to 9/11.* The path shows Clinton distracted by the Lewinsky scandal and feckless when his staff seeks a decision on whether to attack bin Laden. It also shows Bush's miscues. Bush has not complained, but Clinton is furious. Hence back in New York and Washington his reliable drudges, seasoned by their boss's two contentious terms in office, are publicly protesting, demanding revisions, and—behind the scenes—calling on ABC to pull the show. ABC assents to revisions but goes ahead with the series, and on September 12, hours after it begins, the Associated Press will report on the revisions. The surgery did not help much. Clinton still looks feckless and distracted by scandal.

Yet I thought most Americans knew that. In fact during his retirement there have been occasions when Clinton himself claimed that he was distracted from his presidential duties by those Republicans who hounded him. Some of the blame for 9/11 thus rests with them. Withal, *The 9/11 Commission Report* does chronicle several instances of his distractedness and of his deferring to his Secretary of State and to his Attorney General who doubted the Administration's legal authority to attack bin Laden. And there is this illuminating passage on page 189, ". . . President Clinton expressed his frustration with the lack of military options to take out bin Laden and the al Qaeda leadership, remarking to General Hugh Shelton, 'You know, it would scare the shit out of al Qaeda if suddenly a bunch of black ninjas rappelled out of helicopters into the middle of their camp. . . .' The President added, however, that he realized nothing would be accomplished if he lashed out in anger. Secretary of Defense William Cohen thought that the President might have been making a hypothetical statement. Regardless, he said, the question remained how to get the 'ninjas' into and out of the theater of operations. As discussed in chapter four, plans of this kind were never carried out before 9/11."[1] So that Clinton was in a muddle prior to 9/11 is irrefutable.

Here is another press controversy that Clinton did not need to provoke. A lesser controversy was perhaps unavoidable. The former Boy President, known two decades ago back in Arkansas as the Boy Governor, has been widely reported to be in the dumps about turning sixty. At an International AIDS conference just before his August 19 birthday party he publicly lamented that, "In just a few days I will be sixty years old. I hate it. . . . For most of my working life, I was the youngest person doing what I was doing. Then one day I woke up and I was the oldest in every room."[2] Those lachrymose lines were reported in a *New York Post* story headlined "Bill Turning Into Grumpy Old Man." Well, the headline's spiteful tone is what we might have expected from the "right-wing" Murdoch press. But if not "grumpy," Bill is clearly gloomy, and again his public response stands in contrast to that of his cogenerationist, Bush. When the forty-third president turned 60 in July he enthused to *People* magazine, "I really do feel young." Most American sexagenarians share his equable state of mind. Seventy-seven percent polled by the American Association of Retired Persons (AARP) claimed to be "satisfied" with where they were in life. Given the apparent fullness of his life, Bill's gloom is perplexing.

As I entered the carnival atmosphere of the Royal York's lobby I wondered about the retired president's glum admission. For six years he has been traveling the world at a manic pace, gone for days, talking himself hoarse into the wee hours with friends, perfect strangers, anyone whose ear he might bend. At first he was raising money to pay his legal bills—over $11 million—and for the two houses he and his wife have acquired. He also had to raise funds for the Clinton Library. More recently, he has been raising funds for his William J. Clinton Foundation, his fellow Democrats, and, of course, his increasingly swank lifestyle. Here in Toronto he has already raised $2.5 million in table sales, and more will be raised during the evening when Spacey raffles off events with Clinton and "the stars." Canada's *Globe and Mail* has already questioned the "dignity" of Clinton's moneygrubbing retirement, comparing it to the retirement of his predecessors. The newspaper mentioned Harry Truman and Richard Nixon, who it said "never took a dime in public speaking fees after his presidency." The story also mentioned Dwight Eisenhower, "who, after warning us about the menacing military industrial complex, retired to his golf and simple family life."[3]

Along with my curiosity over Clinton's spirits, my dominant emotion through the next few hours surrounded by hundreds of Canadian FOBs was, I would say, mild apprehension. Through the years, my relations with the Clintons could best be described as strained. We have had our disagreements. In the limousine ride over to the Royal York my apprehension spiked when fellow partygoers told me that my ticket for the evening was a gift from the Magna Corporation, as was this cavernous limousine. The Magna Corporation is controlled by the Stronach family, the Canadian family whose daughter, Belinda, is a Clinton intimate, as you will read later in this book. In retirement Bill has coached her political career (again, you will be briefed later). The two have been photographed dining in Manhattan. As our limousine rolls up to the Royal York, a blue security bracelet is strapped on my wrist (rather *too* tightly). I am now recognizable as a VIP, and into the vast "Clinton Foundation Event" we are swept.

Gawkers and paparazzi stand at the entrance of the ballroom. Within, the happy FOBs sip their drinks. Gleeful organizers of The Event welcome us. "Where are you from?" I am asked. "Washington," I mumble. And so the evening begins. Twenty minutes or so later, a cheerful Magna executive notifies my companion, who recently had assisted Bill with another fundraiser of some sort, that we have been invited into a more select reception. We are to be photographed with "the President"—*gulp!*

This could be the end. Bill and I have met before. Stepping over television cables and around a rope line, my companion and I enter a smaller room. Some of "the stars" of the evening are introduced to us, all being ardent FOBs. First is the comedian, Billy Crystal, who is not at all the jovial fellow I would have expected. In fact, he looks a bit ill. Then we meet Paul Shaffer, who is decidedly saturnine. Maybe he wanted to be at the Film Festival down the street. Next we meet Paul Band, "an aide to Bill" I am informed. Later I discover that he bears the title "Counselor to President Clinton." "Where are you from?" he asks. "Washington," I reply . . . *oh, oh.* "Where do you live?" comes next. "Northern Virginia," I venture.

President Clinton's counselor likes Northern Virginia, and he banters on: something about his travels with the boss, plans for a fundraiser here, a fundraiser there. I am reprieved. We are going to hear about the Clinton Foundation's fundraising and Band's many exciting trips abroad. No one has yet to ask me what I *do* in Washington. But over my shoulder I see standing about ten feet away a solitary Bill Clinton bleached in lights. He is waiting to do photo ops with the short line of VIPs to his right. Just as

I am enjoying Band's stories, apprehension spikes anew as our friend from Magna rushes us to the head of the line for pictures with my dinner companion's famous friend.

My last personal contact with him had not gone smoothly. Reporting on it the next day, the *Washington Post* spoke of the President's going "ballistic." Actually when the *Post* interviewed me about the controversial meeting I got off a pretty good line. I insisted that the petulant chap whom I met the night before was only a Clinton impersonator: "He seemed too weak to be the president of the United States."[4] What actually happened was this. President Clinton and his wife were dining a few blocks from the White House at the elegant Jockey Club, and I was a few tables away with one of my young daughters. Through the *maître d'* he invited me to his table to thank me for a couple of bottles of champagne that I had sent over. After coffee my daughter and I headed for his table from which he bounded, big, ebullient, and vital, his hand outstretched. He flooded my daughter, age fourteen, with questions about her summer vacation and revelations about Chelsea's in Colorado. Behind him, at his deserted table, Mrs. Clinton only glared. She is not as trusting as her husband. Still all went well until I asked for the president's assessment of a piece I had published the week before in the *Spectator*. *Bam*, his sunshine vanished.

"You should be ashamed," he erupted, and as his complaints piled up and became repetitive, I noticed Hillary's growing agitation. The place was becoming dangerous. I suggested he return to his table before his evening was spoiled irreparably. To my surprise, the president submitted. Now here we were in Toronto about to meet again, and rumors were spreading that Hillary was scheduled to fly in within the hour.

There was no need to worry about our impending confrontation. My attractive companion fetched Bill's eye, and as they gabbled pleasantly, I maneuvered around behind him, positioning myself on his left for the photograph. When he turned to me I wished him a hearty "Happy Birthday, President Clinton." We shook hands. His blue eyes betrayed no hint of recognition. We turned to the camera. *Click, click* and mission accomplished! My companion and I returned to the ballroom. An aide assured us that our pictures would be ready after dinner.

I had hoped to share this historic photograph with you but inexplicably, the Clinton Foundation denied my request for permission to publish it—hence the empty frame below. Perhaps the original is being saved for the Clinton Library.

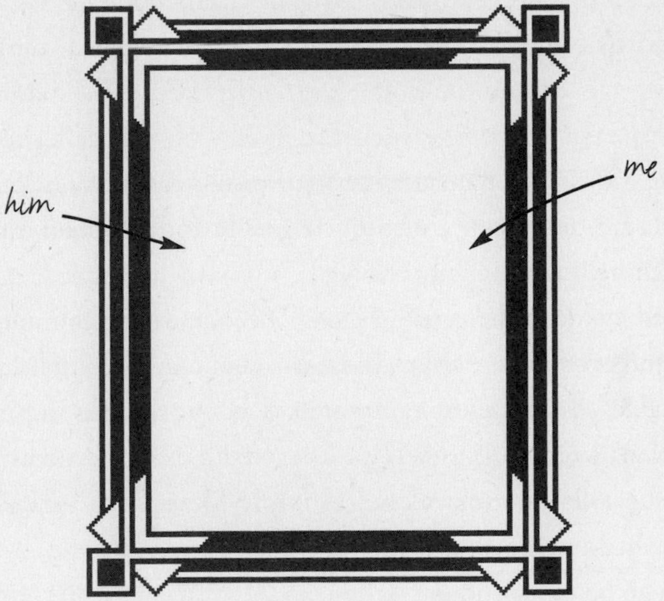

The dinner proved to be at first festive, if ultimately grueling once the raffle broke out. For now the band struck up. I am seated with some American FOBs and a couple of chatty Clinton aides. They work the room, returning to our table for sustenance. One is very amusing with tales of his failed love life in New York. Spacey commences the entertainment. Crystal continues it, along with the singers. The focus always returns to Bill. "More peace and wealth than under any other president," Spacey declaims. "We miss Bill Clinton like we have missed no other president," Crystal attests. The inflation increases. "The last *elected* president of the

United States," Taylor solemnizes, and then he sings a suitably melancholy song from his famous melancholy repertoire.

"Where are you from," guests coming and going from our table ask. "Washington," I reply with increasing polish. They probe no deeper. On my left is an American, who is somehow linked to the trendy Nobu restaurant chain, and between us sits his attractive Irish wife, a Dubliner. She is a minor television figure on a household goods station somewhere in America. To my right is Amed Khan, "Office of William J. Clinton," according to his card. The Irish lady and I chat about friends in Dublin, an actress I knew from the Gate theater and her uncle, a respected BBC personality. "Where are you from," she finally asks. "Washington," I reply. But this time that is not the end of it. "What do you do there?" No one all evening from my limousine ride on has asked this potentially disastrous question. I admit to being a writer. She goes further: "What have you written that I might have heard of?"

By this point in the evening I had been exposed to an hour or more of risible preposterosities from "the stars" about a retired politician whom they all agree is "the most famous man in the world." My mood has turned playful. "*Finnegans Wake*," I heave off. "Oh, he wrote *Finnegans Wake*," she tells her smart-ass husband. "*Finnegans Wake*," he nods approvingly. Maybe next time I go to a Nobu restaurant the corn beef and cabbage will be on the house.

Khan spoke breezily of how he follows up after each fundraiser to ensure that the checks are collected. He boasts of these fundraisers as a Texas oilman might boast of the deals he has struck. Khan, like Band, is fully immersed in fundraising with Bill. He is an agreeable little man who served the Clinton White House abroad somewhere (Africa, I believe) during what he refers to mischievously as the "events" or the "unpleasantness" of the late 1990s. Now he has returned to his boss's service as a bagman. After tonight's chaotic raffle he is going to be kept very busy chasing down an additional $21 million raised in the raffle: a couple of brokers shelled out $1.3 million to travel with Bill to Africa, a Swedish-born commodities merchant kicked in $10 million for more quality time, and so it went.

Khan is effervescent but a hush of awe enters his voice when he mentions his boss's fabled human touch, his "sympathy" with the have-nots, particularly those in Africa to whom his foundation ministers. Khan's attitude toward his boss, whom he refers to usually as "he" or "him," brings to mind earlier conversations I have had with others who served the Clinton mission, usually the lesser fish: his early bodyguards, the Arkansas state troopers; nannies; White House staffers, who kept the household safe and reasonably clean. The attitude is one of condescension, actually *amused* condescension. These aides like Bill, but they do not respect him.

My perception was reinforced upon returning from Toronto and reading an endless glorification of the retired president published in the *New Yorker* and titled "The Wanderer." In it, the writer, David Remnick, chronicled weeks spent traveling with Clinton in Europe and Africa earlier in the summer. Remnick writes of how Clinton's young aides "do" him.[5] That is to say, they mimic his quirky mannerisms. The spectacle is undignified. Clinton, after all, was the president of the United States. I can recall no earlier ex-president being mimicked by aides, at least not mimicked for his goofiness. Khan turns solemn on one point: "his health is fine." About the time Khan said this, "the most famous man in the world" took the stage.

Bill promises to be brief, and commences a *tour d' horizon.* The horizon is gruesome: poverty, AIDS, global warming, rainforests, terrorism—a topic about which he is vague. Considering his insistence on how ardent he was to apprehend or kill bin Laden, this vagueness is surprising.

Clinton's sermonic comes to total confusion when he broaches "the human genome" and geneticists' discovery that "all of us are 99.9% plus the same genetically." From this he concludes that the history of man's conflicts—and most emphatically today's conflicts—are utterly frivolous. Maybe Bill is as eloquent as "the stars" insist that he is, but in retirement he often lapses into the inscrutable, such as this from

Toronto: "In other words, we relate to each other as if what we have in common is more important and all of the other problems that we have are rooted in the arrogance of believing that our differences are more important than our common humanity." Which I guess brings us back to the "99.9 percent-plus the same genetically." On Bill rambles, epitomizing one of the major conceits of his public life, to wit, that talking about problems solves them. It is a conceit shared by other boomers of his political inclination.

If there were ever any discipline to Bill's *tour d' horizon* this evening it dissolves halfway through into sheer gibberish. He smiles and cocks his head as he has done so many times before, but as he speaks he seems listless, his voice hollow. Thinking back on our handshake of an hour or so ago, I recollect none of the vigor he had radiated at the Jockey Club. Here in Toronto his eyes are vacant, his hand seemed boney. His skin is no longer ruddy but pink, and his hair is white. The collar of his shirt hangs round his neck. On stage he smiles wanly. The words roll along, but the vigor of yesteryear is gone. Maybe his health is as good as Khan says; but, boy, has he aged!

After his speech both my companion and I make a break for the restrooms. The lobby is packed with Canadians but subdued. After all, the action is back on the stage with "the stars." My companion notes that Bill has wandered in behind us. Frankly, he looks lost. Security seems light. The polite Canadians give him his space, but my companion is an Israeli by birth and energetic. Besides, she knows him from fundraising, now his main public endeavor. She renews her conversation with him from the reception line. I follow along, a bit more confidently now. "We are with you in this battle against AIDS," I say. "Thank you," he smiles, but the face remains vacant. The forty-second president looks drawn and shrunken. I would say he has lost thirty pounds from the last time we met. He hesitates in the lobby. This time I am positive; he has no recognition of me. If I needed more evidence, a minute or so later he is following me into the restroom.

If the usual Secret Service detail is around, it is unusually inconspicuous. When the former president appears in the mirrors as he heads toward the toilets, the men washing their hands and adjusting their ties pay little attention. It is sad. I never would have thought I would feel sadness for this irrepressible ham.

There was a joke going around Washington during impeachment and the last months of the Clinton administration depicting Clinton in retirement as a greeter at one of the Las Vegas casinos. He would be like the ex-heavyweight champion Joe Louis, burned out, a physical ruin from too many punches and too many reckless years. The joke was funny; but here in Toronto, as I see this relatively young retiree shuffling through the crowd, the joke is not so funny. He is alone, diminished, surrounded by a staff of smug young hustlers, all as self-absorbed as he ever was but much less clever. They are utterly oblivious of the world around them and of the responsibility of preserving the dignity of a former president. Their minds are set on deals to make, trips to take. Surely in the old days Bill's Carvilles and Begalas kept a keener eye out for their boss, and he moved a lot faster in those days.

The whole Clinton road show has an air of unreality to it. "During his administration," reads the boilerplate handed out by the Clinton Foundation to the press, "the United States enjoyed more peace and economic wellbeing than at any time in its history . . . lowest unemployment rate in modern times, lowest inflation rate in thirty years, highest home ownership in U.S. history . . . declining crime, reduced welfare rolls. . . ." Where can such rodomontade originate? Did one of the oblivious aides with whom I have visited this evening dream it up, or is it from the boss himself? In retirement he has made claims spiraling beyond the limits of the credible and into the vapors of the bizarre.

In the aforementioned *New Yorker* article he claimed that the Democrats' 2004 presidential candidate, John Kerry, "should have challenged Bush and Cheney to a town hall debate on their respective Vietnam records. Bush and Cheney were like me—they didn't go."[6] Of course, neither left Bill's paper trail, documenting the frantic scheming of an obvious draft dodger; and Bush actually flew National Guard combat jets. Here is another controversial remark best left unsaid.

Yet maybe the hulk I encountered in Toronto on the evening of September 9 has a need for these controversies. Maybe they get his adrenalin flowing once again. Throughout his retirement he has erupted in angry outbursts, often outbursts that suggest he lives in a fantasy. In the middle of press interviews or public appearances he has suddenly lashed out at those whom he believes spoiled his presidential record: independent counsel Kenneth Starr, or "the right-wingers," as though they created Monica Lewinsky or Osama bin Laden or his campaign finance irregularities. For his grievances now go beyond impeachment. Among the historians there is a growing consensus over his lax governance.

Just two weeks after his Toronto festivities he exploded in the face of a startled Fox News interviewer, Chris Wallace, when Wallace asked if he thought his presidency could have done more against bin Laden. Wagging his finger at Wallace and jabbing at the interviewer's notes, Clinton harangued, "You've got that little smirk on your face, and you think you're so clever." Continuing in the taunts of an adolescent, he accused Wallace of a "nice little conservative hit job" and attempted a rebuttal laced with false statements that Clinton's opponents then spent days exposing. Again, here is a controversy that can only tarnish his legacy.

Yet the controversies have their purpose. They rewrite his eight years of inconsequence for the credulous who might be listening. They bring back fire to his tired bones. They keep his fantasies alive. In Toronto at the observance of his sixtieth birthday, Jon Bon Jovi sang what he told us is Bill's "favorite song." It was Conway Twitty's 1950s hit, "It's Only Make Believe." When I heard it, I wondered who aside from me grasped the irony, certainly not the guy from Nobu restaurant who dines with "the stars," one of whom in Toronto was the author of *Finnegans Wake*.

ONE

FROM RAGS TO RICHES

Scandal is not unknown to the American presidency, but even a scandal-prone president is usually well-organized, punctual, cleanly. Even the Warren Gamaliel Harding of comic memory was punctual. Harry Truman, though as bemanured by scandal as Harding, probably presided over a more orderly White House than that of his venerated predecessor, Franklin Delano Roosevelt. As Truman approached retirement, he perhaps smoldered with as many grievances as President Bill Clinton. Yet, he left the White House on time and decorously.

When Clinton left the White House all was a shambles. For months the press had been proclaiming him a "rock star," and like a rock star he exited the premises. That is to say, he trashed the place. Here was another of his trademark chaotic endings. It was bedlam, and within hours observant Americans recognized that the scandal-prone Clintons had just chalked up two more lulus, Pardongate and the Pilfering of the White House.

Today we again have a well-organized president at 1600 Pennsylvania Avenue. President George W. Bush is up at 5:30 a.m., in bed by 9:30 p.m. In between he runs like a clock: no missed meetings, no meetings running overtime, and no meetings of which Mrs. Bush would not approve. President Bush is Truman without the cronies and without

Truman's near-death ratings—a 23 percent approval rating at the end of a presidency that fellow Americans now rightly revere.[1] President Bush's ratings, at least in his second term, have rarely been robust for long; and they have been feeble at times, but he is a normal American president—moral, law-abiding, and efficient. Clinton was not a normal American president. He was a lax and surprisingly passive chief executive, often allowing his aides to overrule him, as they did every time he sought action against Osama bin Laden. What is more, he was a rogue.

After every exposé, he and his aides laid down the alibi, "They all did it." In truth, no previous president "did it," certainly not with the combination of monotony and impudence that Clinton did. Only President Lyndon Johnson could match his coarseness and promiscuity, and he too entered retirement with a heart on the fritz. On the other hand, no one could ever accuse Johnson of being passive or disorganized; and he retained the respect of those around him, including political aides such as Jack Valenti, members of his Secret Service detail, and his military aides. Clinton's security and military aides were revolted by his goatish behavior, as we shall see. Former Clinton staffer George Stephanopoulos was the most outspoken of Clinton's many disappointed political aides. Once they had hoped he would be the next epochal Democratic president, a Roosevelt or a Kennedy. After half a dozen years of scandals, Stephanopoulos spoke for them all when he wrote that Clinton, "lost the battle with himself, tarnished his presidency and all of us associated with it. If I knew everything then that I know now, of course I wouldn't [have worked for him]."[2]

The lasting image of the 1960s generation's first president is that of a smiling, pouting, hulk of a man—an overgrown adolescent. The world was his stage and journalists—many of them cogenerationists—likened him to a rock star. They thought they were complimenting the President of the United States, and he did, too. From the 1960s to the 1990s something had changed in American culture. In the 1960s both Johnson and John F. Kennedy had an eye for the fair sex and plenty of celebrity, but I cannot find one of their contemporaries comparing them with the rock star of their day, Elvis Presley. Over the next two decades something went haywire in American popular culture.

Clinton's presidency was the long-delayed aftershock of the 1960s generation, particularly that sector of the generation absorbed with Pot and Protest. He was followed in office by a president from the competing sector of the 1960s generation, a cohort more concerned during college days with Beer and Beach Parties. This sequence, in part, explains the enormous bitterness of today's politics at the national level. An intra-generational confrontation is taking place between those young conservatives of the 1960s who thought America should be as America had always been, free and bourgeois; and the young radicals, who thought America should be like one or two late 1960s Beatles albums that now are slipping into memory's well. Clinton and the others from this sector of their famous generation—wife Hillary, Dr. Howard Dean, Al Gore, Jean-François Kerry—were troubled adolescents, indignant and self-absorbed. Now despite hair loss and wrinkles, they pretty much remain adolescent, indignant, and self-absorbed.

By the 1990s normal Americans had wearied of the endless self-promotion and thumbing-of-the-nose from these aging 1960s brats. But the brats' influence remained disproportionately vast. Through their preponderance in the media and in academe they befouled American popular *kultur* with politics—their politics. They replaced bourgeois American culture with *Kultursmog*, complete with hints of the European coffeehouse, dim notions of class struggle, and various occult therapies. The *Kultursmog*, belching from America's newsrooms, editorial offices, and faculty lounges assisted both Clintons in riding out every White House scandal. Mind you, the scandals actually transformed Bill Clinton—and Hillary, too—into celebrities with all the moral dispensations granted to celebrities in celebrity-crazed America. The bad-boy athlete, the slutty actress, the rock star—all are adored; and after each fails a urine test or reports a corpse on the premises, the *Kultursmog* provides willing apologists to exonerate them.

The Clintons have had a whole press corps of apologists. These truckling defenders have had to play their sorry role so frequently that they have become a phenomenon unique to the Clinton era and worthy of their own historic designation. History might remember them as the "Episodic Apologists." In the New Deal, dependable supporters of the president from academe were labeled Court Historians. As the Clintons have proceeded through Bill's shabby retirement and Hillary's quest for higher office, the Episodic Apologists have continued to go through their contortions in defense of the Clintons' accumulating blunders and brushes with the law. There has been nothing like it in American history, but then there has been nothing like aging 1960s radicals and their byproduct, a *Kultursmog* that disguises every misdeed.

Both the *Kultursmog* and the Episodic Apologists will be revisited in future chapters. For now we need only note that by the 1990s society's icons had changed. In retirement, the Boy President was hardly ever likened to an elder statesman. Rather, the comparison used most frequently was rock star. During his retirement Truman had been likened to an artillery officer, which, in World War I, he had been, and an elder statesman, which he was. Harding, by the time of his death, was likened to a Roman senator. Americans in the 1920s admired ancient Rome. Harding's was a Roman profile. He may be an easy laugh today, but in his time he was adored. The memorial built for him in Marion, Ohio, is the most beautiful presidential memorial outside Washington, D.C. Locals will tell the occasional tourist that it is also the largest presidential memorial outside Washington. Annually it attracts several thousand visitors, presumably only a handful of whom could pass a breathalyzer test.[3]

Harding—with his bossy wife, his energetic golfing, his cronies, and the girlfriend thrashing amidst the galoshes in the Oval Office closet—is the American presidency's closest approximation to Clinton. Lyndon Johnson's heirs can rest easy. Of course Harding died before going into retirement and running the risk of further scandal. As for that other scandal-plagued president, Truman, his retirement was quiet and dignified. He lived within the bounds of the law. He read history and groused about his perceived enemies. A comparison between Truman's retirement and Clinton's reveals how America has changed.[4]

At first Truman's retirement was painful and lonely. He tried to influence his party but got nowhere. He was financially fragile with but an army pension of $112.56 monthly and none of the vast government resources for security details, secretarial help, and logistics that Clinton in retirement has today. Truman rejected "consulting fees" or a rich ride on the rubber chicken circuit. He would not, as he put it, "commercialize" the presidency.

Our Boy President did the opposite. In his first four years out of the White House he earned over $43 million *after* expenses and living costs. By comparison sources close to former President George H. W. Bush speculate that his income in his first four years of retirement was but a quarter of Clinton's sum. Moreover, as the chart in chapter two demonstrates, Clinton's retirement annually costs taxpayers more than any previous president—and by a lot. Though he has gone from rags to riches on the speaking circuit, the American taxpayer still pays the travel and hotel costs of his security detail. Another globe-trotting former president, Richard Nixon, absorbed those costs, having given up his Secret Service detail early in retirement. Not Clinton. And the extent of Clinton's globe-trotting has been stupefying. In his first year alone he spoke for voluptuous fees practically every other day in thirty-minute exhalations to any group that would foot the bill, no matter how unseemly. He hit up universities, religious groups, and giant corporations (some with government contracts signed during his presidency) for colossal fees. In Britain he even hit up the out-at-the-elbows National Society for the Prevention of Cruelty to Children for $100,000.

In foreign countries, where the prying eyes of the American press rarely gaze, the spectacle became even less edifying than at home. One day he might be fronting for Beijing, as he did in Sydney, Australia, on February 22, 2002, pocketing $300,000 from the Australian Council for the Promotion of Peaceful Reunification of China, a notorious Chinese Communist front. On another venue he might simply be shilling for BMW, as he did in Auckland, New Zealand, three months later, earning $137,000. A few days before that payday he was flogging condominiums in the pay of JingJi Real Estate Development in Shenshen, China, for $200,000. The Pacific Rim had a ceaseless allure to the forty-second president. On one day early in his retirement, he spoke twice in Hong Kong, flying home with half a million dollars. For that matter the Persian Gulf and the Gulf of Oman had a powerful allure, too. There he has prospered as a lecturer; in Dubai he even picked up a couple of luxury apartments under controversial circumstances, as we shall see in chapter three. (See Appendix I.)

Truman, like most of the modern presidents following him, was temporarily bereft once the motorcades and the smart salutes of the Marine guards ended. Truman's Kansas City friend, Tom Evans, reported that "he was utterly *lost*."[5] But upon returning to Missouri he soon got to work on his presidential library. Its projected cost was $1.5 million. Clinton's Taj Mahal cost $165 million, and it did not contain Truman's trove of documents from such momentous undertakings as his consolidation of the New Deal and from the launch of the Cold War. Rather the Clinton Library contained documents indicating that his administration had pretty much preserved the Reagan Revolution and engaged in a huge political campaign to protect him from impeachment for lying under oath and obstructing justice. Truman's library, unlike Clinton's, was respectful of the history its namesake made. When it came time to write a memoir, Truman wrote two volumes that are reasonably accurate and crackle with his tart partisanship. In the end Truman did all right. When historians took a second look at his achievements in office they ranked him as "near great" and forgave him his flawed appointees and the scandals they brought.[6] For that matter even the unloved Nixon lived a dignified retirement, writing books on statecraft and earning the title of "elder statesman." He took no fees from the lecture circuit.

Every morning of his presidency Truman had arisen even earlier than the current president. He was up at 5:00 a.m., hailed his Secret Service detail, and undertook a brisk walk of one or two miles, all at the army marching pace of 120 steps a minute. Afterwards he retired to his residence (Blair House much of the time, as the White House was under renovation) for a rubdown and a morning nip, one shot of bourbon—no more. Yes, Winston Churchill is not the only modern English-speaking statesman to begin his day with a light libation. By seven Harry was at his desk, documents and newspapers spread before him, no intern in sight.[7]

Clinton is not known to have ever begun a day at 1600 Pennsylvania Avenue with a morning nip, and if he was up at 5:00 a.m. it was likely that he was still up from the night before—then and now he sleeps only a few hours a night in unscheduled catnaps, making life supremely hectic for his staff, particularly those in his security detail who have to be constantly at his side. As for receiving Truman's matutinal rubdown, that would be one of the Boy President's few sensual pleasures still unchronicled. Perhaps a morning nip of bourbon would have settled him down for a few hours, though he probably would have needed another and another. There are springs in Clinton's system that are obviously difficult to control. What has been recorded about him, and in copious detail, is his lack of discipline. In fact, history will remember him for being the most undisciplined president of the modern era and the least ethical.

In his retirement things did not improve. Whether on the speaker's circuit or in any other pursuit—for instance, in writing his memoir—he has been chronically late. During visits to Ireland, where Clinton spent a surprising amount of time early in his retirement, his tardiness became legendary. I interviewed a theater impresario in Dublin who knew Clinton through his friendship with one of Clinton's buddies, the Irish singer, Bono. The Irishman was still stung by the American's helter-skelter appearance at a local charity fundraiser. Though late for every event on the schedule, he had charged his hosts an honorarium in the neighborhood of $100,000. Nonetheless, when the theater impresario tried to move the hand-shaking former president along, all he got was an outburst of Clinton's famed temper.[8]

Running late was not Clinton's most notorious imperfection. History records more serious offenses: lying when a lie is not necessary and telling a whopper when a little white lie would suffice. Even under oath Clinton has told gratuitous lies. He has also abused his power and obstructed justice frequently, usually to cover up the unseemliness of his signature recreation, girl-hopping. As president he also became known for his very loose interpretation of campaign finance laws; for globalizing presidential fundraising, particularly with agents of Beijing, and, of course, for lapses in taste—the most lurid of which have been recorded in that modern Rabelaisian masterpiece, *The Starr Report,* which along with its companion volume, *The Evidence,* made Clinton's the most talked-about presidential penis ever. The clinical term for its condition is Peyronie's Disease, causing wits to joke that President Clinton's anatomy when turgid shared a likeness with the Leaning Tower of Pisa. Harding never suffered such undignified comparisons, nor did Johnson.

Moreover, Clinton had a surprisingly cavalier regard for national security. As *The 9/11 Commission Report* has demonstrated and as this book will elaborate, his neglect injured American security interests at home and abroad. On terror he was a no-show. In his mammoth autobiography, *My Life,* the forty-second president devotes precisely one paragraph to airport security measures taken during his administration, though he had ample warning that plots were being planned similar to our modern-day Pearl Harbor on September 11, 2001. For instance, the 9/11 Commission reported that on December 4, 1998, Clinton received a President's Daily Brief whose headline read, "Bin Laden Preparing to Hijack U.S. Aircraft and Other Attacks." The passive Clinton remained inert.

According to the *New York Post,* the briefing contained "information indicating that bin Laden and his allies were preparing an aircraft hijacking and other attacks in the United States to free three jailed Arabs, including the mastermind of the 1993 World Trade Center bombing, Ramzi

Yousef and 'Blind Sheik' Omar Abdel-Rahman."[9] Airport security was not tightened. At the time Clinton was admittedly facing impeachment and "distracted," as his defenders plead. On the other hand, President Richard Nixon was also "distracted" by an impending impeachment. Still, in October 1973, the month that the House Judiciary Committee accepted impeachment resolutions against him, Nixon retained sufficient focus to stand by Israel in one of the Cold War's most deadly rounds, resupplying Israel nine days into the Yom Kippur War, confronting the USSR's threat of unilateral action by putting our armed forces on worldwide alert, and negotiating a ceasefire between Egypt and Israel.

Yet if disorderliness and tardiness have not been Clinton's most grievous defects, they have often been his most amusing defects. With comic consequences they usually accompany the culmination of what should have been the most serious undertakings of his life: for instance, his Rhodes scholarship's final requirements, his presidency's final days, the completion of his memoir. The drama is always the same. Aloof in his colossal narcissism, he fritters away his time in show-off proceedings or in scheming to cover up the scandals that result from that narcissism. Then comes his mad dash to make up for wasted time. As a coda to the burlesque, his Episodic Apologists can always be relied upon to follow up with a chorus of lamentations to "talent wasted" or to his "missed opportunities."

One sees the pattern beginning at Oxford in the 1960s where he partied, "networked," traveled to foreign parts (behind the Iron Curtain to Czechoslovakia and the Soviet Union), squandered time in bull sessions, and wasted Rhodes scholarship money in politicking. His last year was spent mainly in London organizing demonstrations against American foreign policy, a favored tactic being to scatter marbles beneath the hooves of police horses and enjoy the equine mayhem. Then it was back to Oxford and a feverish round of negotiations with professors for his degree and pulling every available string with administrators. All failed, and he became the rare Rhodes Scholar to leave without a degree.[10]

His habit of dilly-dallying and procrastinating continued right up to the writing of his memoir. After signing what was billed as the largest advance for a presidential memoir ever (another public deceit, as we shall see), he departed for months of public appearances and paid addresses that rang up millions of dollars of income but left his memoir to a team of overtaxed researchers. Their task was to render coherence to a mound of autobiographical interviews he had taped while president and some twenty chaotically scrawled spiral-bound notebooks he had filled more recently. Another challenge facing his writers was to make his narrative at least plausible. With his deadline approaching, he returned to scratch into the unfinished manuscript self-indulgent anecdotes and equally self-indulgent charges against his opponents. Consequently, *My Life* is the most slovenly and unreliable presidential memoir ever written. It abounds with howlers, some of which are apparent on the face of it, others having been exposed by courts and grand juries after careful and very public deliberations. The archipelago of lies strung through the book is easily recognized by anyone familiar with Clinton's life and conscientious about the truth.

At one point in *My Life* the oblivious memoirist repeats a delightfully absurd deceit that his wife was caught out in years ago. Connoisseurs of the Clinton claptrap had a good laugh then, and they had an even better laugh the second time around. The first laughs came when Hillary, during a trip to New Zealand in the 1990s, sought to establish an intimate link to the antipodal New Zealanders by informing them that her parents long ago (in 1947) and faraway (in blustery Chicago) named their only daughter after New Zealand's most famous adventurer, Sir Edmund Hillary, conqueror of Mt. Everest. Almost immediately poor Hillary was set upon by those stalkers who have harassed her for so many years, the Fact Checkers. They noted that Sir Edmund, an obscure beekeeper at the time of Hillary's birth, did not climb Mt. Everest until *after* she was born—six years after! Mrs. Clinton's bogus christening is but another instance of a Clinton suavely passing on a gratuitous lie and getting clobbered. Nonetheless, in writing his memoir Bill could not resist this fib just one more time. Not until the autumn of 2006 did the Clintons come clean about this amusing little lie. Hillary's Senate campaign staff made the admission. "It was a sweet family story her mother shared to inspire greatness in her daughter, to great results . . ." explained Jennifer Hanley, the campaign's spokeswoman.[11] So through adulthood and three decades of public life, the Clintons kept on lying. Yet why come clean in the middle of a Senate campaign that Hillary could not lose? Well, that will be one less lie that Hillary might have to confront in a 2008 presidential race.

Another previously exposed mendacity that Clinton could not resist depositing anew in his memoir is the tale of his heroic confrontation with his violent stepfather. Historians will thank one of Clinton's first biographers, Arkansan Meredith Oakley, for the spadework here. The fib originated in 1992 when candidate Clinton sat down with *New York Magazine* reporter Joe Klein. He told Klein about his stepfather's frequent abuse of his mother, which doubtless occurred. Both were heavy drinkers and boisterous partygoers. But then came Clinton's gratuitous lie. He claimed that he, though still a young boy, battered down a barricaded door and ordered a cringing Clinton *pere* never to abuse his mother again.[12] The confrontation was almost certainly fabricated for Klein's wonderment. While writing her 1994 biography, Oakley scrutinized young Bill's testimony in his parents' 1962 divorce papers and found that, though Bill had called the police on his drunken stepfather, "Nothing in his testimony indicates that young Billy was able, or even attempted, to stop Roger Clinton's beatings."[13] Yet the vainglorious confrontation survives in *My Life,* along with howlers that are even more easily dispatched.

One is Clinton's contemptible claim that his business partners in the Whitewater scam, the McDougals, might not have been found guilty at all had the Whitewater jury known of the "connections to my political adversaries" of David Hale, the leading witness against them. Clinton elaborates: "The jury didn't know about the money and support Hale had been receiving from a clandestine effort known as the Arkansas Project."[14] Truth be known, these charges were fully investigated by an Arkansas grand jury *five years* before *My Life* was published. The grand jury found the charges, as the public statement from government investigator Michael E. Shaheen Jr. concluded, "unsubstantiated or, in some cases, untrue."[15] I shall return to the Arkansas Project in this book's Epilogue, as it has become one of Clinton's minor obsessions, and I played an amused role in the so-called project. It is sufficient to note at this point that a grand jury has investigated it fully and denied Clinton's claims. Possibly Clinton ignores this grand jury finding in keeping with his demonstrated contempt for grand juries. On the other hand, this act of dishonesty and all the abovementioned deceits are probably symptoms of Clinton's peculiar mindset. He believes his own lies. That is characteristic of a sociopath.

Even that claim of his about signing a historically unprecedented publishing contract turns out to be a lie. My review of the millions he raked in from 2000 to 2003 shows not a penny advanced by his publisher, Alfred A. Knopf, though at his signing Clinton claimed an advance of $10 million. Mysteriously it grew to $12 million the following year. The same *New York Times* journalist reported both the $10 million advance and the $12 million advance a year later with no explanation for the increase. Actually the "advance" was no advance at all. Rather it was a guarantee against future royalties, a way for the populist president to avoid paying taxes during his high-income days on the speaker's circuit until later years when his income would not be as great.

Clinton's most carefully documented chaotic ending was his final departure from the White House during which he attempted to make up for eight years of lost opportunities and racy escapades in one mad rush to completion. The administration ended as it began, disorderly and uncouth. At his first Inauguration in 1993, Clinton had arrived thirty minutes late for the traditional coffee with his outgoing adversary, George H. W. Bush; and he brought along two uninvited guests, his Hollywood pals Linda and Harry Thomason. Now, eight years later at the White

House coffee for Bush's victorious son, George W. Bush, the Clintons were more punctual. Yet Clinton still brought controversy with him. He had just granted a historically unprecedented riot of presidential pardons. Official Washington was appalled, and Pardongate soon overshadowed the incoming president's arrival in office.

"I've never seen anything like this," lamented Roger Adams, the United States pardon attorney at the Justice Department. "We were up literally all night as the White House continued to add names of people they wanted to pardon." Adams added, "Many on the list didn't even apply for pardons."[16] Obviously the Boy President had been up all night too, as the bags sagging beneath his bloodshot eyes proclaimed. The Clintons' 2001 departure from the White House was to be the most chaotic since 1814, when President James Madison left with the redcoats coming up the road.

During their final White House days most outgoing presidents can be seen quietly if sadly packing their bags and preparing a farewell address to the nation. One can understand Truman's sadness, given his huge unpopularity and the reports of grafters thriving among his administration's tax collectors and at his Reconstruction Finance Corporation. On his last Thursday night as president at 10:30 p.m. Truman broadcast a farewell address now recognized as his finest speech. Clinton's was to be among his worst.

Truman wanted to explain to a nation that had rejected him the historic decisions he had made. Clinton could not really explain the historic decisions he had made. In number they were few, and the most momentous were the consequence of zoo sex on government property—not a topic to be discussed during primetime when the FCC is all ears. Truman's decisions had set in motion the policies that would win the Cold War four decades later. Clinton's decisions were mostly the expedients forced upon a lout. As for the war he was facing, now called the War on Terror, it was another responsibility he left for others to handle. During his years in office he handed terrorism over to lawyers—National Security Adviser Sandy Berger and Attorney General Janet Reno—who, unlike Clinton's personal lawyers, were not what you would call proactive. They adjudged military action *malum prohibitum* and passed on.

In Truman's farewell address he reminded his audience that he had continued his recently deceased predecessor's plan for the United Nations. Next, Truman oversaw Germany's surrender. Then came his preparations for the Potsdam Conference where he, a novice, would sit down with the two remaining giants of the Second World War, Winston Churchill and Josef Stalin. Next, Truman ordered that an experimental atomic bomb be exploded in the New Mexican desert, whereupon he ordered that two more be dropped on Japan, ending the Second World War. Those were just the decisions he faced in his first four months! There were later decisions of equal gravity. He reminded his audience of his decision to go to war in Korea and to fight the Cold War. "But," he presciently concluded, "when history says that my term of office saw the beginning of the Cold War, it will also say that in those eight years we have set the course that can win it. . . ."[17] With that summation Harry ascended to the family quarters of the White House and went to sleep.

On Clinton's last Thursday night in the White House his farewell address was comparatively brief. He littered his remarks with economic statistics, sang his well-known jingle about entering the twenty-first century, and vanished from the television screen. Unlike Truman, however, he did not go to sleep. Rather he trundled off to a closed-door meeting with staff members to weigh pardon requests for hundreds of felons, some of whose names soon became household words. The pardons would haunt his early months of retirement, and at least one provided him with seed money for his grandiose presidential library. Changing into a sweatshirt and jeans, he then stayed up into the early morning, packing his effects and reminiscing with nocturnal staffers and Harry Thomason, who had returned from Hollywood for the funereal proceedings. Thus began one last all-nighter at the White House for these arrested adolescents, still so fondly linked to 1968.

Friday, Clinton's final full day on duty, was one of the busiest days of his presidency. Desperately pursuing a respectable legacy, he got on the telephone early, importuning Prime Minister Tony Blair and the leader of Northern Ireland's Catholics, Gerry Adams. In another series of calls he leaned on Israeli Prime Minister Ehud Barak and Palestinian Liberation Organization chairman Yasser Arafat. In both instances he called on the contending parties to produce peace agreements that might cleanse impeachment from his legacy and bejewel it with a Nobel Prize for Peace. Along with these international calls there were calls to his lawyer, David Kendall, who was negotiating with independent counsel Robert Ray to prevent the forty-second President's imminent prosecution for Whitewater-related matters. Another of Kendall's concerns was to preserve Clinton's Arkansas law license. Ray was dangling a noose before Clinton and his overworked lawyer. The prosecutor demanded immediate action. To encourage that action Ray had impaneled a new grand jury and readied it for testimony.

Kendall and Clinton also had to contend this day with the Arkansas Bar Association, whose members wanted Clinton fined and his law license suspended for five years because of lies and evasions committed while he was under oath during the Paula Corbin Jones proceedings. Later, Clintonistas would argue that Ray was motivated by a desire to run for the Senate. Perhaps he was, but how do they account for the tenacity of the Arkansas Bar? An unsung heroine here was the Bar's representative, Marie Miller, an African-American Arkansas lawyer. Once a nun, she was indifferent to Kendall's high-powered tactics. Acting independently of Ray, she and the Bar were deeply offended by Clinton's offenses and wanted him fined and denied his law license, all before he left office. Clinton wanted to settle for a two-year suspension and to delay an agreement until after leaving office. On this chill Friday morning, an agreement was forced on him. Clinton accepted a $25,000 fine and a five-year suspension of his legal license. He also agreed that he had given false testimony about Monica Lewinsky. The announcement was made at White House press secretary Jake Siewert's last press conference at 2:00 p.m. after which

Siewert deadpanned, "On Monday, January 22, 2001, from 9:00 a.m. to 4:00 p.m., the president will be awaiting the arrival of the Westchester County cable guy."

Actually, it might have been better for the Clinton legacy had he left the White House that afternoon and met with the "cable guy." He would have been out of sight during the evening news reports of his false testimony, his $25,000 fine, and his suspended legal license. Moreover, he would have been safely away from the trashing of the White House that was about to take place. Finally, no one would later have grounds to suspect that he met late on Friday with the ex-wife of Marc Rich, the fugitive financier who was about to become the most controversial recipient of a Clinton pardon. Secret Service logs show the ex-wife, Denise Rich, arriving at the White House around 5:30 p.m. with her friend, Beth Dozoretz, formerly finance chairwoman of the Democratic National Committee.

Whether the ladies were cutting a deal for Rich's pardon has yet to be established, but several weeks later both invoked the Fifth Amendment when Clinton's pardon orgies were under investigation before the House Government Reform Committee. Sources have linked Mrs. Rich romantically to Clinton, as we shall see in chapter four. Secret Service logs reveal that she visited the White House perhaps as many as nineteen times while Clinton was president and public records reveal over $1 million in donations from her to the Democratic National Committee, at least $450,000 to the Clinton Library and $100,000 to Hillary's Senate campaign. The ladies' visit during the chaos of the president's last hours surely must have raised eyebrows around the White House, assuming that eyebrow fatigue had not yet set in.[18]

As for the trashing of the White House, it followed a 6:00 p.m. champagne engagement party hosted by Hillary for one of her staffers in the Roosevelt room. When staffers suggested to the First Lady the possibility of leaving a few practical jokes in the offices of the incoming Bush administration, Hillary reportedly had a brainstorm: "Wouldn't it be hysterical if someone just happened to remove all the *W*s from the computer keyboards?"[19] There ensued a modest rampage that left sixty computer keyboards disabled, desks glued shut, file cabinets vandalized, lewd messages on answering machines, doorknobs stolen, and a presidential seal gone.

This was not the first time Clinton staffers had acted up. There had been earlier mischief. When they were on the USS *George Washington* during a 1994 D-Day ceremony, Clinton staffers were accused of stealing towels. There would be reports of White House staffers' misbehavior right up to the end. After Clinton's petulant departure for New York from Andrews Air Force Base on Saturday afternoon, his companions on Air Force One filched everything removable from the famous plane, from napkins to china to toothpaste—anything with that coveted presidential seal or some other mark of presidential grandeur. Some of these collectibles appeared on an eBay auction. Others doubtless even now add to the interior décor of various Clintonista residences.

Friday night's party was not Clinton's last White House stop. He went on to more consultations regarding pardons. At midnight he and Hillary took in their last movie in the White House theater, *State and Main.* Then Bill pulled that last presidential all-nighter, packing his effects and nostalgically padding through his empty offices with the indispensable Thomason, reminiscing and BS-ing as power slipped away. This lasted until 4:00 a.m.

No wonder he looked a wreck Saturday morning. Only then did he complete his list of pardons. In his last two hours as president he granted 140 pardons and 36 commutations. One of the pardons went to Susan McDougal, his old business partner and another of his ephemeral *horizontales.* Back when independent counsel Kenneth Starr had jailed her for refusing to testify as to whether Clinton had told the truth during her Whitewater trial, Clinton scoffed when asked if he might someday grant her a pardon. Now anticipating the forgiveness or perhaps the amnesia of the media's Episodic Apologists, he did just that. At 10:05 a.m. he left the

Oval Office. Pocketing a pen and some golf balls, he galumphed off to coffee with the Bushes. By 11:05 the two couples were en route to the inauguration in the presidential limousine. President Bush took his oath at noon and intoned his inaugural address. Beyond the eyes of the cameras a military aide discreetly moved "the football," the forty-five-pound attaché case containing the Pentagon's launch codes, from Clinton's side of the dais.

Doubtless the aide felt relieved. The disorderly Clinton was not always fastidious about the country's nuclear codes. In 1999 he had hastily left a high-level diplomatic meeting in Washington without telling the military aide responsible for the football. Abandoned, and without security, the poor man had to hotfoot it back to the White House alone through the streets of the capital, football in hand. That story was widely reported. Less widely reported, Clinton actually lost his personal set of nuclear codes when the Lewinsky scandal broke. His security detail turned the White House upside down but never found those codes.[20] Maybe someday they too will turn up on eBay or on a Clintonista's coffee table.

In the limousine on their way out to Andrews, the Clintons got their first taste of life as private citizens. For the first time in eight years their car had to stop at a stoplight. Once at the airport the emotions of the last few days ignited publicly.

During Truman's last afternoon in Washington, after he had suffered through Eisenhower's inauguration (both men had come to hate each other), he lunched quietly with former cabinet members at the home of his secretary of state, Dean Acheson. During the Clinton cabinet's last afternoon in Washington, its members still hankered for the glitz of their rock star.

Again, times had changed. Members of the Clinton cabinet joined a motley crowd at the airport in a vast hangar with Clinton's staffers and hundreds of defiant supporters. A stupefying spectacle ensued. Cameras and microphones were everywhere. For more than an hour Clinton shook hands at a boisterous pep rally that some speculated was scripted to distract attention from that embarrassing deal he had signed with the prosecutor. Then he delivered his second nationally broadcast address of the day, his first having been his regular Saturday radio message. The address this time was more personal. Directed to his overwrought admirers, it was a typical Clintonian mixture of bathos and defiance: "You gave me the ride of my life and I tried to give as good as I got." Then looking out at a placard he mused, "You see that sign there that says 'Please don't go'? I left the White House, but I'm still here. We're not any of us going anywhere." Then he left—another promise broken. Upon landing at Kennedy Airport the Clintons provoked another emotional eruption. This time Senator Clinton led the sobs. Finally they went home to their new address in Chappaqua.

Friends of the Clintons had for a long time worried about their fate *après* Washington. During the previous summer's Republican National Convention in Philadelphia, late one evening I fell in with a boozily reflective Rick Kaplan, Clinton's friend who was then at the helm of CNN, and Kaplan's CNN colleague Jeff Greenfield, who had months before pitted me against Al Franken in a show that was supposed to demonstrate how we two wags had joked about Clinton's miseries from our different perspectives. Franken's humor was of the "dark" variety, almost bleak. I was much merrier, for to me this hayseed huckster has always been amusing. Franken was self-pitying and a useless defender of Clinton; though he never admitted the obvious, namely, that Clinton had taken him for a ride. To this day Franken remains a Clinton defender and a former humorist.

Now on this night in Philadelphia the whole Clinton Saga was approaching its end, and as Kaplan, Greenfield, and I reflected on its lurid dramas Kaplan surprised me. He expressed foreboding as to the scandals that might await a retired Boy Clinton finally freed of presidential responsibilities. Greenfield shared his pessimism. I was frankly astounded. How could they be so candid in the presence of a well-known Clinton critic? Could this be the end of the Episodic Apologists? Bereft of power would Clinton also be bereft of apologists? Not at all, as we shall see.

TWO

SUNRISE IN CHAPPAQUA

It may have been the most elaborately planned exit from the White House ever—two full months of executive orders, exit interviews, farewell speeches and valedictory celebrations for President Bill Clinton. One week after the former president and Hillary Rodham Clinton left the White House, there is widespread acknowledgement even among close Clinton aides over how that planning ended: in a public relations debacle.

—*Washington Post,*
January 27, 2001.[1]

Rick Kaplan's premonitions of his scandal-prone friend's future were to be realized not *after* he left the White House but *while* the Boy President was vacating the premises with his lovely wife, Bruno. The moniker bespeaks a certain thuggish side to her political praxis that has been spotted by all law-abiding Clinton-watchers who have followed her rise from Arkansas to Washington. The Clintons did not retire from the White House. They absconded!

If Kaplan read the above report published in the *Washington Post* a week after the pardoning, pilfering, and trashing of the White House, my guess is that he recognized that the Clintons' historically unprecedented exit constituted something more than the "public relations debacle" noted by the *Post.* To a seasoned Clinton-watcher these reports of last-minute presidential pardons and stolen White House property must have adumbrated still more congressional investigations, perhaps even a Justice Department inquiry, possibly criminal prosecutions.

This first week out of office proved to be a gruesome one for the former first family, and things were not to get better for months. On Sunday, the day after Bill and Bruno made their dramatic flight to New York, the *Washington Post* revealed that the Clintons, "faced with multimillion-dollar houses to furnish here and in suburban New York, left the White House yesterday with an unprecedented $190,027 worth of gifts received over the last eight years."[2] Within hours, the news media carried additional reports, this time of damage done to the White House and of the petty theft on Air Force One.

On Wednesday, Andrea Mitchell of NBC News reported that the Clintons had established a "gift registry" weeks before, where donors were asked to buy them presents for a national housewarming party in circumvention of Senate ethics regulations that were about to cover Senator-elect Clinton. According to Mitchell, "Mrs. Clinton registered her choices last November, just like a new bride. A spokesman said, 'Because friends wanted to give her special farewell presents.' But donors tell NBC News a very different story. They say they were solicited by Clinton Beverly Hills contributor Rita Pynoos. Told to send a $5,000 check to the store quickly before the Senate ethics deadline [*sic*]. The donors also say they have no idea what their money purchased. Pynoos did not return calls." Mitchell went on to report that "one of the most generous donors, New York Clinton supporter Denise Rich [donated] $7,300 for two chairs and two coffee tables."[3] Denise was the former wife of fugitive Marc Rich, the beneficiary of a recent Clinton pardon. We shall discuss both later. But the revelation was tough on the Clintons.

Senator-Elect Clinton had to beat a similar ethics deadline in signing a contract for her memoir and she did. On November 15, 2000, Simon

& Schuster announced that she had signed a contract for $8 million, despite being in the critics' chorus six years earlier when House Speaker Newt Gingrich's book contract was for a paltry $4.5 million. As howls rose, Gingrich returned the money. Bruno never did, despite protests from her Episodic Apologists in a *New York Times* editorial.*

As for the pilfering of the White House, the moving trucks rolled up to the mansion on January 19 and spirited away such White House property as china, silverware, furniture, and three television sets. Soon both Clintons were being assailed. What has yet to be reported is that Mrs. Clinton's mother, Dorothy Rodham, was deeply involved in the heist. According to a White House staffer who stayed on to work for the Bushes, Mrs. Rodham was furious when the Clintons subsequently returned $28,000 of the controversial take and wrote an $86,000 check in restitution for the rest.[4] Truth be known, early reports of the heist were inaccurate. The congressional committee that soon set about investigating the matter discovered that the Clintons had undervalued their booty. A conservative estimate came to $362,000.[5] Nor was it accurate to report that the pilfering had begun in January. It had been going on for months, as the press's Episodic Apologists might have known had they paid attention a year before when the *American Spectator* reported the Secret Service's alarm that the Clintons, as early as March 2000, were carting off property that was not theirs.[6] At the time, the Apologists were again giving the Clintons the benefit of the doubt. Clinton had survived impeachment, so once again his Episodic Apologists were full of hope. They foresaw Mrs. Clinton heading towards a seat in the Senate and possibly the presidency. The forty-second president was on the road to a dignified retirement, his

*The *Times'* December 22, 2000 editorial was a classic specimen of the Episodic Apologists' years of indignation: "We are sorry to see Hillary Rodham Clinton start her Senate career by selling a memoir of her years as first lady to Simon & Schuster for a near-record advance of about $8 million. The deal may conceivably conform to the lax Senate rules on book sales, though even that is uncertain. . . . Only a few years ago Newt Gingrich, at that time the House speaker, accepted an ethically dubious $4.5 million book deal with a publishing house owned by Rupert Murdoch. . . ."

scandals behind him. Perhaps he would become another Jimmy Carter. In the *Kultursmog* Jimmy has been exalted as "America's Greatest Ex-President." Bill's elevation to this bizarre rank was on track. Carter built homes with Habitat for Humanity. Bill might build whole cities.

In her memoir, *Living History*, Hillary explained the allegations of grand larceny as the consequence of a simple "clerical error." Simple "error" is a frequent explanation for many of the Clintons' intermittent scandals. The firing of the employees at the White House Travel Office (Travelgate) was attributed to error as was, presumably, their subsequent harassment by the Justice Department. The unfortunate appearance in the White House of the FBI files of over 700 Republicans (Filegate) was a "bureaucratic snafu," or so Hillary explains in *Living History*. "Errors" and "snafus" aside, the Clintons' lives have followed a pattern of disregard for ethics and the law that began the moment they entered public life, and "public life" began for these 1960s eager beavers sometime during grade school. Bill's thwarting of the draft is well-known. Less well-known, perhaps, is that immediately after law school Hillary's service for the House Judiciary Impeachment Inquiry then pursuing President Richard Nixon was marred by so many acts of excess and impropriety that the committee's Democratic counsel wrote that he "could not recommend her for any future position of public or private trust."[7]

Down in Arkansas the pattern continued. No impropriety committed by the Clintons in the White House or in leaving the White House is without a precedent earlier in their lives. The Clintons' reckless fundraising in the 1996 reelection campaign that welcomed foreign contributors into the president's mansion was preceded by reckless fundraising that welcomed shady figures into the governor's mansion in the 1980s. The Clintons' gubernatorial campaigns involved so many dubious loans that they were still being investigated in the early 1990s.

Even the grand larceny perpetrated during their final White House exit had an Arkansas precedent. Twenty years before, when defeat in the 1980 election forced Governor Clinton to leave the governor's mansion, the Clintons committed at least petty larceny. I.C. Smith, the FBI's Special Agent for Arkansas, recalls that the petty larceny came about when Hillary, "out for revenge" after her husband's defeat, "took all the food and beverages from the governor's mansion to their private residence. I was told that not only did they empty the mansion cupboards, but completely depleted the funds appropriated for entertaining, leaving incoming Governor Frank White with no money for that purpose."[8] The Clintons are what law enforcement officials call "repeat offenders." Only the forgiving nature of their friends and supporters has saved them from oblivion or perhaps from criminal charges.

Smith's revelation brings to mind another embarrassment that threatened the Clintons' last days in the White House and early months in Chappaqua. Unreported still, a problem developed with the president's Secret Service detail. Many of its members did not want to leave with Hillary whom they hate or with Bill whom they hold in amused contempt. Hillary's tantrums toward staff and toward their principal, her husband, should by now be well-known to the reading public. Perhaps less well-known is that these conscientious, patriotic, security personnel and similarly right-minded military aides have felt cheapened by the Boy President's goatishness with the fair sex. Guarding a bedroom while their principal is rutting within atop some dim tart is not what they expected upon entering their respective proud services. One of Clinton's former military aides told me of the sheepishness of members of Clinton's Secret Service detail when they had to turn him away from a hotel bungalow where he tried to deliver a telephone message for the president. One of the agents told him disgustedly, "You don't want to go in there."[9] Such scenes have taken place with Clinton in office and in retirement, and they are an insult to the pride of men dedicated to protecting the life of the country's chief executive.

During the Lewinsky scandal, when offensive details of Clinton's indoor recreations were becoming public, military aides and Secret Service guards were made particularly uncomfortable as he continued his recreations with subordinates despite the heightened danger. One military aide even proposed resignations en masse. The move was never seriously pursued, but, if anything, Clinton's military aides were even more uneasy about Clinton than the Secret Service. One officer had to counsel a tearful Air Force enlisted woman after Clinton cornered her in a galley on Air Force One and fondled her breasts and bottom. The Secret Service agents had seen it all, and few wanted to follow the disreputable couple into retirement. During Clinton's retirement, an unusually high number of agents have turned in their papers early.[10]

By the end of the Boy President's tenure many of those acquainted with him had come to recognize that Bill was a rogue. Even the famed Friends of Bill (FOBs) recognized it, as the frankness of Kaplan and Jeff Greenfield suggests. Still, in the emotionally intense politics of the early twenty-first century, for a Democrat to acknowledge the coarseness of the Clintons has usually been a psychological impossibility. Doing so would put them uncomfortably close to the hated Republicans. Once again, the bows and the bunting of American politics fall to the floor, to be swept away by the janitorial staff. Rather than addressing issues or ideas, our politics frequently address the psychological needs of its clientele, that is to say, the psychological need for heroes, for enemies, for venting one's dispendious wrath. American politics in its essence usually addresses angers, not ideas.

Bill and Bruno have known this for years. They are geniuses at whipping up illogical and petty angers. By preying on the psychological disorders of their fellow Democrats, they have become the Roosevelts and Kennedys of the present without ever providing a New Deal or New Frontier. Rather, the Clintons have filled the minds of their credulous supporters with visions of conspiracy, ruin, and "Clinton-haters." The term was born in the Clinton era and applied to anyone gauche enough to take note when a Clinton uttered a bald-faced lie or breached a public trust. By the time of the forty-second president's retirement from office, *Clinton-hater* had entered the lexicon of American hate terms along with such familiar slurs as *McCarthyite* or *homophobe*.

From the Clintons' earliest scandals to Pardongate and the pilfering of the White House, more and more Clinton supporters were becoming aware that the Clinton-haters had a point. Yet they faced a psychological barrier against admitting it in public. Thus siding with the Clinton-haters was an impossibility. The Clintons had mastered mob psychology. As a consequence, by 2005 the mob was again enthralled by Bill and Hillary. The Democrats and their stenographers in the media were likening Bill to Elvis Presley. His wife had become the Democrats' leading contender for their presidential nomination. This has been the couple's greatest comeback. If an even greater one awaits them it will have to be engineered from behind jailhouse walls, which, if you think about it, is not unimaginable.

Waking up in his private residence in Chappaqua the day after signing those pardons and relinquishing the presidency so mawkishly, Clinton now had psychological needs of his own to address. Bewildered and blue, he had not been in such a Clintonian funk since being booted from the governorship precisely twenty years before. On that dismal day he was only the third Arkansas governor of the century to have failed to win a second term. Politically he was on the rocks. No longer did he have the stately governor's mansion with its silver and antiques, its staff and official cars, its generous domestic budget. Out of office, the Clintons were reduced to a little yellow and white clapboard house in Little Rock.

Hillary, in her hippie raiment, her insolent radicalism having helped to land them in this dump, was scolding him for his defeat and filling the tiny house with dreadful used Victorian furniture: huge brooding wooden monsters that gave the décor the ambiance of a haunted house. She was its resident witch, and there was no place for Bill to hide. Boy, had she become difficult! Having moved from the Northeast's power corridor to Hicksville and now facing the prospect of Hicksville *sans* political power, she was "mad as hell."

The ex-governor was really low. He was also angry. And he was sputtering with grievances. Depression, anger, and grievance—these are the constituent elements of a Clintonian funk. From 1981 to 2001, after every Clinton slip-up has come the Clintonian funk. His post-gubernatorial funk is still remembered in Little Rock. On election night in 1980 the defeated governor was spotted on the floor of the governor's mansion writhing in anger and tears.[11] In the months ahead he did some heavy drinking, an indulgence he was to cut back on in the later 1980s. In one lurid incident, at a small but popular Little Rock bar, The Afterthought, he engaged in an act of public indecency, oral sex with a female journalist.[12] People in Little Rock began spotting him standing around shopping malls and grocery stores, forlorn and dazed. At one point he stood by a checkout counter, alternately apologizing and seeking advice. He mixed humility into the Clintonian funk then, for he probably recognized that voters are fetched by it. In 1981 he still saw each and every one of his fellow Arkansans as a potential vote.

In 2001 the ex-president was again really low, but there was no humility in this Clintonian funk. His political prospects were nil. Agents on his Secret Service detail would later report that he mused about a possible campaign for Secretary-General of the United Nations. His friends planted stories in the press that he was interested in a run for mayor of New York. But for now politics was out. This funk contained only depression, anger, and grievance—no humility. His anger and grievance in the aftermath of the 1980 defeat had been against the press and against those Arkansas politicos who he thought had abandoned him. This time he directed his anger and grievance at the media and a new bugaboo, "the Right" or "the Far Right."

By the end of his scandalous presidency Clinton had developed an explanation which he believed explained each slip-up. The forty-second president was a victim of "the Right." In retirement he elaborated on the theme until it became a historical fact—at least for him and the Clinton faithful. One finds the explanation advanced in his earliest post-presidential interviews. He repeats it in his memoir, *My Life*, where he seems obsessed, reiterating the plot even on the book's last page, a page that might more appropriately envision hopeful tomorrows, perhaps Chelsea's first run for office. Clinton's presidential library devotes an entire exhibit to grousing about "the Right's" conspiracy against him.

According to Clinton, his presidency suffered its scandals because of a synergy between the Right and the mainstream press. The Right fabricated stories of scandal, and the mainstream press dutifully passed them on. This explanation was first tried out on the public in 1994 when Clinton's political adviser, James Carville, described the occult process as a "Media Food Chain." By 1997 White House staffers had composed, presumably at taxpayers' expense, a 331-page report on the Food Chain. Titled "Communication Stream of Conspiracy Commerce," it depicted the flow of these shocking fabrications, advancing from their point of origin on the Right and heading into the mainstream press. The Right's sources were identified: London's *Sunday Telegraph*, Richard Scaife's *Pittsburgh Tribune-Review*, the *Wall Street Journal*, the *Washington Times*, and the *American Spectator*. In an early post-presidential interview Clinton explained to *Newsweek* magazine, "We live in an historical period when the fanaticism of America is on the right, and it has an apparatus to support it."[13] For all his public smiles Clinton is an angry man; and throughout his retirement he has frequently given vent to this anger, often at odd moments.

A year after Clinton moved to Chappaqua, one of his Episodic Apologists, Jonathan Alter, asked him in the abovementioned *Newsweek* interview, "how low did you go in the months just after" the pardons. "I was just angry," the former Boy President repined, "that after I worked so hard and after all that money had been spent [by the Independent Counsel] proving that I never did anything wrong for money ["money" was not part of the Independent Counsel's charge; and Clinton had, indeed, admitted to wrongdoing by signing independent counsel Robert Ray's January 19, 2001 agreement], that I'd get mugged one more time on the way out the door. People are free to say that they disagreed with this or that part of the decisions I made, but there wasn't a shred of evidence that it [granting 140 pardons and 36 commutations] had been done for any improper motive [other than enriching relatives and possibly paying off contributors]."[14]

This typical Clintonian sophistication will give historians a sense of the difficulty journalists and prosecutors have had with this rogue. In Clinton's response to the credulous Alter, he conflates the issue of his pardons (many obviously with an "improper motive"; see chapter four) with the issue of lying about sex with an intern. In chapter one we have seen that independent counsel Ray proved Clinton had given false testimony regarding Monica Lewinsky. In fact, Clinton admitted as much in signing his agreement with Ray. Pressured by Ray and the Arkansas Bar's representative, Marie Miller, he accepted a five-year suspension of his law license and agreed to a $25,000 fine. Forty-four percent of those polled by *Newsweek* judged the punishment "about right." Thirty-three percent thought he should have been punished more harshly. A decade before Clinton trotted out this sophistry to the vulnerable Mr. Alter, then-Senator Bob Kerrey struck a resonant note in the country's political culture by describing Clinton as "an unusually good liar." Actually Clinton's strength has not been that of a good liar but that of an inveterate liar whose friends and constituents do not particularly mind being lied to by him. Considering the frequency with which he has been caught, it is more accurate to say that he is simply a crude and constant liar.

Back in 1981 as the then defeated governor, Clinton fortified his wobbly spirits by tirelessly telephoning around the country seeking advice on his next political move. This incessant telephoning has been a conspicuous feature of the Clinton lifestyle, particularly late into the night—no Clinton political aide sleeps far from the phone. Now alone in Chappaqua twenty years later, he turned to the telephone in despair. The sudden bad press was imperiling his speaking schedule, which his money-hungry wife had helped arrange months before. He contemplated doing a $2 million commercial during the Super Bowl. There were anticipated half-million dollar paydays ahead. Now the paydays were in doubt.

Moreover, to reward his wife's loyalty during the Lewinsky scandal he had committed himself to a future political career for her. That was in trouble, too.

The press was now reporting her role in Pardongate, and the roles that her brothers played in winning—for a price!—pardons for drug dealers and other scoundrels. She and her staff were being blamed for the "practical jokes" played on incoming Bush staffers and for the missing furnishings. Now Hillary's future looked no more promising than Bill's. Both faced huge legal bills—$11 million, possibly more. Always relying on the funds of others, the Clintons had set up fundraising groups to extinguish their legal debts and would rely on such fundraising despite their accumulating millions.

The dreadful headlines were threatening Bill's debt-free future and Hillary's anticipated return to the White House. Thus he relentlessly dialed up friends and members of his old White House attack team, including former chief of staff John Podesta and press secretary Joe Lockhart. They held conference calls. By February and March they were holding regular meetings reminiscent of the 1992 presidential campaign's "war room." It was like old times. The Democratic Party's best political minds were at work covering for another of the Clintons' slip-ups.

This was a desolate time to be with Clinton in his Chappaqua refuge, a century-old nicely renovated Dutch Colonial at 15 Old House Lane, snuggled behind government vans with network camera crews maintaining their vigil. Basically only the Secret Service was within and some domestic help. Hillary had her senatorial duties to distract her from the stormy news. Her absence might have been for the best. In bad times she has rarely been a source of consolation—damage control, yes, but not consolation. The tirades and flying objects directed by her at Bill's defenseless skull are not fictions invented by Clinton-haters. They are historic events, as Eleanor Roosevelt's public rebukes of Franklin were historic events and Nancy Reagan's dreamy gazes toward Ron. As we shall see, there would be more spousal abuse during Clinton's retirement when his amours threatened Hillary's political longevity. Indignation and recrimination are her fortes.

Interviewed for this book, Terry McAuliffe admitted the profound funk into which his friend had fallen upon leaving the White House.[15] McAuliffe had been a colossal fundraiser for Clinton in the 1990s, owing to his contacts with labor unions and his keen eye for deals that less reckless dealmakers might pass up. Moreover, there was his chutzpah. In her historic cattle futures deal Hillary had seen a $1,000 investment transubstantiate into $100,000. McAuliffe, during the ethical Renaissance that was the Clintons' 1990s, saw a $100,000 investment in Global Crossing swell to an $18,000,000 killing when he cashed out before the fly-by-night operation went bust and its CEO, Bernard Ebbers, went to prison. Yet when his windfall was exposed, he avoided Hillary's mistake. She greeted exposure with icy silence. He greeted it with a full frontal attack on the Democrats' most prominent enemy, President George W. Bush, whom McAuliffe implicated in the Enron scandal without benefit of evidence. The press took up the chase, utterly forgetting McAuliffe's Global Crossing payday.

Audacity of this magnitude explains Clinton's admiration. He made McAuliffe chairman of the Democratic Party despite the Democrats' qualms. Clinton saw to it that McAuliffe remained chairman even after Senator John Kerry won the 2004 nomination. The Democrats' apprehensions over McAuliffe stemmed from his role in the Democrats' 1996 fundraising scandals. He had been a strong advocate of White House "coffees" and "sleepovers" in the Lincoln Bedroom. During congressional hearings into these dubious fundraisers, then-DNC chairman Don Fowler identified McAuliffe as the genius behind them. For Fowler's candor, Clinton replaced him with McAuliffe.

Now on Clinton's first day out of office Chairman McAuliffe arrived at 15 Old House Lane, checked in with the Secret Service, and joined the ex-president for his first lunch as a private citizen. Over tuna sandwiches they talked. "It was a very difficult time for him," recalls McAuliffe in our interview. McAuliffe and Clinton mulled over the pardons. "I said at the time. It was a mistake, and he realized it was a mistake," McAuliffe remembers. "The public beating he took was tough on him. . . . Every paper was writing about it. He had just left the White House. He was trying to get his life together, figure out what he was going to do." McAuliffe's next recollection is one that every Clinton friend or acquaintance confirms to me. Clinton, despite his troubled tenure in office, *hated* being out of office. In fact, wherever he is right now, whatever he is doing, you can be certain that he would rather be at 1600 Pennsylvania Avenue. Retirement even on that turbulent morning in Chappaqua left him "dejected." That is McAuliffe's word for it. Months later, whether I was interviewing Clinton's friends and acquaintances in America or abroad, they would always mention this longing. They mentioned it even more frequently than they would mention another of Clinton's peculiarities. An amazed Arkansan from his first administration put it this way: "He really does like women."[16]

There is nothing surprising about that last revelation, but Clinton's longing for a return to the White House is bizarre. Perhaps it is a consequence of his 1960s-engendered adolescent megalomania, but I have never seen this longing in any president I have known in retirement. Nor have I read of such post-presidential cravings. Neither Ronald Reagan nor George H. W. Bush ever expressed a desire to be president again; at least no one who heard them ever recorded it. The president I knew best in retirement, Richard Nixon, spoke of the White House with a slight wistfulness, for he obviously wished he had handled Watergate differently. Yet he betrayed no ardor to return to power. Clinton has from the day he left. "He loved being president," McAuliffe emphasizes. "He loved all eight years of it. He loved every single day of it." Every single day, even with "the Right" and its agents in the mainstream press peeking into his bedroom and his White House hideaway, can the thing be true? So those who have known him say. "Let's be honest," McAuliffe went on, "one day you're running the world and the next day you're trying to figure out how to use an ATM card. He hadn't used an ATM card. I guess he had had them before that. But it was sort of alien to him, the concept of an ATM card. You're the president. You live in a bubble."

Actually I doubt Clinton had ever used an ATM card. Clinton has "lived in a bubble" nonstop since his second term as Arkansas's governor. This house in Chappaqua was only the fourth private home he and his wife had ever owned. After being exiled to the little yellow and white house in Little Rock, he regained his bearings and retook the governorship in 1982, moving back into public housing where he indulged himself at taxpayers' expense for the next two decades, first in the governor's mansion, then in the White House. McAuliffe's reference to Clinton's unfamiliarity with ATM cards brings to mind another of this surprisingly passive politician's amusing foibles, one known to every Clinton insider who has ever seen the soup stains on his shirt. He is a hopeless klutz. He has been all his life.

At twenty-two, when Clinton served as driver for Senator William Fulbright during Fulbright's 1968 Senate campaign, the senator was desperate to rid himself of the garrulous young political enthusiast. Clinton was a menace behind the wheel and as incapable of maintaining the car as he was of maintaining silence during the senator's naps in the back seat. Years later, the Arkansas troopers guarding Governor Clinton laughed aloud at his inability even to turn a Mr. Coffee machine on or off. One Saturday morning in the governor's mansion in the 1980s, state trooper Larry Patterson explained the machine's operation to the boss in laborious detail, only to have to explain the phenomenon to him again the very next day.[17] By the time Clinton got to the White House he remained all thumbs even with a computer. Its elementary tasks defeated him.

A truth worth establishing here and now is that Clinton has lived like a pampered rich boy from his earliest days. The claim that he is from an impoverished background is an absurd exaggeration. Curiously, having recently amassed a fortune he now admits as much—at least occasionally.

During his retirement he has been curiously inconsistent with the legends he spins about his life.

In *My Life* he actually jokes about duping voters into thinking him the creature of a log cabin upbringing and boasts of his financial success. The claim long made by supporters that he is as uninterested in money and luxury as a Hindu holy man is utter nonsense. The truth is that Clinton has never needed to earn money to live life at the Ritz. In the governor's mansion he had a large household staff, a grounds crew, chauffeurs, and a nanny for Chelsea. Some staff members were convicts from Arkansas penitentiaries who worked as gardeners and handymen at the mansion. They also worked at the home of Hillary's parents, which might explain Mrs. Rodham's sense of entitlement to White House furnishings.[18] At least one of Chelsea's nannies was listed in the state budget as a "courier," though the Clintons used her to mind their daughter while claiming a child-care tax credit, a clear, if petty, case of tax fraud.[19] Though Clinton has always boasted of the meager salary he took as governor, the claim is misleading. He always had comfortable entertainment budgets and travel allowances that allowed him to travel the country and even the globe pursuing his destiny. Once in the White House things became even better, save for the increased public accountability that earned the Clintons so many unenviable headlines. It took the Clintons years to recognize that in the White House, public scrutiny is more rigorous than in one-party Arkansas.

Clinton's comfortable lifestyle began in his youth. He was hardly ever impoverished. That the myth of his poverty has endured years of public scrutiny through all his campaigns is another example of Clinton's playing to the psychological needs of the credulous. The typical Clinton supporters need to think of themselves as champions of the underdog. They believe in the up-from-the-log-cabin political career of their messiahs, no matter how illusory the log cabin or how hedonistic the political savior. Clinton's log cabins were often not far from a country club. A glance at his résumé reveals his attendance at the finest schools: Georgetown, Yale, and Oxford. Even back in Arkansas he attended a private school.

Admittedly, during his first few years, before his mother married into the Clinton clan, Bill lived a working-class life with his mother's parents, but after she married Roger Clinton, ample funds were always available for her son's upper-middle-class lifestyle. He never had to take a summer job and apparently never did. His enthusiasm for golf was not acquired while struggling in Dogpatch. As a student at Georgetown, he drove a late-model Buick convertible. While squandering his Rhodes scholarship money he traveled widely throughout Europe and, despite the Cold War's restrictions, visited Moscow and Prague, where he stayed with a family famous, I discovered when I interviewed them in October 1993, for its role in founding the Czech Communist Party.[20] When I visited them, they were still Communists! Anyone who examines young Bill's cunning exertions to beat the draft will recognize that he must have had powerful connections in the Arkansas political establishment to devise such strategies.

The source of those powerful connections was also the source of his comfortable life, namely, Uncle Ray Clinton, owner of Buick dealerships. In the Arkansas of the 1950s and the 1960s, a Buick dealership was more lucrative than a grain elevator or a pig farm. Future historians, who in time are going to expose Clinton's secrets as joyously as did the historians and journalists who penetrated the veils around John F. Kennedy decades after his death, will clap their hands when they see the role that Buick dealerships played in Boy Clinton's rise. Those dealerships were as critical to Clinton's comfort and clout as Ambassador Joseph P. Kennedy's bootleggers were to JFK's pursuit of the presidency, and Uncle Ray's dealerships were perfectly legal. One of the irrefutable facts—one of the *rare* irrefutable facts—in Clinton's curriculum vitae is that his stepfather really was a drunk and a ne'er-do-well. On the other hand, his stepfather's brother, Uncle Ray, was a force to conjure with in old Arkansas. There was so much money available in the Clinton family that after young Billy's hard-drinking stepfather bungled his own Buick dealership he could still move his family to a 400-acre farm. That the farm did not have indoor plumbing was an asset that candidate Clinton would spin for years as yet more evidence of his hard lot.

By 2004, along with the globe-trotting lecturer's riches came an unrestrainable sauciness. In public speeches, most memorably the ex-president's speech to the 2004 Democratic National Convention, Clinton crowed of his wealth. For some reason by then he began to joke about how he had hoodwinked the credulous with tales of his barefoot youth back in jerkwater. After years of deception Clinton comes clean in his memoir and describes an upbringing that is frankly upper-middle class. When he comes to that 400-acre farm with the outhouse he jokes: "Later, when I got into politics, being able to say I had lived on a farm with an outhouse made a great story, almost as good as being born in a log cabin."[21] Yes, he actually wrote, "born in a log cabin"! Bill knows his customers!

In retirement he acquired two log cabins. A year after buying the $1.7 million home in Chappaqua, the Clintons bought their $2.85 million brick Colonial on a leafy cul de sac in Washington's Embassy Row. The purchase of the first house attracted temporary controversy when McAuliffe offered to put up $1.35 million as collateral. The controversy was twofold. First, was McAuliffe's $1.35 million a gift and therefore taxable? Second, had the Office of Government Ethics "legally approved" it, as Hillary gratuitously declared to the press? The head of the Office of Government Ethics publicly denied he had, and went so far as to say he had warned the Clintons about this interpretation. Here on a small scale are the constituent elements of most of the Clintons' large-scale scandals: a reckless end run around the law, a brazen lie, and all for petty gain. McAuliffe prudently withdrew his offer.

The second house created less of a controversy; and it has become the Clintons' political headquarters, a center for the fundraising that goes on ceaselessly, and for political soireés to guide Hillary to the 2008 presidential nomination. By contrast with the swirl of politicking at the Washington manse, the five-bedroom home in Chappaqua often has the lights out for days and nights on end. Once Bill got his "life together," as

McAuliffe puts it, he was rarely there. Hillary has been there a bit more often but not as often as might be expected. Though she is a dutiful senator, her visits to New York are comparatively rare for a junior senator. She has an agenda that demands she be a national figure with an eye to 2008. When she is in New York she prefers to stay in Manhattan, usually at swank hotels, often the Plaza before renovation began, where security personnel report that her rudeness with the staff became legendary.[22]

An investigation of stores in Chappaqua shows that the Clintons have no charge accounts in town and are rarely seen there, though when early stories of the recently retired president's arrival were published he claimed that he would be making a daily forty-five-minute commute to his office in Harlem, another New York venue he rarely shows up at. No nearby church, by the way, has any record of the Clintons as regular attendees despite their claims to deep spiritual wellsprings. In fact, my investigations into the Clintons' Chappaqua lifestyle cast a net across a thirty-mile radius of the hamlet and found not one church where Bill is even a casual visitor.

The Chappaqua house seems to have been purchased hastily late in 1999, so that Hillary could duly claim residency for her senatorial race. In 2000 the Clintons would both pop up mainly for photo ops. An early shot has the President and the First Lady moving their belongings in from a large, nondescript van. Other pictures show candidate Hillary Clinton reading in her cozy library. Naturally on Election Day 2000 she and her husband were pictured voting and smiling warmly to neighbors. Months thereafter those neighbors have reported few Clinton sightings either in town or at their residence. At Clinton's office in Harlem it is much the same. The locals rarely see him. Initially Clinton wanted to rent offices on pricey West 57th Street in the Carnegie Hall Tower—at $89 a square foot it would have been over $800,000 a year and more than the government was paying for the offices of Gerald Ford, Jimmy Carter, Ronald Reagan, and George H.W. Bush combined!

The news caused an uproar with a public still vexed by the Clintons' unseemly White House exit. The controversy over his 57th Street office revealed something else about Clinton that would be vividly observable in his early months of retirement. To wit: At some point late in his presidency Boy Clinton had become as ravenous for luxury as . . . well, as a rock star. At times this apolaustic impulse threatened his political instinct. For now, the political instinct reasserted itself. As the uproar over Carnegie Hall Tower grew clamorous, Clinton made a bold political stroke. He announced he was taking more modest offices in Harlem, and with the attendant rejoicing the uproar was forgotten. Clinton, the man novelist Toni Morrison called America's "first black president," would retire to Harlem! His offices were to be located at 55 West 125th Street on the fourteenth floor. The 8,300-square foot space was leased for $346,128 annually—half a million dollars of savings for the American people! Harlem's indigenes were thrilled. The neighborhood would be reborn! Though, as is so often the case with a man of Clinton's checkered past, there was irony. In taking the panoramic top floor of 55 West 125th overlooking Central Park, Clinton was supplanting space held by the city's child-protection agency.

Though Clinton has lived handsomely at the public trough, he is not known for his charitable giving. In fact, as the *American Spectator* reported years ago, back in Arkansas the Clintons even took a tax deduction on old clothes—underwear!—that the family had donated to charity.[23] As a retired president, he has lived exuberantly well. His annual pension at the time he left office was $171,900. His transition allocation for office, staff, communications services, printing, and postage came to $1.83 million for his first seven months out of office. From friends and prospective business contacts he took every freebie available, dinners, hotel accommodations, trips on corporate jets—the Delta Shuttle was a frequent indulgence.[24] He has become the most costly ex-president ever—see the chart opposite for fiscal year 2002.

Financially, Clinton's retirement was going to be very successful. Still, on that first day of retirement, sitting there with McAuliffe over their tuna fish sandwiches, the Great Pardoner had reason to doubt his future. The press was blistering him. Worse was to come.

Over the next few months, journalists found that members of the Clinton family had received large sums in payment for negotiating presidential pardons. Pardons had gone to unrepentant arms dealers, drug dealers, and Arkansas cronies. The reputations of both Clintons went into free fall. Even fellow Democrats were castigating them. Reports McAuliffe: "It's a hard transition for any human being to leave the most powerful job in the world. . . . Then you had the firestorm of the pardons. It was very difficult with editorial after editorial attacking you."

ALLOWANCE	FORD	CARTER	BUSH	CLINTON
Pension:	$165,000	$165,000	$165,000	$171,000
Staff Salaries:	$ 96,000	$ 81,000	$ 96,000	$150,000
Staff Benefits:	$ 23,000	$ 0	$ 40,000	$ 54,000
Travel:	$ 35,000	$ 2,000	$ 43,000	$ 35,000
Rental:	$110,000	$102,000	$169,000	$354,000
Telephone:	$ 21,000	$ 25,000	$ 14,000	$ 28,000
Postage:	$ 6,000	$ 20,000	$ 14,000	$ 22,000
Other Services:	$ 11,000	$ 71,000	$ 13,000	$ 80,000
Printing:	$ 0	$ 5,000	$ 12,000	$ 15,000
Supplies:	$ 9,000	$ 6,000	$ 11,000	$ 24,000
Equipment:	$ 4,000	$ 9,000	$ 36,000	$ 36,000
Total:	$480,000	$486,000	$613,000	$969,000

Two days after McAuliffe lunched with his woebegone leader, the *Washington Post* published the kind of editorial McAuliffe had in mind, asking, "What conceivable justification could there be for former president Clinton, on his last morning in office, to have pardoned fugitive financiers Marc Rich and Pincus Green?" Their pardons had been among the first to attract the media's opprobrium. In 1983 Rich and Green had fled the country after being indicted for an oil deal that had defrauded the U.S. Treasury of over $48 million. For seventeen years they lived in Switzerland, free of prosecution and growing ever more prosperous from international financial dealings, often in arms, usually with enemies of the United States. When pardoned, Rich ranked sixth on the outstanding fugitive list maintained by the Justice Department.[25] He and Green had never served a day in jail or made any restitution. Both lived luxuriously and openly in Swiss estates, to the frustration of American prosecutors whose U.S. marshals had tried to nab Rich at least twice on European soil. The public outcry over these pardons intensified when news sources reported that Rich's ex-wife, Denise, a Manhattan socialite and songwriter, was a major donor to the Democratic Party, to Hillary Clinton's senatorial campaign, and to the Clinton Library Foundation.

The *Post* continued: "The Rich pardon is not the only one of the president's 176 parting clemency actions that raises questions. Mr. Clinton commuted the sentences of three Hasidic Jews in New York, convicted of defrauding the federal government of millions by setting up a phony Yeshiva and garnering tuition grants. They come from a community important now to New York Sen. Hillary Clinton. Was there a better reason for mercy? Whitewater felon Susan McDougal, who became a celebrity for thumbing her nose at Kenneth Starr's grand jury and refusing to answer legitimate questions, won a last-minute pardon. . . . Mr. Clinton has diminished the integrity and grandeur of the pardon power just as surely as he diminished the various privileges he abused by invoking them to defend his tawdry conduct in office. What a way to leave."[26]

The moral indignation displayed by the nation's liberal elites after each Clinton scandal has always been a thing to marvel at, but never had the indignation reached such a boil as after Pardongate. In fact, it became so furious and contagious that, for a while, it appeared that this time Boy

Clinton was not going to make another of his vaunted "comebacks." Even Democratic leaders peeked up from their parapets to inveigh against him. For those of us who had been implicated by Bill in the "Media Food Chain" and by Hillary in the "Vast Right-Wing Conspiracy," it was a voluptuously satisfying intermezzo of outrage.

The Episodic Apologists actually began to compliment us on our prescient comprehension of the Clintons' roguish essence. No longer were we simply Clinton-haters. Now the *New York Times* glimpsed in us a sophistication verging, it seemed, on cosmopolitanism. We were "cynical critics" whose "low expectations" of the Boy President could now only be criticized for being insufficiently low. Calling for congressional investigations, the *Times* editorialized that "the former president . . . seemed to make a redoubled effort in the last moments of his presidency to plunge further and further beneath the already *low expectations* [!] of his most *cynical critics* [!] and most world-weary friends."[27] The *Times* speculated sadly that its editors might "never understand the process by which a departing president and his wife come to put sofas and flatware ahead of the acute sense of propriety that ought to go with high office."

For my part, the most memorable vindication came from the *New York Observer*, another redoubt of the Clintons' Episodic Apologists now undergoing an episode of indignation: "Now with Mr. Clinton stripped of the power and protection of the presidency, his supporters see him exactly as he is. And *the image that presents itself is terrifyingly close to the caricature his enemies drew of him. They were right, after all. Mr. Clinton was, in fact, an untrustworthy low-life who used people for his own purposes and then discarded them. How could they have been fooled so badly?*"[28] The italics are mine, but I think that I answered the *Observer*'s exasperated question earlier in this chapter. The Clintons recognize their loyalists' psychological needs, among them the need to become morally indignant, the need to have enemies, and the need to feel superior to the bourgeoisie at Wal-Mart or perhaps standing next to them at Bergdorf Goodman. Even journalists at the *Post*, the *Times*, and the *Observer* have these needs.

The former president took all of these angry editorials quite hard. He was set to launch his first speaking tour, and the outcry against him made the Secret Service uneasy. The colossal intensity of the reaction against the Clintons' White House exit is probably explained by the contortions Democrats had so recently put themselves through in defending Clinton from impeachment. During impeachment Senator Joseph Biden rose to the demands of the moment and purred, "I think [Clinton] has been a great president. I agree with him ideologically on almost everything." Yet after Pardongate the senator blew his top. He judged Clinton "totally indefensible."[29] During impeachment Charles Schumer, at the time a congressman, asseverated, "Censure or rebuke is the appropriate punishment; impeachment is not." After Pardongate Senator Schumer huffed, "To my mind, there can be no justification for pardoning a fugitive from justice."[30] During impeachment former president Jimmy Carter declared: "I would say a lot of damage has been done, but not in any case fatal or permanent damage." After Pardongate, said Carter, "I think President Clinton made one of his most serious mistakes in the way he handled the pardon situation the last few hours he was in office. . . . I don't think there is any doubt that some of the factors in the [Rich] pardon were attributable to his large gifts. In my opinion, that was disgraceful."[31]

Disgraceful! No justification! Indefensible! Things were getting out of hand. Clinton's most reliable Episodic Apologists from days gone by were now sounding like Clinton-haters of the worst sort, that is to say, humorless Clinton-haters insensate to the full comic dimensions of the Clintons' burlesque. *Wall Street Journal* columnist Al Hunt forsook eight years of alibiing for Clinton and condemned him as the "albatross" of his party, adding a gratuitous invitation for him to "drop dead."[32] William M. Daley, the Clinton administration's secretary of commerce and Al Gore's campaign chairman, adjudged the pardons "terrible, devastating," and "appalling."[33] Robert Reich, the administration's secretary of labor, opined, "Clinton is utterly disgraced."[34] Congressman Barney Frank, too, was "appalled," the pardons being "so insensitive to what is right and wrong."[35] Finally, *New York Times* columnist Bob Herbert arrived at a conclusion that I had been ever so gently trying to suggest to him and his peers ever since 1992: "Bill Clinton has been a disaster for the Democratic Party. Send him packing." And, "It's time for the Democratic Party to wise up. Ostracism would be a good first step. Bill Clinton should be cut completely loose." Whereupon Herbert, too, vindicated the Vast Right-Wing Conspiracy, reporting that "some of Mr. Clinton's closest associates and supporters are acknowledging what his enemies have argued for years—the man is so thoroughly corrupt it is frightening."[36]

Both Clintons were under pressure to fade away. The role of the Hasidic Jews and of Hillary's brothers in Pardongate implicated her deeply. She and her aides were perceived as the culprits behind the plundering and vandalizing of the White House. A late February press conference proved to be a disaster when she implausibly denied any knowledge of the pardons and amateurishly professed to be "heartbroken" by her brothers' venality. Donna Brazile, Gore's campaign manager, wrote in the *New York Times*, "It's time to let Bill Clinton go—go on and live the rest of his life and allow a new generation of Democratic leaders to renew their fight on behalf of working families in America."[37] The aforementioned editorial in the *New York Observer* was particularly severe toward Hillary: "It is clear now that we [New Yorkers] have made a terrible mistake, for Hillary Rodham Clinton is unfit for elective office. Had she any shame, she would resign." The paper called the Clintons "this coarse and manipulative couple."[38] Through more than a decade of eating their words as dessert after every Clinton scandal, the Clintons' Episodic Apologists had become fat. Now they were crapulent.

They gave themselves over to the moralistic excess that has become characteristic of the liberal mind. Their orgies did not bode well for the Clintons' future. Three months into retirement Clinton was still dropping in the polls. A *New York Times*–CBS News poll found his approval rating had thudded to the lowest level since he was first sworn into office. From the 50 plus percentage points he enjoyed during much of his second term, he was down to a 38 percent approval rating.[39] An NBC–*Wall Street Journal* poll measuring his wife's favorable rating showed that she had dropped from 50 percent in January to the low 30s by March. Sixty percent of those polled thought she had lied during her February press conference.[40] Hillary busied herself in legislative activities. She would bury herself in her work and hope that congressional investigations into the pardons would run out of steam. Bill had no such shelter. He was more in the public eye. He was beginning his lecture tour, and wherever he spoke questions might be asked about his infamous last days. According to news reports, sponsors were withdrawing from some of his planned engagements.

How bad had things gotten? Consider the testimony of a theretofore obscure public opinion expert, Avdal A. Dosky, the street vendor down the block from the White House. Mr. Dosky's specialty was photographing tourists as they stood next to cardboard presidential likenesses. By March 2001 he had pulled Clinton's likeness from the lineup. Some corporations might still be willing to fork over $100,000 to hear the disgraced president talk, but tourists would not give Mr. Dosky $6 to be seen with Clinton in public. "The first couple of years were okay," Mr. Dosky confided, "but with the Monica Lewinsky scandal, business died."[41] After the pardons, business was nonexistent.

As we all now know, eventually Clinton's critics within the Democratic Party gravitated back to their rock star. By the second half of 2001 he and his wife were being enlisted by McAuliffe to host fundraisers in their Washington home. Probably there were coffees. Possibly there were sleepovers. "The guy was still a huge star in the party. He did a lot of events for us in 2001 and 2002," McAuliffe glows. "He was still revered in the party."[42] Sure, sure, but this time it took a little longer for the Clinton faithful to forgive, forget, and focus their moral indignation again on the Clinton-haters. For some it actually took months.

Such undying loyalty is not without precedent in modern celebrity-mad America. Other stars have enjoyed it—for instance, the televangelists

Jim and Tammy Faye Bakker and Jimmy Swaggart. In the more profane world of pop entertainment the embattled image of Michael Jackson springs to mind. The similarities between the King of Pop and the Democrats' rock star are striking.

When Jackson returned to his Neverland Ranch after being charged with seven counts of "performing lewd or lascivious acts on a child under 14" and two counts of "administering an intoxicating agent," fans and friends rushed to his support. Off they went to Neverland. Stars such as Serena Williams and MC Hammer were there for him. Perhaps James Carville showed up, too. After all, that other famous Clinton advocate, Mark Geragos, was there. He had defended Clintonistas during tough times. He was Susan McDougal's lawyer. I once saw him on cable TV divulging that the Arkansas Project had given millions of dollars to the Clintons' enemies, that being the official Clinton position. At Jackson's trial Geragos naturally testified for the defense. As Michael has not lived through as many scandals as the forty-second president, his apologists cannot really be called Episodic. Yet there they were outside Neverland's great gate during his trial waving signs very similar to signs I have seen defending Bill. "Michael is Innocent" some proclaimed, or "Leave Him Alone." Responding to Michael's accuser, these Jacksonistas even employed the all-purpose Clintonista explanation that the accuser was "in it for the money." Perhaps that was Geragos' idea. Whatever the case, both Clinton and Jackson walked.

Early in 2001, with Clinton's American lecture tour off to a bad start, he headed abroad. "He traveled the world," says McAuliffe. "That helped him on the world stage. It's one thing to see him here. You ought to see him overseas. When he goes to a foreign country it is something."[43]

THREE

THE GHOST SHIP

If upon retirement the forty-second president of the United States was rarely to be found in his suburban New York home, if he was only an infrequent presence on the fourteenth floor of his Harlem office, if he was almost never at the side of Senator Hillary Rodham Clinton, then where was he? The jovial, white-haired retiree was in an airplane—a private jet 80 percent of the time, usually one owned by a corporation or a tycoon, or paid for by an event sponsor. He was often in plush hotel suites or in the guest quarters at a private estate—always paid for by a sponsor or some other benefactor. (The Clintons are cheap! Historian Nigel Hamilton writes that they did not even pay for their wedding reception, leaving it for a young friend of Hillary to pick up the tab.[1]) Perchance Bill was at a cocktail reception, looking dreamily into the eyes of some pretty thing who had just bathed in thirty minutes of a Clintonian sermonette. As likely as not, he was out of the country.

Back in his Arkansas days, once the Boy Governor had chatted his way through a reception, schmoozed with legislators, or emerged from a more intimate rendezvous, his state troopers recall that an upbeat Clinton would ring out with a favorite command: "Let's hit it." Off they would motor to the next stop on his itinerary. His whole adult life has been an itinerary. Since entering adulthood he has been constantly on the move, and never more so than during these first years out of office. Members of his Secret Service detail today describe an ex-president who is less reckless than he was in Arkansas. Then state troopers even had to hustle him out of parties where cocaine was out in the open and he an occasional user.[2] Often the host was his financial supporter Dan Lasater, and if the parties never earned Clinton a drug charge they were part of a pattern of recreational behavior that led to Lasater's conviction for cocaine distribution along with Roger Clinton, the governor's half-brother.[3] Roger received one of Clinton's last-minute pardons in 2001 while peddling pardons himself, one for a Mafioso. Lasater had won his pardon years before from then-Governor Clinton, who claimed to be moved by Lasater's plea that he needed his hunting license reinstated. A man has to feed his family!

Clinton's recent assignations have also been more discreet than during his White House years. If he ever brought a cutie back to Chappaqua during the first years of his retirement I have no report of it. After his memoir came out he took a few more chances, picking up with a hot Chappaqua divorcee in her early forties—admittedly a little long in the tooth for him—and repeatedly meeting, according to sources close to the Secret Service, with Canadian heiress Belinda Stronach at her Manhattan pad, which we shall get to later.[4] Those guarding him report that his current *modus operandi* usually involves one-night stands in the arms of a hostess during a lecture tour or brief liaisons abed with a groupie. This fits with his frenetic post-White House tempo. In the early years of his retirement the former president was probably more on the go than at any other time in his life.

In his first fourteen months out of office he averaged a speech practically every other day, nearly 200 in thirty countries on six continents.[5] (See Appendix I.) Faced with the uproar over his indecorous departure from the White House, he traveled the world. McAuliffe is right: Clinton was treated grandly abroad, and never more grandly than in Australia, where a Beijing front organization often footed the bill; in Hong Kong, where even more Chinese money flowed; and, of course, in the United Arab

Emirates, where he picked up lavish fees and properties. Nor were his hosts the only ones footing the bill: the American taxpayer covered the costs of his security detail, their salaries, travel costs, and hotel accommodations. Two thousand one would prove to be a successful year for the former Boy President, but it got off to an inauspicious start.

At first the press echoed with allegations and recriminations. By February investigations had begun on Capitol Hill. As we have seen, the Episodic Apologists were stewing through their longest episode of disappointment, longer than post-Monica, longer than post-grand jury. All this bad news had its maleficent effect, especially with the corporate world. Almost unique among modern presidents, Clinton was asked to join no corporate boards when he left the White House. Rumors that he would be invited to the board of Oracle Corporation, the software provider, drew a public demurral from Chairman Larry Ellison, "I think the President is quite busy right now."[6] As late as the spring of 2005, Clinton's Manhattan office could not tell me of any corporate board on which he served. God knows what has happened since.

Worse, corporate sponsors who had agreed months before to host his speeches got cold feet. An early February 2001 speech for Morgan Stanley Dean Witter for $100,000 drew such widespread disapproval from clients that the company's chairman publicly admitted his invitation to the controversial former president had been "a mistake." At another $100,000 payday that month, this time at New York's Grand Hyatt, a cosponsor, Credit Suisse First Boston, withdrew its name from the program and from press releases. "In light of current events, we have reduced our involvement," Credit Suisse's spokeswoman, Victoria Harmon, explained; though, she added, the bank remained the event's "cosponsor and will honor its financial obligations."[7] Before February was extinct, Oracle was under fire from investors for a speech arrangement it had with Clinton, reportedly for $125,000; and from London came word that the banking firm of UBS Warburg was withdrawing its sponsorship of a New York speech—another $100,000, *sayonara.*[8]

This retirement was not meeting the retiree's expectations. Even his social life was disappointing, particularly his nocturnal social life with the anticipated cuties. During his second administration, as revelations from his sexual harassment suit were made flesh and dwelt among us—in the ample flesh of Monica and the less plentiful flesh of Paula (soon to be pictured in her underpants in a men's magazine)—Hillary seethed.*

Contrary to her theatrics, Hillary had, of course, known about Bill's earlier infidelities. Clinton had been unfaithful to her as early as his courtship while she was in Washington working on the impeachment of President Richard Nixon. Bill was then campaigning for Congress in Arkansas. Hillary sent her father and brother down to keep an eye on him. In fact they married with the understanding that Hillary's husband would be wayward, as recent biographers such as Nigel Hamilton make clear. By 1981 she began hiring private investigators, a practice that was to lead by the 1990s to strong-arm tactics against his paramours and even against his political opponents and prosecutors. Hillary's ruthlessness should alarm political observers.

It is when Hillary's lawless side is glimpsed that the nickname Bruno commutes from mere jest to objective assessment. Even in the White House, Bruno had her informants keeping an eye on things. One was Evelyn Lieberman, Deputy Chief of Staff, who kept her informed of Monica and the rest in her husband's White House harem. Hillary also had a couple of bruisers on the White House staff. At the Office of Personnel Security she stationed the comic Craig Livingstone, an ex-bouncer whose Falstaffian rotundity evoked laughter throughout Washington when he was exposed, and Anthony Marceca, an ex-cop who was less amusing. It was Livingstone and Marceca who gathered the Republicans' FBI files for the Clinton White House.

Bruno's practice of maintaining private investigators began with her

---

*Earlier there had been the fleshy Gennifer (whose very dirty memoir of energetic sex with Bill is not to be missed).

employment in 1981 of Ivan Duda to catalogue her husband's women. Some suspected that she was going to use his catalogue of adulteresses to divorce Bill. Actually she was gearing up to return her husband to the governor's mansion. So wanton had his dissipations been after his 1980 defeat that Hillary feared personal morality would be an issue in the 1982 campaign. According to Duda, Hillary "wanted to be prepared for any charges that might come up" regarding scandal.[9] By 1992 Hillary's private investigators composed a small team of thugs who charged the Clinton campaign more than $100,000 to discredit and harass her husband's former girlfriends.[10] The Clintons expanded such operations throughout the 1990s against political opponents, prosecutors, and members of Congress, hiring the likes of Terry Lenzner, Jack Palladino, and Anthony Pellicano, the last of whom was sentenced in January 2004 for possession of military-grade plastic explosives and two hand grenades that had been fashioned into homemade bombs.

Though the Clintons' lawyers deny that the Clintons paid him, Pellicano assisted the Clintons as early as 1992, when he attempted to discredit Gennifer Flowers. By 1998 he was tapped to discredit Monica Lewinsky.[11] In early 2006 Pellicano was again in the news, this time as the chief thug in a scandal involving some of Hollywood's most celebrated personages. As a consequence he was indicted on wiretapping and conspiracy charges, instigating still more news stories, few of which ever mentioned his Clinton connection. Once again the Episodic Apologists suffered episodic amnesia.

Of course, neither Pellicano nor any of Hillary's other private investigators could shut down Monicagate or impeachment, though they did practice their arts in the shadows. A former independent counsel has told me that thugs threatened one of his colleagues, Kenneth Starr. My source admitted to being menaced himself on the streets of Washington, usually at night but at least once in daylight. The prosecutor took to carrying a gun.[12]

The lurid details of Monicagate posed a hazard to Hillary. By 1998, and contrary to what she deposits in her memoir, she was planning a political career of her own. With the counsel of her old crony, Harold Ickes, she had set her sights on a New York Senate seat. Bill's sexual exploits and his impeachment, however, had complicated matters. When she finally did decide to run, in November 1998, she laid down the law in a fortissimo that would haunt her husband's retirement. According to those familiar with the story, she announced that Bill's sordid past was about to be history. Never was he again to endanger her prospects for higher office with further scandalous liaisons gumming up her news cycles. As we shall see later in this chapter, testimony chronicled in *The Starr Report* will cast a shadow over her ultimate prospects for the presidency for years to come. Nevertheless, in late 1998 Hillary, with her political future in mind, issued her edict to Bill: No More Spectacular Sex Scandals. In retirement, Bill knew that Hillary had him under watch. It introduced into his life apprehensions he did not need—not good for the ticker or for his self-esteem. Bill has had to be careful.

At first he pushed his luck. He attempted flings with ladies of a higher class than the comfort women from the White House. That was imprudent. The White House *horizontales* were usually old girlfriends from Arkansas and various interns. Hillary was never as angered by these prosaic types as by the more glamorous, accomplished types that Bill might occasionally hook up with. When they entered the picture during Bill's early retirement she was furious. Moreover, this was her first year in the Senate. Another sex scandal could devastate her political future. Hillary's colossal rage, combined with Clinton's ongoing post-Pardongate headlines and the threatening congressional investigations, forced Bill to shove off for foreign shores.

Still jovial on the outside, Bill was angry within and adamant that, as always, he had "done nothing wrong." Yet, Boy Clinton is conflict-averse. We saw this as he quietly accommodated a Republican Congress and ducked the provocations of Osama bin Laden. And friends of the Clinton family can tell you he is *never* more conflict-adverse than when confronted by an angry Bruno.

So in March of 2001, off he flew to foreign parts in one of those spacious jets, talking points in hand: Vancouver, $150K; Maastricht, $150K; Baden-Baden, $250K; Copenhagen, $150K; back to America for a clean shirt and a change of linen; then Salem State College in Massachusetts, $125K. Soon it was off to Toronto, $125K; Hong Kong, $250K, and hours later, $250K more—on that one day, May 10, 2001, in Hong Kong, Bill had two gigs and half a million dollars (according to my researchers). However, in Hillary's Senate Financial Disclosure Report, only one Hong Kong appearance is recorded for May 10. Discrepancies, discrepancies, a Clinton trademark! Four days later, thousands of miles more on his odometer, and he was in Kysaker, Norway, $150K. (See Appendix I.) On he went, a forlorn Bill Clinton, a flesh and blood modern-day reenactment of *The Flying Dutchman*, that spectral ship of legend, that roams the world from port to port, a dreadful curse upon it. Though in Clinton's case, it was not so much a curse that was upon him as a ringing in his ears: Hillary's rant: "Avoid Rich Babes!"

Sir Walter Scott, in his note to *Rokeby*, sees the ghostly vessel as a ship plying the seas, bringing eerie calamity to those it encounters. Clinton, too, was a *Ghost Ship*, driven from home by an angry wife and an irate public. As for calamity, both Clintons have a history of having brought eerie calamity to friend and foe alike.

There has always seemed to be a strange curse attending the Clintons. So many of their friends and associates have suffered instant catastrophe. The sad fate of the McDougals, one dead and another in the clink, is grim evidence of this Clinton Curse. So is the fall of Webb Hubbell from high office in the Justice Department to jail and disgrace. Hillary's old law partner was not even repristinated with a last-minute pardon. Another of her law partners, Vince Foster, was the Curse's most tragic victim. Once Hillary's lover, he found himself overwhelmed and rejected in the turbulence of the Clinton White House.[13] Fearing he had failed his friends as White House lawyer, and doubtless stung by Hillary's coldness, he killed himself. Almost all the Clintons' Arkansas pals went down. Even some of their White House staffers suffered the Clinton Curse. As for the Curse's effect on the Clintons' enemies, I leave that for chapter four.

It has long been a conceit indulged in by Clinton and his friends that, of all modern presidents, the one he most closely resembles is John F. Kennedy, his boyhood hero. To be sure, the 1990s playboy president had JFK's capacity to charm, though JFK's was the charm of a matinee idol from Hollywood's golden era. Clinton's is more that of, well, of a rock star, one of the seedier ones, say, Jerry Lee Lewis. Both Kennedy and Clinton are remembered for their sense of fun and their power to connect with the public. Both were easily fetched by the fair sex, though Kennedy's women were usually chic, while Clinton's tastes have been, well, broader. Turning to their performance in office, arguably a similarity is perceptible there, too, if not in foreign policy where Clinton was comparatively inert, at least in domestic legislation where both presidents' legislative records are negligible.

Still, Kennedy was always the *soigné* gent. Clinton has been most notoriously the rogue, perhaps a big lovable lug to some, but still a rogue. Among recent presidents, a closer likeness to Clinton than JFK was struck by Clinton's fellow Southern *rastaquouere*, Lyndon Baines Johnson. The likeness begins with childhood and exists right down to their dismal retirements. Both shared shabby hayseed origins, though with more money in their families in their early days than either would admit while campaigning among their rube constituents. In childhood, both Billy and Lyndon lived in unhappy homes with dominant mothers and derelict fathers. Both were clever boys, possessed of a relentless drive for affection and for political advancement. Probably Johnson's libido was as excitable as Clinton's. Possibly he treated women as coarsely—although he was never publicly accused of rape, as was his Arkansas successor. Johnson was a vastly more effective president and for that reason, a worse president. His Great Society was an economic and social blight on the country, though arguably his civil rights legislation struck the greatest blow for racial equality since the presidency of Abraham Lincoln. Clinton essentially continued the Reaganite formula for prosperity under the pressure of a Republican Congress. Still the liberals rarely complained, again demonstrating the Clintons' mastery of their supporters' psychological needs. By the 1990s the liberals were in greater need of enemies and conspiracies to ponder than of public policies to legislate.

During Clinton's second administration when his sex life became, so to speak, fully exposed, his apologists argued that other modern presidents "did it" too. They mentioned FDR, Eisenhower, and Kennedy, but never Johnson. Neither Roosevelt nor Eisenhower deserves the charge. In his dying days Roosevelt, with his daughter's encouragement, reestablished a platonic friendship with an old flame, Lucy Mercer Rutherford. Sexual intimacy would have been physically impossible. This is not adultery. As for the apologists' charge against Ike it depends on conflicting evidence about an attractive enlisted woman who was his driver in the European theater during World War II. This is hardly the promiscuous sex Clinton pursued. It is amusing that the historically minded apologists never include Johnson in this list of presidential Casanovas. The forty-second president's likeness to Old Beagle Ears is understandably discomfiting.

In some ways Johnson's lonely retirement prefigured Bill's. Johnson went back to the ranch and contended with powerful emotions: anger, bewilderment, fright. Unlike Clinton, Johnson had no need to raise a fortune in retirement. He had acquired his own extensive holdings while only a senator. Moreover, at the end of his presidency he did not have Clinton's $11 million in legal bills or a grasping wife with presidential ambitions. Like Clinton, however, Johnson fretted over his legacy, fearing that his controversial presidency was likely to attract historians to the fetid corpus delicti. Both men wanted to get their side of the story out.

In writing his memoir Johnson, like Clinton later, brought in outside assistants. One was a twenty-five-year-old Harvard Ph.D. candidate known today as the historian Doris Kearns Goodman. The president met her in 1967 when she was a White House Fellow. From his retirement in 1969 to his death in 1973 the young researcher remained in tender intimacy with the ailing politico, working on his memoir and noting his decline. The stories she has related of Johnson in retirement bring Clinton's retirement to mind. In their retirement years as in their years spent hustling the limelight, both men were prodigious BS-ers and not just any kind of BS-ers but BS-ers of that classic type, the college-boy braggart. Clinton BS-ed a multitude of implausible achievements: reading "five or six books" a week while in the White House, reading hundreds of books while at Oxford, and, most famously, his fabulous achievements on the golf course, which the national press soon recognized as nonsense.[14] Typical of his easily refuted college-boy BS-ing was his claim during a 1996 radio address to "vivid and painful memories of black churches being burned in my own state when I was a child."* A day later, on June 9, the *Arkansas Democrat-Gazette* set the record straight. No such thing happened in Arkansas during the Boy President's childhood.[15]

Johnson's BS-ing was just as rich. Goodwin tells the delectable story of Johnson's histrionic complaint to her that he merely misspoke when in 1966 the journalist Hugh Sidey disapprovingly recorded Johnson's boast to our troops in Korea that his great-great-grandfather died at the Alamo. "God damn it," Johnson exploded to the young researcher as they researched his memoir, "why must all those journalists be such sticklers for detail? Why, they'd hold you to an accurate description of the first time you ever made love. . . . The fact is that my great-great-grandfather died in the Battle of San Jacinto, not the Alamo. When I said the Alamo, it was just a slip of the tongue." And he went on to recall his ancestor as "the hero" of San Jacinto.[16] Unfortunately, the rascal was in the presence of an aspiring Harvard historian. In due course she discovered that Johnson's great-great-grandfather died peacefully in bed having never served a day at San Jacinto. He served his country as a real estate salesman and probably a damn good one.

*It was an election year, and the Democrats, hoping to turn out their black supporters, confected a series of inflated stories about arson in black churches. Some of the arsons had taken place. Some were fabrications. None was racially motivated.

Despite his similarities with Clinton, Johnson's brief retirement before his heart gave out was grimmer than anything Clinton experienced even during bypass surgery. At least it was grimmer than anything I have detected in the travels of Clinton's *Ghost Ship*. The nubile Kearns tells us that by 1970 she would fly down from Cambridge to the former leader of the free world's ranch and find the sixty-two-year-old man in a hell of a heap: "His hair whitened; wrinkles appeared on his skin; hollows deepened beneath his eyes; the backs of his hands flecked with spots of brown . . . chest pains returned." He had become moody and occasionally disoriented. Now the old BS-er's tales had shifted from war stories to reveries of childhood. Will anything so pathetic as the following overtake Clinton?

"A curious ritual developed," Kearns recalls. After fitful sleep, Johnson was awakening at 5:30 a.m. "Terrified at lying alone in the dark," he would knock at Kearns's door, she reports, and in robe and pajamas shuffle into her bedroom. She attests that she began to anticipate these arrivals and got up even earlier, made her toilette, and seated herself—fully clothed (!)—in a chair near the waiting bed. Soon he would enter, and repair, to the bed. He would pull the sheets, she writes, "up to his neck" and they would talk. "In those dawn talks, I saw him as perhaps few others, except his wife and close friends, had seen him: crumpled, ragged, and defenseless. He spoke of the beginnings and the ends of things, of dreams and fantasies. His words seemed to flow from some deep well of sadness, nostalgia, and longing."[17]

No one with Clinton, even during his *Ghost Ship* drear, reports seeing him in such a state; but sources close to the Secret Service report that in retirement he does hate to be alone. His first months in Chappaqua were the worst, but even today he is lonely. In early 2001 a telephone was often at his ear, frequently late at night. In 2002 Julia Payne, a Clinton spokeswoman, told a *Newsweek* reporter, "One night last year he called about 1:00 a.m. ranting and raving about something. And I said, 'Sir, are you watching Fox again?'"[18] He had become restless and often irritable, at first lumbering around his property, then lumbering around the world. Journalistic accounts of his BS-ing into the early morning hours with trapped staffers and writers were commonplace by 2005 and 2006, so much so that readers presumed he was a drinker. Not so; Bill is not even a modest tippler.

For a born klutz, this lumbering could be dangerous. While president the big lug was known for one fall in particular, the time he tore up a knee, supposedly after tripping on a stairway at golfer Greg Norman's Florida mansion. (Actually, he damaged the knee in a poolside fall while pursuing a cutie.[19]) In the first week of his retirement he suffered another famous fall after going out on the driveway at Chappaqua to throw a tennis ball for Buddy, his chocolate Labrador. Still the clumsy kid forever teased by his Arkansas classmates (his public jogs during the presidency were always studies in slow motion), Clinton tripped over the dog and fell to the ground. "You guys got a good shot," he whined to nearby reporters. "That's the first time he's knocked me down in all the time we've been together."[20] Well, most probably it was not the first time; but it may have been the last. A year later, almost to the day, Buddy, having been abandoned by his absentee owners, was hit by a car after bolting from the house. Only the Secret Service's backup team was around to take the ex-presidential dog to the Chappaqua Animal Hospital. There Buddy, a fixture in the Clinton family since joining it as a pup just before the Lewinsky scandal broke, was pronounced dead. Even the animal world is not exempt from the Clinton Curse. At the time, the Clintons were in Acapulco. Soon thereafter Buddy's bereaved owner was off to Dubai, $300K; Cairo, $175K; back to Dubai, $300K; on to Tel Aviv, $150K. After Tel Aviv he returned home briefly, then on to Palo Alto, $125K, and to Santa Barbara, $125K. There he ended the sad month, dogless but much closer to the millions he envisaged.

Clinton's $600,000 paydays in Dubai (January 17 and January 20) deserve further reflection, for his relations with Dubai highlight another irregularity of Clinton's retirement. Just as no president ever became so dependent on foreign campaign contributions during his presidency (as we shall see regarding the Chinese in chapter five), no president became so dependent on foreign money in his retirement or so willing to rent his influence illegally to foreign powers. When, in early 2006, a political firestorm arose over the takeover of some United States port operations by a Dubai company, Dubai World Ports, questions followed over whether Clinton had acted as an agent of the United Arab Emirates (UAE) without following the law and registering as an "Agent of a Foreign Principal." His rewards from Dubai have been munificent. After his $600,000 take in January of 2002, he had another $150,000 payday in June for speaking at Dubai's American University. UAE officials also donated between $500,000 and $1 million to the Clinton Library. A source in the UAE government reports that he earned another $300,000 in 2005. Another source has told me that in Dubai Clinton has been given two luxury apartments.[21]

In February of 2006, as news of the ports deal hit the headlines, it was reported by columnist Robert Novak and by the *American Spectator*'s "Washington Prowler" that Clinton was making calls on Dubai's behalf and cutting such Clintonistas as former press secretary Joe Lockhart and Vernon Jordan in on the deal. By March, lawyers at the Department of Justice's Office of Legal Counsel were beginning to review whether Clinton had registered as an "Agent of a Foreign Principal." According to federal law, anyone doing political or public affairs work on behalf of a foreign country, agency, or official must register and update his status every six months. Clinton had not. Yet the same source that informed me of Clinton's fancy pads in Dubai told me that when the ports crisis blew Clinton called a high-level UAE official offering his services. And just to make this a typical Clinton scandal, Hillary weighed in, telling the press that she had no idea of her husband's involvement in Dubai. She was then leading the Democrats' opposition to the deal. It was another gratuitous and easily dispatched lie. "She was also very much aware of President Clinton's financial arrangements with the UAE," a former Bill Clinton staffer told the Washington Prowler. "We're talking about more than a million dollars, some of it paid out soon after they left the White House. That income helped the Clintons buy the properties that allow them to live both in New York and in Washington." Or perhaps the senator does not read her own financial filings.

The Clintons have been a trial for the Secret Service. Other presidents and vice presidents have usually developed splendid rapport with their Secret Service details, taking pride in the Service's high degree of professionalism, loyalty, and, of course, courage. The agents reciprocate, often assisting their principals beyond the call of duty consistent with their regulations; for instance, those regulations governing integrity and their readiness for protective action—two areas the Clintons seem to have especially disdained in their dealings with their Secret Service guards.

I recall a particularly poignant instance of the Secret Service's loyalty when I was a consultant to Vice President Spiro Agnew. He wanted me to serve as a speechwriter and, after I begged off, he hired me as a consultant, allowing me to travel a bit with him and get a sense of the White House. Then, overnight he was transformed from being vice president of the United States to being ex-vice president and the vilified signatory to an embarrassing *nolo contendere* for tax evasion. Agnew, the paladin of the "Silent Majority," was, of a sudden, out on his ear and soon to be relieved of Secret Service protection. Yet a bond of friendship had grown up around the agents and their disgraced boss. They volunteered when off duty to move his effects out of his office in the Old Executive Office Building and into his temporary offices on Lafayette Square—years later at his death the same agents prevailed on his wife to expand the small funeral service she had planned so that they could pay their respects. Such bonds between members of the Secret Service and the family they protect are not unusual.

Regarding the Secret Service, I admit to a prejudice in their favor. In my library hangs a huge picture of Abraham Lincoln bearing a bronze plaque:

Presented To
P.D. Tyrrell, U.S.S.S.
—By—
Robert T. Lincoln
April 14th, 1887
For Loyalty And Service To His Father
Abraham Lincoln

P. D. Tyrrell is my great-great-grandfather, who, though born in Dublin in 1831, rose to head the Secret Service in Chicago where the agency's work mainly involved breaking counterfeiting rings, one of which planned to steal Lincoln's body from its crypt in Springfield, Illinois, bury it in the Indiana dunes by Lake Michigan, and ransom it for $200,000 and the release of an accomplished counterfeiter, Benjamin F. Boyd, whom Captain Tyrrell had already landed in Joliet State Prison. Before ambushing the body snatchers as they approached the crypt under cover of darkness, Tyrrell explained his intent to the dead president's son, Robert. Body snatching not being precisely a counterfeiting case, Tyrrell's Secret Service involvement was unorthodox. In his new book, *Stealing Lincoln's Body*, Thomas J. Craughwell writes that Lincoln "remained exquisitely detached" as he listened to Tyrrell describing what the agent called "such a horrible and Damnable an act." Impassively, Lincoln offered "assurance that Tyrrell could count on him for any assistance" in what was surely the Secret Service's earliest involvements in presidential security.[22] After the culprits were arrested, Tyrrell's reward was the picture and the plaque—a private gesture that would be illegal today.*

When I traveled with the vice president to Chicago before his fall I regaled his aide, David Keene, with tales of P.D. Tyrrell, "the Sherlock Holmes of his day," as I put it. Keene turned to an old Chicago agent

*George Washington's remains had been the target of an 1830 plot by a body snatcher who either wanted the First President's body for a relic or for scientific inquiry.

accompanying our party and asked, "Ever hear of him?" "That would be Pat Tyrrell," the old boy said, "my predecessor here." The anecdote suggests another characteristic of the Secret Service, its institutional memory. In 1988, when members of President Ronald Reagan's Secret Service detail visited my Virginia home, in preparation for a dinner the Old Cowboy was to attend there, one agent, Special Agent Daniel J. Sullivan, espied the Lincoln picture and declared me a "member of the Secret Service family." He gave me a pair of Secret Service cuff links to seal the bond. My admiration for the Service solidified.

No first family has ever been known to treat its detail as rudely as the Clintons (though in researching this book I found to my surprise that the Gore family also was known to treat its Secret Service detail shabbily). The Clinton stories are always the same, treating their agents like menial servants, disregarding their procedures, placing them in compromising situations. An FBI agent familiar with the problem from his investigations of Arkansas corruption notes that the Clintons' mistreatment of bodyguards began back in Arkansas, where they treated their state troopers even worse than they were to treat the Secret Service. Apparently they came to trust some of these troopers. According to my FBI source, when the Clintons came to Washington they planned to bring Arkansas troopers to the White House to supplant the Secret Service.[23]

Hillary felt it best to have a cordon of trusted troopers around the family when she blew her top at her husband. Such explosions had been regular events at the governor's mansion, causing the cook, Miss Emma, after an especially sulphurous eruption, to lament, "The devil's in that woman." As a trooper recalls the story, Hillary accosted the governor screaming, "mother f---er, c--- sucker, and everything else."[24] Recalling the Clintons' hopes to replace their Secret Service detail with proven loyalists from the Arkansas state police, the FBI agent concludes: "Same as the Travel Office scandal. They wanted to bring in what in Arkansas would be called 'our people.'"[25]

Equally fantastical, the Clintons wanted to put an Arkansas state trooper in charge of the "football," the attaché case containing the Pentagon's launch codes referred to earlier in chapter one, which Clinton treated so negligently. Naturally the launch codes are entrusted to a seasoned military officer. The troopers were never brought into the White House either as bodyguards or to carry the football; but the Clintons, particularly Hillary, were never comfortable with the higher professionalism of the Secret Service, or, for that matter, of their White House military aides. In Arkansas she could send her bodyguards to run errands—a trooper has recalled purchasing tampons.[26] With the Secret Service that kind of indulgence was more difficult to pull off. So, too, was her habit of ordering bodyguards to carry her bags. By protocol Secret Service agents are to keep their hands free for instant response to attack. But those idle hands always tempted the First Lady to treat her Secret Service guards as bellboys. If an agent refused her importunities, all hell might break loose. I have talked with some who did refuse. They were soon reassigned to more serene duties. Bearing in mind both Clintons' lifelong interest in government at the highest level, it is astounding that they would continue to risk controversy over such trivial demands.[27]

Beyond regularly cursing at military aides and Secret Service agents, there is at least one account of Hillary assaulting an agent. Prone as the impulsive Clintons were to spur-of-the-moment schedule changes, they might, of a sudden, request the presidential limousine without warning, and woe to the driver who arrived late. On one occasion Hillary actually beaned her driver from the back of the car with a book as the Clintons drove off to a hastily called dinner.[28] At least one military aide took revenge. In the mid-1990s, he began leaving his issues of the *American Spectator* lying around where the Clintons would see them. Of course, he was careful to remove his address label.[29]

The consensus explanation offered by Secret Service agents and by military personnel who suffered these indignities is that the Clintons, though immensely learned in the logistics of politics, simply had no idea how the White House actually worked. The White House has, as one of

Clinton's military aides told me, a military infrastructure of over 2,500 individuals tasked with everything from daily meals, to communications, to all the responsibilities attendant with the football. Eight years later, when the Clintons left, the consensus was that they were only marginally better informed, albeit they had become more adroit in concealing their blunders. Years from now one can imagine a school of revisionist historians arguing that the Clintons' White House scandals were often a consequence of their failure to learn the standards and practices of the presidency. If the revisionists take into account the Clintons' character flaws, especially their 1960s narcissism, they may have a point.

The couple's treatment of the military and the Secret Service never improved. In the hallways of the White House both military aides and Secret Service agents were instructed to avoid making "eye-contact" with the Clintons. In fact, they were told to make themselves scarce.[30] As mentioned earlier in this book, during the Clintons' post-White House years there was an unusually high turnover in their Secret Service detail. Many agents found the Clintons' rudeness even more difficult to endure after they became the ex-First Family. A typical example of this rudeness occurred when a sudden rainstorm hit Chappaqua in mid-2001. Scurrying from the downpour, the agents took shelter under the eaves of the Clinton house until Hillary spotted them. Typically, she exploded; and they were ordered to trudge back through the rain to their guardhouse.[31]

Not surprisingly, agents who have worked for the Clintons detest Hillary, while holding a slightly amused, if condescending, appraisal of the ex-president. Hillary's problems with the Secret Service have continued on into her Senate career, where she has created and exploited antagonisms between her Secret Service detail and the U.S. Capitol Police charged with guarding Senate offices. The Secret Service's relations with Bill are more cordial. He is friendlier, less demanding, and naturally entertaining. Where Hillary is hostile—even violent—and cold towards them, Bill is easygoing and, if not considerate, at least usually amiable.

The Clintons' domestic rows have always caused problems both for their bodyguards and for their sorely pressed public staff. Three months after his first inauguration the president appeared in public with what *Newsday* described as a "two-inch gash" on the right side of his face. There was a second wound on his neck. Then began the cover-up—always a Clinton specialty. The White House press secretary explained the wound as the result of a shaving accident. Unfortunately, in this cover-up not everyone was "on message." The victim dismissed his disfigurement as having been incurred during a playful wrestling match with his daughter, then thirteen years old. Reporters brought the discrepancy to the attention of Communications Director George Stephanopoulos and heightened tensions with questions about recent rumors that Hillary had walloped the president with a Bible or perhaps an urn. Stephanopoulos attempted a change of subject. Controversy heightened.[32] Today the marriage is more serene, perhaps because the Clintons are rarely together. Sources close to the Secret Service, however, do report that dreadful altercations have erupted several times: in September 2001, January 2002, August 2002, April 2003, and May 2004.

Always, according to one source, it has been "verbal violence between Hillary and Bill on his sexual escapades. The issue in all cases was that she does not care what he does as long as he maintains secrecy. The 'verbal violence' includes yelling, screaming, throwing of soft and hard objects, breakage of vases and glasses and just plain nastiness."[33] There is nothing new here. Such hostilities have been reported throughout their marriage. Their response is the same as it is to most indelicate stories about them, to wit: all are "lies" or "exaggerations" or "old news," fashioned by political enemies. Yet the persistence of such "lies" and "exaggerations" surely constitutes some level of validation. No other First Family has suffered them. In fact, there are no reports of domestic violence in the rocky marriages of the Kennedys or the Johnsons to say nothing of the more conventional marriages of the Trumans, the Eisenhowers, the Nixons, the Carters, or in either of the Bushes' marriages. The Reagans' marriage was an extended love affair. Even Gerald

Ford's anxious days with Betty were unaccompanied by reports of facial lacerations, flying vases, or obscenities.

Historians chronicling the Clintons' lives will have spent more time interviewing lawyers, prosecutors, police officers, and federal agents, than historians chronicling the lives of any other first family, though earlier historians might have had similar interviews if the presidential ambitions of Aaron Burr had been realized, or if Warren Harding had sweated through a second term. And, considering all the law enforcement officials that historians of the Clinton Saga will have had to interview, will any ever stumble across this bizarre and ribald fact? With the exception of their fundraising scandals and that famous real estate venture known as Whitewater, every other Clinton scandal was the consequence of that sempiternal turbulence in Bill's pants.

Born without a libido, Clinton would have presided over a much different presidency. To be sure, it would have had an abundance of lesser scandals, for Clinton's fundamental problem is low character not high testosterone. The scandals, however, would have been more prosaic. While interviewing law enforcement personnel charged with either protecting him or with investigating him, I have been amazed at how often they were telling me of intrigues, abuses of power, misdemeanors, and occasional felonies, committed because Clinton had suffered sudden sexual arousal.

As I mentioned earlier in this book, the coarse nature of Clinton's sex life seems to offend these law enforcement types. I think it explains why so many around him have so little loyalty to him. JFK's liaisons were discreet. He was a gent. Bill was a dog, and his bodyguards look down on him. In fact, as a field hound's entire anatomy is animated by its energetic nose, likewise the forty-second president's entire anatomy has usually been animated by only one organ. That this particular organ so frequently decided the course of American history in the 1990s is an inescapable fact. How this fact will be taught to the nation's youth is an intriguing question. Perhaps the presidency of William Jefferson Clinton will figure in their sex education courses. At a December 7, 1998 press conference during the Lewinsky drama, a reporter, citing the national incidence of various sexually transmitted diseases ("three million new cases of chlamydia, 650,000 new cases of gonorrhea"), asked press secretary Joe Lockhart, "Has the Secret Service, in their obligation to protect the president, asked that Monica Lewinsky be tested?"[34]

A few choice revelations contained in *The Starr Report* should demonstrate what I mean when I refer to Clinton's sex life as being coarse. Along with other revelations from the *Report* (some of which I shall quote at length later in this chapter), they should adumbrate why Hillary cannot be altogether confident that her political future can be insulated from her Animal House years at the White House. Even if Bill follows her edict, No More Spectacular Sex Scandals, there is still this historically unprecedented period of deviant behavior.

It was a blustery Sunday afternoon, January 7, the first day of the Blizzard of 1996. Young Miss Lewinsky was snuggled up in the warmth of her Watergate apartment. A call came from the White House. "This," she remembered to prosecutors, "is the first time he called me at home. . . . And I asked him what he was doing." The President of the United States told his twenty-two-year-old intern that he was "going into the office soon." She replied, "Oh, do you want some company?" Said the president, "Oh, that would be great."[35] Now, this is not so bad. The Boy President could have replied, "*Cooool.*" When Lewinsky asked him what he was doing, he could have said he was "*just hangin' out.*"

At any rate, the two made plans to meet that afternoon at the door of the Oval Office. They got past Secret Service Uniformed Officer Lew Fox and reposed for a brief chat on a sofa in the Oval Office before repairing to the lavatory. As *The Starr Report* pithily puts it, "she and the president kissed, and he touched her breasts with his hands and his mouth. The president 'was talking about performing oral sex on me,' according to Ms. Lewinsky. But she stopped him because she was menstruating and he did not. Ms. Lewinsky did perform oral sex on him."[36] This is not good, but there is more. In the *Report's* Notes, note 28 records, "They engaged in oral-anal contact as well."[37] Turning to the *Appendix to the Starr Report* for amplification, we see that the prosecutor, Karin Immergut, questions Lewinsky further on this matter. The questions and answers have been redacted in the *Appendix*, but sources familiar with the questioning recall that Lewinsky said that the president proceeded to masturbate—a frequent practice of his during their White House trysts, so not unusual—and she licked his anus.[38] Well, after all, his pants *were* off.

It is with clinical precision that I have termed the sexual contacts described in *The Starr Report* as zoo sex. Compared with this president and his intern, the monkeys on Monkey Island at the zoo are more fastidious. Though the male monkeys are usually more aggressive. A careful reading of *The Starr Report* reveals this president, once again, as being amazingly passive. His lover—if that is what we call her—made all the initial advances. In fact, she seduced him. He simply sedentarily received her ravenous attentions. Actually, he is lucky that he was not injured. After responding to Immergut's questions, Lewinsky expressed discomfort that her parents might find out about this incident but no discomfort at telling it to the assembled prosecutors and support staff, which reveals an additional problem the Clintons had during the Lewinsky scandal, to wit: Monica was an incontinent blabbermouth.[39] She would tell the prosecutors *everything* and in *graphic detail.* I have discussed her depositions with seasoned sex offense investigators. Most agree Lewinsky was unnecessarily forthcoming about her sexual encounters with the president. In some ways these two narcissists, though born a generation apart, were cast from the same mold.

It is almost impossible to conceive of any of America's handful of promiscuous presidents engaging in such behavior, certainly not in the White House—not JFK, and probably not LBJ. Possibly the pathetic Harding would, but then Harding would at least have been deliriously in love.

The Secret Service agents attached to Clinton in retirement have not been faced with the security problems encountered earlier by the state troopers and later by Secret Service agents in the White House. They have not had to turn away military aides tasked to bring messages to the president because he was copulating behind closed doors. Nor have they been threatened with termination by his secretary, Betty Currie, for incautious moments with Lewinsky. That regrettable contretemps took place when Lewinsky was fuming in the guard booth at the White House's northwest gate. Clinton had delayed her visit with him, claiming he was meeting with lawyers. When an agent let slip that the president was not actually with his lawyers but rather with the leggy Eleanor Mondale, there was a dreadful blowup.[40]

Even after the Lewinsky scandal broke into the open, two past military aides, a retired Secret Service agent, and two permanent White House employees report, Clinton would be "consoled" by two other White House interns.[41] During the Lewinsky scandal, my researchers at the *American Spectator* gathered a list of seven White House staffers, five of them interns, whom Clinton used as comfort women. None would go public. One was at some point accosted in a D.C. coffeehouse, supposedly to silence her.[42] Arkansas state trooper L.D. Brown, one of Clinton's bodyguards with whom he built up a genuine, if short-lived, friendship, predicted that Clinton would compromise the Secret Service much as he had compromised the Arkansas state police. It never got that bad, but frequently Clinton put the Secret Service in difficult situations.

The retired Clinton is more circumspect. According to a source close to the Secret Service, "Clinton has changed his behavior in the sense that he is extremely publicity- and security-conscious and will go to extremes to hide his activities from Hillary, the media and even from his detail. The reduced media attention in recent years has also been a great assistance to him. This has allowed him to pursue various females without creating a high attention level. Secret Service sources—with a somewhat more relaxed approach to his security (i.e., dramatically reduced advance work)—report on a private basis that he will occasionally spend the night at houses of hosts where he was only expected for dinner." Most of his one-night stands have taken place during his foreign trips, often with hired hostesses. "He has purchased gifts clearly aimed at females, including string bikinis (in Rio), perfume (in Sydney), embroidered towels (in Paris), and sent roses (yellow, two dozen each time) on two occasions from a hotel in London."[43]

Clinton's nightlife does remain at least somewhat reckless. He is known to flout warnings from security personnel against entering the kind of off-the-beaten-path nightspots that the nocturnal Clinton has gravitated to since his early public life in Arkansas. Sources in the New York Police Department's Dignitary Protective Unit, which scouts public accommodations before the former president arrives (they call the work "farming"), report that he is an ongoing problem for them. His affinity for "off-the-beaten-path" night spots means members of the Dignitary Protective Unit have to do advance work to anticipate security problems, which they report to his Secret Service detail. They have, over the last few years, notified the detail of compromising conditions, namely, the propinquity of fast women and drug users. Invariably Clinton and his party go anyway. As a consequence of his recent prosperity, Clinton is now fond of small obscure restaurants on Manhattan's posh Upper East Side that are frequented by the young set. The joints present the Secret Service with additional security problems because they are often a few steps down from the sidewalk.[44]

If Clinton's sex life in retirement is less apt to break into the headlines, that does not mean his sexual recreations will never make headlines anew. Hillary and Bill surely know that the day may come when world attention fastens again on Clinton's most intimate ruttings. This time the news stories are likely to be even more graphic than Lewinsky's testimony to the independent counsel. There are tapes.

We know how disclosures from Nixon's Oval Office tapes have continued to bring fresh disrepute to the thirty-seventh president decades after Watergate. What will happen if the tapes of President Clinton's phone sex with Monica (and probably others) make their way into the public domain, perhaps after being sold or leaked by the foreign intelligence agents who almost certainly have them? *The Starr Report* states that Lewinsky "spoke on the telephone with the President approximately 50 times, often after 10:00 p.m. and sometimes well after midnight." It gets worse: "On 10 to 15 occasions, she and the President had phone sex.* After phone sex late one night, the President fell asleep, mid-conversation."[45] But did foreign intelligence eavesdroppers—most likely from France, Israel, and Russia—fall asleep? Intelligence experts know that the aforementioned countries had the capacity to snatch these calls from the airways, which summons another thought. The most controversial recipient of a Clinton pardon, Marc Rich, was close to agents from at least one of these countries, possibly all three.

It is a problem that should haunt the forty-second president's retirement. His March 29, 1997, cavortings with Lewinsky as chronicled in *The Starr Report* are relevant here:

> According to Ms. Lewinsky, their sexual encounter began with a sudden kiss: "This was another of those occasions when I was babbling on about something, and he just kissed me, kind of to shut me up, I think." The President unbuttoned her blouse and touched her breasts without removing her bra. "He went to go put his hand down my pants, and then I unzipped them because it was easier. And I didn't have any panties on. And so he manually stimulated me." [The inestimable value of a sound sex education for service in government is manifest here, no?] According to Ms. Lewinsky, "I wanted him to touch my genitals with his genitals" and he did so, lightly and without penetration. Then Ms. Lewinsky performed oral sex on him, again until he ejaculated.

*"Phone sex," as defined by the authoritative *Starr Report* on page 416, "occurs when one or both parties masturbate while one or both parties talk in a sexually explicit manner on the telephone."

> According to Ms. Lewinsky, she and the President had a lengthy conversation that day. He told her that he suspected a foreign embassy (he did not specify which one) was tapping his telephones, he proposed cover stories. If ever questioned, she should say that the two of them were just friends. If anyone ever asked about their phone sex, she should say that they knew their calls were being monitored all along, and the phone sex was just a put-on.[46]

There is evidence throughout Clinton's public life that he is a very intelligent fellow, but then there is the above.

Bill Clinton's *Ghost Ship* was launched across the seas by scandals that he and his wife had perpetrated in the last days of his presidency, by his hope to make a fortune, and by his fear of Hillary. This fear differs from his earlier apprehensions about Hillary. The marriage has changed.

Some have always concluded that the Clinton marriage has been a marriage of convenience, she being his enabler, he being her political ticket to the future. The marriage has been that, but it has been also something more colorful, to wit: a typical European playboy's marriage. Given its Arkansas provenance, this might seem incongruous; but remember that Bill and Hillary began dating at cosmopolitan Yale, and Bill went on to Oxford, from where he made wide-ranging excursions across the continent. There the playboy's marriage features: 1) a rascally playboy bringing fizz to his life by chasing skirts and hoodwinking his ever-vigilant wife, and 2) a busybody, sternly maternal wife, bringing huge self-esteem to herself by patrolling her husband's recreations. All things considered these are satisfying marriages for both spouses, though there is always the threat of flying china and lacerations on the face and neck.

By the end of the Clinton presidency, shadows had crept upon these happy two. Hillary had struck out on her own with her own political career. Dick Morris, the Clintons' longtime political adviser, claims it has always been "the deal" between the Clintons that after Bill's political moment had passed, it would be Hillary's turn. In 1990 they explored the possibility of her campaigning for the governorship, though the idea wilted as his presidential plans took shape.[47]

Notwithstanding all the scandals of Bill's governorship, the Clintons had decided to seek the 1992 Democratic presidential nomination. One of the legends of the Clinton Saga is that throughout their marriage they planned Bill's run for the presidency. Actually, as their open marriage entangled them in ever more scandals, there were years when they all but gave up hope. Purely by accident, I had sources around them and Hillary in particular grew pessimistic in the 1980s. David Marannis reported in the mid-1990s that Clinton's political adviser, Betsey Wright, convincingly warned him against a 1988 presidential campaign because of the governor's lurid escapades with women and with the Arkansas troopers, who procured them.[48] By 1992, however, the Clintons had overcome their hesitancy. Some will perceive this as evidence of their political shrewdness. More likely it is a sign of their arrogance. The scandals of his past repeatedly became national headlines during his primary campaign. All that saved him was a cultural shift that even the Clintons did not appreciate.

American culture had shifted into the hands of their fellow 1960s "kids." The new generation of journalists in the newsrooms and profs in academe shared their prejudices and sympathies. Any prior presidential candidate with such a record of corruption and personal failings would have been booted from the race halfway through the Clinton exposés. Documents detailing Clinton's draft evasion? Tapes of Clinton coaching Gennifer Flowers to lie to the press? Clinton was always reprieved, and once in the White House the Clintons' character flaws instigated more scandals than any previous presidential administration. Ironically, every time a Clinton scandal was exposed throughout the 1990s, sources told me that the Clintons expected the worst. Every time the worst never came. Thus halfway through the second term Hillary was readying herself for her own crack at high office—once again, arrogance. Beyond their turpitude, it was Hillary's egregious political judgment that accounted for the mess they had made of things. Yet she entered the political arena anyway.

Travelgate and Filegate could be traced to her. Her refusal to release Whitewater documents got the Clintons their endless adventures with independent counsels. Her refusal to accept a relatively painless settlement in Paula Corbin Jones' sexual harassment lawsuit triggered the discovery process that turned up Lewinsky. Through most of their marriage, Hillary's political judgment had been downright dangerous. Yet throughout 1998, as Monica babbled on and Bill further ensnared himself by lying under oath, Hillary began to contemplate a Senate seat—again arrogance.

One of the earliest public mentions of Hillary running for the Senate from New York came in a Jack Anderson column written by his partner Dale Van Atta in late November.[49] Earlier in the month Senator Daniel Patrick Moynihan announced his plans to retire as New York's senior senator in 2000. On November 6, 1998, the day the announcement was leaked to the public, New York Congressman Charles Rangel called the White House urging Hillary to run for the open seat. In her memoir, *Living History,* she claims she considered the suggestion "absurd." She claims that it would take months before she made a decision and then only after an irresistible public clamor for her candidacy had arisen throughout the Republic. Here is another of her gratuitous lies, perpetuated, I assume, out of contempt for the public—again, arrogance.

Actually Van Atta's sources told him she had probably decided to run for Moynihan's seat within days of his retirement announcement. Among the friends who encouraged her to run was Secretary of Health and Human Services, Donna Shalala; and Hillary had another advocate. Somewhat surprisingly, the former secretary of defense in Richard Nixon's cabinet, Mel Laird—a friend of Hillary's from her Republican youth—had reviewed her prospects at Shalala's behest. He was optimistic and predicted to Van Atta that Hillary would run and win.

After some typical Hillary missteps, she proved to be a competent campaigner, then a capable senator. She sensed the country's drift towards center-right and adapted to the times. But, as mentioned, her marriage has dramatically changed. After laying down the law to Bill about Spectacular Sex Scandals, Hillary has immersed herself in Democratic politics. The Clintons live pretty much isolated from each other. Bill is counselor and fundraiser. Periods pass with no communication. When they do talk, it is on the telephone and then usually about politics and her advancement.

Clinton will come to Washington and not even enter their Embassy Row residence, sleeping elsewhere. This can cause embarrassment. Early in 2004 Clinton arrived in town for a Democratic unity dinner. His New York staff created mild panic in requesting that the featured speaker be given a suite at the hotel where they assumed the fundraiser was being held. The venue was the National Building Museum, which had no guest suite. Though a Democratic National Committee organizer of the event recognized, as he said, that a suite "was a standard request for them," he assumed that as the Clintons' Washington home was but four miles away all would be well. Informed by the Clinton staff that their boss preferred a hotel room, the event organizer insisted, "I guess he's got to go home."[50]

Two scenes provide color and light on these two unusual politicos. The first takes place in June of 1999, when Hillary is still playing the disingenuous role of unwilling candidate—seven months after her decision had been made. She is toying with some of her most devoted friends. The second scene reminds us of the hard-boiled pol that Bill's libido has helped her become.

It is a mellow June evening in 1999 at 1600 Pennsylvania Avenue. Hillary is aglow. She has retired to the glass-enclosed third-floor solarium. Below, a dinner-dance for her thirtieth Wellesley class reunion continues. The Boy President has remained for the dance and the conviviality. True to form, his less gregarious wife has slipped away, changed into casual clothes, and settled in with a half-dozen old friends.

All are spending the night at the White House. These friendships go back decades. Hillary's old Wellesley mentor, political science prof Alan Schechter and his wife have been assigned the Lincoln Bedroom. Jan Piercey, a longtime confidante and former Wellesley roommate, now Executive Director of the World Bank, is here with her husband, Glen, and their precocious ten-year-old daughter, Lissa, who is fulfilling her dream of a night in the White House. Johanna Branson, another college roommate, now a Boston art professor and historian, has brought along her husband, Jock Gill.

One by one they depart the dance and repair to the solarium, wine and soda glasses in hand, knowing that this is the way their old friend would like to end the evening, quietly and with friends she trusts. This "very private First Lady" might want to ruminate on the past and contemplate her future, which at the time was the stuff of Washington rumors. It is about 10:00 p.m. as the old friends fall into talking—shoes off, coats off, with blonde Lissa snuggling under Hillary's arm on the beige couch.

It is Hillary who raises the subject no one else dares to raise: her possible run for the U.S. Senate in New York. "Jan thinks this is a crazy thing I'm contemplating," says Hillary, baiting her friend.

"I never said that, Hillary, because I'd never give you political advice," Jan responds. Gill plays devil's advocate, throwing out all the reasons that Hillary should not subject herself to more political abuse. After the White House she could be enjoying the closest thing to *noblesse oblige* that America offers its demiroyalty. Has she considered the opportunities?

She had and was particularly fetched by the offer of a philanthropic foundation that some wealthy benefactors offered to set up to promote her causes. "But," Hillary laments, "I would always be viewed as *former First Lady*. It would be 'former First Lady said such and such. . . .'" Her friends got the message. Hillary was now ready to stand on her own and earn new stature. Gill was persistent that night. Why attempt a political career? Politicians had already treated her to enough discourtesy. "I just feel so committed," Hillary said firmly. "I'm not satisfied with what we've done. *I'm* not done." Gill perseveres. He mentions the intrusiveness of the New York press, its willingness to dig up the muck of all those past Clinton scandals. Possibly it will discover new scandals.

"I know that. I'm aware of it. I've been through it, and I am prepared for it," is her firm response. "You know, for years—for *decades*—I have written legal briefs. I have given speeches. And I have lobbied Congress. I have been standing *outside*, knocking on the door, while they set policy and pass laws. I'd like to be on the inside making the case. I've been on the outside too long," replies the former First Lady of Arkansas and the most politically involved First Lady in Washington since Eleanor Roosevelt.

But why New York? Hillary's response that night should have made clear that this campaign train had already left the station. She admitted to having looked "at some other possible states. But they have a number of very-qualified people running who worked hard and long to be congressional candidates." In New York the only other Democratic contender, Congresswoman Nita Lowey, had telephoned that very afternoon to say that the field was open for Hillary. Lowey would not run. This was candidacy-by-acclamation, explained Hillary. "I'm being drafted. It is so rare to be drafted in this way. The nature of politics is such that you have to seize the moment when and if it comes, or it may never come again."

Her friends that night felt they had witnessed a historic moment. Unspoken then, but uttered since, was their collective conclusion that this New York race could be her springboard to the presidency. It could come as early as 2004, if a Republican were to win the White House in the next year. The idea of President Hillary had been with Hillary and her Wellesley friends for thirty years, ever since she gained national prominence as student body president for delivering Wellesley's first graduation speech by a student. She had been featured in *Life* magazine. "A lot of us thought then that Hillary would be the first woman president," one of her old classmates attests. "I thought if ever in my lifetime there is a woman president, it would be her."[51]

Well, possibly, but in a second scene worth reporting it becomes apparent that Hillary's future has many shadows on it. She is not the ingénue she played that June night in the solarium. And she does have baggage from Bill's presidency. In August 2001, in an unguarded moment of conversation with Congresswoman Nancy Pelosi, soon to be House Minority Leader, a currently serving Capitol Hill police officer standing two feet away heard Hillary snap, Bill "f---ed" Denise.[52]

The reference was to Denise Rich, the former wife of Marc Rich, the most controversial recipient of a last-minute presidential pardon. A generous Democratic supporter, Denise had given $1 million to the Democratic Party and at least $450,000 to the Clinton Library. A month before Senator Clinton's conversation with Pelosi, the sexy Manhattan socialite made it into the gossip columns by boasting during television interviews with Larry King and Barbara Walters of her relationship with the former president. To Walters she confided that theirs was a "*special* relationship." Gail Sheehy kept the controversy alive in *Vanity Fair*, reporting that "Denise's own breathy admissions on national television that 'the president and I have a special relationship' all but spelled out the missing word: intimate."[53] Soon Hillary's friends weighed in. The *New York Post* reported from Washington that "Hillary's defenders—believing Rich was hinting she had an affair with Bill Clinton—railed about her, ripping Rich as 'This starf---er onstage [with Bill Clinton] with her bosoms hanging out.'"[54] Yes, they actually used the quaint word "bosoms."

Let us move on to the Clintons' more seemly post-presidential misadventures, those last-minute pardons.

FOUR

PARDONGATE

Washington, D. C.
February 20, 2001

At the end of a private interview, Vice President Richard Cheney is asked by journalist Dale Van Atta about the controversies regarding Bill Clinton's recent avalanche of pardons.

Van Atta: "There's talk about what the Republican Party should do, if anything, about Clinton now—always being in the news. Off the record, what's your view?"

Vice President: "I don't know—just sort of sit back and [he begins to laugh] watch . . ."

Van Atta: "With great amusement?"

Vice President: "Yeah. I mean, I'm just sitting here now—they just brought me the news magazines for the week. Here's Time, *"The Incredible Shrinking ex-President" with pictures of Bill Clinton about two inches high on the cover. Here's* Newsweek, *'Sleepless Nights and Secret Pardons—Inside Story of Bill's Last Days'—on the cover. Exclusive story there." [In deadpan, almost] "You know the guy is—he's always been unbelievable. He's still unbelievable. And—just the contrast between Bill Clinton and, I*

> *think, what most Americans expect in terms of standards of conduct in a president, is considerable—so self-destructive. . . . It's too bad. No—well, the presidency ought to be treated with greater respect."*[1]

So who really is this Denise Rich? The amusing answer is that she is one of a group of high-profile women, all of whom had their way with the erstwhile Boy President often in the early days of his retirement, leaving him, it seems, dangerously depleted. The historically more consequential answer is that she is the former wife of the international fugitive, Marc Rich, whose carefully engineered pardon during the last hours of Bill Clinton's presidency was the most notorious pardon, though, as we shall see, it probably was not his most reprehensible. Denise facilitated the process.

Yes, Hillary had warned Bill after the Lewinsky disaster to restrain his girl-hopping. Unfortunately in the elite circles that the retired president now traveled there is a disproportionate number of take-charge women such as Denise who often reverse the roles men and women play in the sexual chase. Bill, the sexual predator, became for these ladies their sexual prey. To his fans Clinton may be a rock star, an "Elvis," but no one who has seen him in the flesh has mistaken him for a manly man. Rather he is a man-child, and in retirement he became—alas—a sexual prize, like, say, David Bowie. It proved injurious to his health.

In the course of a modern-day president's tenure it is not unusual for him to age visibly. Jimmy Carter looked positively anile halfway through his presidency, though he seemed to recover in retirement. Even President George W. Bush, the fitness paragon who bench-presses over two hundred pounds and was a sub-seven-minute miler before his knees gave out, grayed rapidly during his first term. Clinton, always battling allergies and his adolescent impulses, aged noticeably while president, but nothing like the ominous deterioration that he suffered during the first four years of his retirement, at the end of which he underwent quadruple bypass surgery, followed by supplemental surgery, medication fit for an octogenarian, and *white* hair—so much for the salubrious benefits of recreational sex and slow-motion jogging.

There is a chilling irony here. Exposed during his sexual harassment trial as a sexual predator, he, in retirement, has suffered role reversal. As governor and president, he preyed on the young and the vulnerable. There were the well-known cases of Paula Jones and Monica Lewinsky, and there were less well-known cases—for instance, the enlisted Air Force woman mentioned in chapter two whom he groped. Another victim of his predatory instincts was Kathleen Willey. She was the White House volunteer, who, under financial pressure and with her husband missing, met Clinton in the Oval Office seeking a government job. He responded with unwanted kisses and by pressing her hand on his aroused genitalia. During impeachment the country also became aware of Juanita Broaddrick, a Clinton supporter in his 1978 gubernatorial campaign. On national television she claimed he raped her in her Little Rock hotel room, controlling her by biting down on her lip. That tactic suggests he had prior experience at this sort of thing and might not have always been the passive lothario he was with Monica.

I have no reports of the ex-president being so forcibly ill-used by the tony women linked to him in the early period of his retirement, but there were several who got by Hillary's edict. Denise was one. Apparently, Lisa Belzberg, the estranged wife of Seagram heir Matthew Bronfman, was another. She lived ten minutes from Clinton's Chappaqua residence at the time rumors about the two began circulating. In June 2002, the *Washington Times*' "Inside Politics" reported that "the pretty blonde socialite" had a seven-week affair with Clinton after they met at a Christmas party: "Mr. Clinton behaved like 'a big old hound dog' and later, trysts reportedly took place in mid-afternoons on the 24th floor of New York's chichi Hudson Hotel."[2]

The Hudson Hotel has indeed been a favorite watering hole for the retired president, though it is not the bar that attracts him. He is not a heavy drinker. Rather the Henry Hudson is a hangout for pretty young things. Before his medical setbacks he was seen there regularly, though employees I interviewed throughout 2005 say he no longer comes in at all. As for his dalliance with Belzberg, sources close to the Secret Service have reported Clinton suffering spousal abuse at the hands of Hillary in January 2002, about the time this affair reportedly began, and in August 2002, about the time that the press began reporting a relationship between Clinton and another high-powered lady, Belinda Stronach, the billionaire CEO of Magna International, Inc., the Canadian auto-parts manufacturer created by her father.[3]

This relationship has gone on for a long time. In fact, Secret Service sources report that Bill was again having trysts with Stronach in her Manhattan apartment in 2005; and, as we saw in our Prologue, Magna has remained a generous supporter. In recent years Stronach has been photographed with the former president leaving late-night haunts on scores of occasions. A former American ambassador to Canada and Friend of Bill (FOB) told me that Stronach considered Clinton a political mentor.[4] Evidence of that came in early 2005, when Stronach made Canadian political history by leaving the Conservative Party (and her former boyfriend, Conservative strategist Peter MacKay) to save the government of Liberal Party Prime Minister Paul Martin, by casting one of the two votes that preserved it in the House of Commons. In so doing she secured the cabinet position of Minister of Human Resources. Her explanation was pure Clinton: "the country must come first."[5] Unfortunately, her political career fared no better than those of the others Clinton has mentored during retirement. As we shall see in chapter seven, most of his candidates lose. Less than a year after Stronach saved the Liberal Party she and her new party were out of power, replaced by the first Conservative government since 1993.

During Clinton's retirement there have been other ladies, though most, according to my sources, have been one-night stands with hostesses on Clinton's speaking tours. Some of these girl-hops, sources report, took place in Ireland, France, Australia, Taiwan, Rio, and London. In London, on two occasions he had two dozen roses sent from his hotel. In Sydney, as we saw, he purchased perfume and in Paris, embroidered towels.[6] Then there was that public buying spree he went on in Rio accompanied by actor Anthony Hopkins, about the time that he was coming out of his post-presidential funk. Sauntering along the promenade at Ipanema Beach, he popped into a beachwear shop and purchased three sarongs and two bikinis, none of which has ever been seen on Hillary.[7]

I do have one more trustworthy account of a Denise Rich-type "hitting" on our rock star president in his *Ghost Ship* phase. Clinton was at the University of Ghent in Belgium on October 30, 2001. The venue was the International Conference on Globalization, featuring antiglobalization activists and moderate globalists, most notably Clinton. The conference was small. Barely 500 people were there, for in the immediate aftermath of September 11, 2001, these orb-obsessed intellectualoids and this particular issue seemed passé. Clinton had even waved his $100,000 fee, so eager was he to find an audience and make his mark in the new post-9/11 world. The antiglobalists were antagonistic. Few people applauded his bromides, but as journalist Richard Miniter recalls, "one of the leading lights of the antiglobalization movement stared adoringly at him." She was blonde and sexy Noreena Hertz, at the time a well-known globalization critic and author of another of the movement's Chicken Little tomes, *The Silent Takeover*. "When Clinton concluded," Miniter reports, "she passed him a note as he passed by. He stopped to make eye contact, touched her forearm, sat next to her, scribbled something, rose, passed it to her, pocketed her note, and walked out to sustained applause. She glanced down at the note and slowly slipped it into her notebook." Not everyone was impressed. Later Miniter asked a reporter from the German weekly, *Stern*, if he saw the exchange of telephone numbers. "That was incredibly stupid," the German sniffed.[8] Three years later almost to the month, when word rang round the world of Clinton's severe heart blockage, one wonders if Miss Hertz felt any sense of responsibility. Doubtless she and scores of the retired president's other spirited female acquaintances were relieved that he had not assumed room temperature while in their company.

Denise Rich's contact with Clinton began long before Hillary confided her allegation to Representative Nancy Pelosi that Bill "f---ed" Denise. *Daily Variety*, the newspaper of the entertainment industry, reported Denise's presence with the president as early as 1993 at a California fundraiser. She, with her then-boyfriend, Dr. Niels Lauersen (a Dutch fertility doctor soon to be convicted of billing fraud), and another couple were "the only ones to have attended both the cocktailer and the sit-down."[9] Presumably she was a hit. Two years later she was in the president's delegation at Yitzhak Rabin's funeral. Her friendship continued throughout the 1990s, reaching a climax of sorts when she told Barbara Walters of her "very special relationship" with Clinton. She included Mrs. Clinton in that "relationship," but Rich had to realize that her choice of words would leave Hillary out of the equation in the mind of the press and cause a stir.

Denise had become a famous donor and fundraiser for the Democratic Party beginning in the early 1990s. By the fall of 1998, her name appeared on a *New York Daily News* "fat cat" list of guests who had slept in the Lincoln Bedroom. She was also listed as a habitué at White House coffees. In the spring of 2001, she admitted on ABC's *20/20* to having visited the White House twelve to eighteen times during the Clinton administration, but denied sleeping in the Lincoln Bedroom.[10] (Secret Service logs set the figure at nineteen.) Among my sources, two senior Secret Service officers have corroborated that she was indeed a frequent guest in the Lincoln Bedroom, at least in 1998. By this time, Clinton and Denise were appearing at public fundraisers for the Democratic Party and for her personal cancer-research charity. In fact, he served as chairman of the charity's dinners in 1998 and 2000.

Denise came from a family of some wealth, but what really put her in the money was her husband Marc, whose international trafficking in commodities and arms made him fabulously wealthy and—for seventeen years before his pardon—one of America's ten most wanted international fugitives.

He had fled to Switzerland in 1983, a few steps ahead of federal indictments on fifty-one counts including tax evasion, mail fraud, wire fraud, racketeering, and trading with the enemy. She joined him in exile, but has long claimed that she knew nothing of the criminal charges against him, only that he had tax problems. Around 1990 she discovered that he also had a young girlfriend, Gisela Rossi. That brought her back to New York. She began divorce proceedings against Marc in 1991, eventually settling for a fortune that has been estimated at between $500 million and $900 million. Whatever the figure, it was sufficient for her to engage a plastic surgeon of great gifts, purchase the largest triplex on Fifth Avenue, and hire a staff of twenty, including a "personal healer." The songwriting career that she began in Switzerland is perhaps what accounts for her presence in Hollywood in 1993. She became friendly with, among others, Bette Midler; and when Midler starred in *The First Wives Club* Denise provided a popular song for the film, "Love Is on the Way." By all accounts Denise is a friendly, likable woman, serious about her songwriting but even more serious about politics, at least the celebrity politics of the Democratic Party.

Denise's political fundraising and proximity to the president, however, were what made her famous with the politically active, with congressional investigators, and with Justice Department prosecutors in the Southern District of New York. As she spread her money around the Democratic Party and helped raise still more, some Democrats and reformers thought it unseemly for the ex-wife of a fugitive from justice, whose riches presumably derived from his ill-gotten wealth, to be distributing those riches throughout the Democratic Party while palling around with the president. In the fall of 1998, after Denise joined Clinton in a fete that raised $4 million, Ellen Miller voiced their concern. As spokeswoman for Public Campaign, a campaign-finance monitor, she grumbled, "The president seems to have no sense of ethical consideration, either in his personal or fundraising life."[11] Well, perhaps this is just an early instance of the Boy President being sorely used by a high-octane socialite. Investigators probing Clinton's 2001 pardons write in their report for the House Government Reform Committee that "Denise Rich was in many ways the key figure in the effort to obtain a pardon for Marc Rich."[12]

She had been a steady donor and fundraiser for the Democrats throughout the 1990s, but her own generosity picked up dramatically towards the end of the Clinton presidency when, according to government investigations and newspaper accounts, her interest in gaining her former husband's pardon intensified. From 1993 to 2000, Denise gave at least $1,100,000 to Democrats, but $625,000 of that arrived between 1998 and 2000. In that same two-year period, she made one of the largest donations to the Clinton Library, $450,000. My sources tell me she may have donated as much as $300,000 more to the library, a donation difficult to verify. After the *New York Sun* published a story on foreign contributions to the library shortly after its opening, a touch-screen computer display of donors' names mysteriously disappeared—the consequence, supposedly, of what library officials claimed were "programming errors."[13] Denise also donated $100,000 to Hillary's Senate campaign, after being generous to the president's defense fund.

As to precisely when she began to campaign for the pardon, that remains uncertain. She may have begun as early as 1996. My source on this, a former White House lawyer who worked on the pardons, said on a "no-name, no-attribution" basis that a pardon for Rich was discussed by Clinton, Denise, and others in 1996. They put the project aside then "when cautioned about" Rich's Iran dealings being "still too fresh on people's minds."[14] Those dealings involved buying oil from Iran while the personnel at our Tehran embassy were held hostage from 1979 to 1981 and defrauding the United States Treasury of over $48 million in tax revenue.[15] They also earned Rich and his partner, Pincus Green, their initial indictments. Another source, a major New York City banker involved in

Democratic fundraising, claims Denise discussed a possible pardon with Terry McAuliffe in early 1996, possibly late 1995.[16]

Certainly by the late 1990s, Denise was deeply involved in obtaining the pardon. Congressional investigators in their report for the House Government Reform Committee note numerous contacts between Denise and Marc Rich's legal team, which by 2000 included Clinton's former White House counsel, Jack Quinn. (Rich's lawyers were not all Democrats; I. Lewis Libby, later Vice President Dick Cheney chief of staff, was a Rich lawyer from 1985 until the spring of 2000.) The investigators' report, *Justice Undone: Clemency Decisions in the Clinton White House*, also quotes from a letter Denise sent to the president dated December 6, 2000: "I support his application with all my heart. The pain and suffering caused by that unjust indictment battered more than my husband—it struck his daughters and me."[17] Months later, in the spring of 2001, the again dismayed Episodic Apologists at the *New York Times* reconstructed the steps leading to Rich's pardon. The *Times* cited Denise's December 6 letter, describing it as an "emotional letter." Then the newspaper reported Denise's "buttonholing him [the president] at a White House dinner on December 20." Still, Denise's husband was an unrepentant fugitive. He had fled justice, rebuffed government plea-bargaining offers, and continued trading with rogue states. How did the pardon come through? Reports the crestfallen *Times*, Clinton agreed to pardon Rich late in January after having "overruled the unanimous opposition of his aides."[18]

If the Rich pardon was opposed by Clinton's aides, there were others in high places who favored it: for instance, the aforementioned ex-White House Counsel Quinn and Deputy Attorney General Eric Holder, Jr. According to investigators for the House Government Reform Committee, Holder was working as "a willing participant in the plan to keep the Justice Department from knowing about and opposing" the pardon.[19] The investigators went on to note that "Eric Holder's support of the Rich pardon played a critical role." Apparently compassion for an unrepentant fugitive was not the Deputy Attorney General's motive. Investigators found that he "was seeking Jack Quinn's support to be appointed as Attorney General in a potential Gore administration."[20]

One of the problems with Clinton's last-minute pardons was that many were given without his conferring with responsible officials, in this instance, officials in the Justice Department. This is not illegal, but it was heedless, and another instance of Clinton's impulsiveness creating grave controversy.

As noted in prior chapters, when word of the pardons hit the headlines, public outrage followed. They were issued Inauguration Day, just two hours before the Boy President left office, and shortly after he had agreed to a $25,000 fine and the suspension of his law license by the Arkansas Bar Association. The newly installed Bush administration played the scandal *pianissimo*, hoping to "move on," that being the cliché popular at the end of the Clintons' shambles. Yet, as noted, this time the Episodic Apologists were in their most stupendous lather ever. They needed time to work through their emotions. As the *New York Times* editorialized in February,

> We think Mr. Bush's desire to simply close the door on the last days of Clintonism may not be possible. We sense a national need to come to grips with the wreckage, both civic and legal, left by former President Clinton. It may not be enough simply to observe that the pardon of Marc Rich is an act so baffling that virtually no responsible member of Mr. Clinton's own party will defend it. . . . Perhaps we can never understand the process by which a departing president and his wife come to put sofas and flatware ahead of the acute sense of propriety that ought to go with high office.

Whereupon the *Times*' editorial called for still more investigations of the now retired president:

> The e-mails from Mr. Rich's lawyers and business associates reflect intense financial and political activity aimed at enabling Mr. Rich's

> main Washington lawyer, Jack Quinn, to advance his request for the pardon and to keep the matter secret from federal prosecutors. A central player in all this, Mr. Rich's former wife, Denise, was in direct contact with the president. . . . A thorough investigation and a reconstruction of the events leading to the pardon are required. At some future point, it may be appropriate for the Justice Department and the Federal Bureau of Investigation to examine whether any laws were violated.[21]

By now the Episodic Apologists were sounding like Republicans.

Characteristically, Clinton responded with the hurt feelings and moral superiority of a recidivist caught yet again. He whined that he had "spent a lot of time on" the Rich pardon and "there are very good reasons for it." The public, he insisted, would understand, "once the facts are out."[22] That, of course, is always a problem in the aftermath of a Clinton slip-up, getting the facts out.

Denise and her apparent abettor in the pardon scheme, Democratic fundraiser Beth Dozoretz, along with numerous other top Democrats, took the Fifth Amendment. "A total of 26 witnesses either invoked their Fifth Amendment rights or refused to be interviewed," according to the House Government Reform Committee report. And there were other difficulties that by now have become staples of a Clinton scandal: "A number of document requests issued by the Committee," investigators wrote in their report, "have not been complied with by their recipients, either because of an invocation of Fifth Amendment rights or an invocation of attorney-client privilege. In some cases the invocation of privilege has been spurious."[23] Consider the case of Hugh Rodham, who was paid over $200,000 to arrange a commutation through his White House contacts for Carlos Vignali, a major drug dealer. Rodham refused every document request from the House Committee, though many were not covered by any attorney-client privilege whatsoever.

Angry as the *New York Times* and other Episodic Apologists were, within a year the Apologists' cycle of indignation, forgiveness, and hope began again. Interviewed by Apologists about his pardon of Rich, Clinton placed the blame elsewhere. Asked by *Newsweek* if he would pardon Rich again, his answer was "Probably not, just for the politics. It was terrible politics. It wasn't worth the damage to my reputation," and he went on to say, "I don't know Marc Rich and wouldn't know him if he walked in the door there. [Actually later that year Rich did "walk in the door" to a room where he met Clinton, as we shall see later in this chapter.] I was very sensitive to prosecutorial abuse because I had seen it."[24] So viewed from the aggrieved Clinton's perspective, independent counsel Kenneth Starr was to blame. The Clintons had employed such impudent blame-shifting to absolve themselves before; for instance, after Filegate or after the Episodic Apologists became so angry with Bill over Lewinsky. On that occasion Hillary laid the blame to the alcoholism of her husband's stepfather. So the stepfather was responsible for Lewinsky's deflowering.

Note that Clinton perceived no ethical problem in granting a pardon to an unrepentant felon whose former wife was distributing money to the president's favorite charities. Rather the problem was "the politics," by which he means public relations. To Boy Clinton—forty-first successor to George Washington—"politics" is public relations. During his presidency, public relations dominated practically every decision. Witnesses as diverse as Clinton's first CIA director, James Woolsey, and "war room" veteran George Stephanopoulos have emphasized the point. Whether the issue was national defense or the federal government's incineration of a cult's compound in Waco, Clinton's primary concern was usually public relations. In Clinton's response to *Newsweek*, he makes it clear, politics is public relations. For some, say, Washington, politics is principle. For others, say, Bismarck or Metternich, it is about the wielding of power. For the first president of the 1960s generation, politics is public relations. It has been a long descent from the first president, whose concern for ethics and precedent governed his every waking hour, to the Clinton squalor, where ethics has been replaced by PR and psychobabble. Moreover, it is a touching example of Clinton's obliviousness that after eight years of scandals he might still express concern for his "reputation."

The presidential pardoning power is the only unchecked power granted a president by the Constitution. It is a residue of monarchy. In fact, when granting a pardon, a president is even less accountable than a monarch. The president leaves office, and the consequences of his pardon leave with him. The responsibility of the monarch's pardon might be borne by his dynasty's successors for generations. When pardoning his secretary of defense, Caspar Weinberger, for Iran-Contra-related offenses, President George H.W. Bush provided a public explanation. He even consulted with Democrats in Congress. Clinton, in his last hours as president, issued pardons and commutations, without consulting Congress, his Justice Department, or any other government agency. He granted clemency to those who had or whose advocates had financially supported him, his wife, and his party, thus inviting allegations of personal corruption. His grants of clemency to persons who had paid off his family members and former staffers invited allegations of indirect corruption. This disregard for conventions was a major cause of the uproar over Pardongate. Another was the roguish nature of those pardoned and of those inveigling pardons. Through the years, one of the main problems hampering the general public's comprehension of the Clintons' misdeeds has been that they frequently involve white-collar crime, the intricacies of which are only hazily understood by the general public. Those who do understand these matters are lawyers, prosecutors, government investigators, and career criminals. The Clintons have attracted the attention of more persons drawn from these ranks than any previous First Family. This, the Clintons complain, is the consequence of a conspiracy. Actually, it is the consequence of the company they keep.

The investigators who wrote the House Government Reform Committee's report made this observation: "While other Presidents had issued controversial pardons and commutations, never before had a President made so many grants of clemency with so little justification."[25]

What the report does not say is that a large number of those granted clemency by Clinton were unrepentant crooks, some still dangerous. The report mentions that Clinton ran the risk of being accused of corruption and of indirect corruption. It might also have dwelt on the picaresque gang his acts of clemency brought together: gunrunners, money launderers, drug dealers, and thirteen Clintonistas convicted during the various independent counsels' investigations. These included seven from the investigation of Secretary of Agriculture Mike Espy, five from the investigation of Secretary of Housing and Urban Development Henry Cisneros, plus Susan McDougal from the Whitewater investigation. Seven separate independent counsels were impaneled during the Clinton administration. One was still at work in 2005, that being independent counsel David Barrett.

Barrett's investigation lasted over a decade, cost over $23 million, and never ended until his report, which had been delayed by some 140 motions from Clintonista lawyers for seventeen months, was published in 2006. The Clintons' allies pointed to its length and expense as evidence of how unfairly the Clintons were treated by this independent counsel. They had leveled the same complaint at the Starr investigation whose length and cost arose from precisely the same cause, the Clintons' obstruction of the investigation. In fact, the length and expense of the Barrett investigation was another example of the Clintons' thwarting legitimate government inquiry and causing the very expense they then deplored. The actual investigation of Cisneros ended in 1999, with his pleading guilty to lying to the FBI, a misdemeanor. It was a minor charge but a humane one in light of the excessive sentence a felony conviction would bring down on him under the government's mandatory sentencing guidelines. Of course, Barrett got no credit for his leniency. What caused Barrett's investigation to continue for over six more years was the nuisance motions from the Clintonistas' lawyers meant to kill his report or gut it with redactions. The final report was printed with 120 pages of redactions, though so successful were the Clintonista lawyers in spreading confusion that the *New York*

Times reported that the report was published in full—only to have to publish a correction days later. Even with the redactions it was clear that Barrett had uncovered serious abuse of power by Clinton's IRS and Justice Department. Unreported was that Barrett was physically harassed, accosted on the street by thugs who warned "we know who you are," or, again "we can find you." Starr suffered threats too and was given bodyguards. Barrett took to strapping a gun on his ankle.[26] The Clintons' disregard for the law has had its unlovely aspects.

Earlier presidents granted pardons, but none to such a discreditable cast of characters as Clinton put together. In Appendix II, I list some of the most colorful beneficiaries of Clinton's clemencies, along with some of their memorable achievements en route to government housing. But consider those felons who sent prosecutors' toupees flying highest. Rich has already been mentioned, and then there is Vignali, for whom the First Lady's brother, Hugh, lobbied. House investigators report that Rodham was claiming Vignali's commutation to be "very important" to "the First Lady as well as others." Vignali had been convicted after a two-year investigation found that he had peddled 800 pounds of cocaine, which was ultimately converted into crack cocaine. His father, Horacio, whom investigators also suspect of drug trafficking, spread hundreds of thousands of dollars throughout the Democratic Party in California to expedite his son's commutation. The $200,000 Horacio paid Rodham was not deposited until three days after his son's pardon. Most of the letters written on the son's behalf, some coming from recipients of Horacio's recent generosity, were misleading and based on false information. The son never admitted to wrongdoing even after his conviction or while his father was pursuing his commutation. Nor did he express remorse. Naturally the Justice Department strenuously opposed the commutation, asserting that it would be a setback for drug enforcement. Nonetheless, Vignali went free.

Another of Rodham's clients was Glen Braswell—a huckster who peddled, among other forms of snake oil, an antibalding miracle. Braswell had been convicted of tax evasion and mail fraud, but was pardoned after paying Hugh Rodham $230,000. While his pardon was being pursued he was under federal investigation for still more criminal acts, a condition that in itself should have denied him a pardon. Braswell got his pardon. When the word spread of Rodham's payment from Braswell, Rodham returned the payment. He also agreed to return the money he got from Vignali, though investigators report he returned only $50,000.

The clemencies Roger Clinton attempted to arrange were equally inconsistent with federal pardon guidelines and would have freed felons even more dangerous than those Rodham fronted for if Roger had been successful. Perhaps the most infamous of his clients was Rosario Gambino, the notorious Mafioso whose heroin deals had earned him a forty-five-year sentence. Roger also pulled in more money than Hugh Rodham and such gratuities as a gold Rolex watch from Gambino's family. Investigators noted that Roger had "received a substantial portion of $225,000 that was swindled from the Lincecum family" for a pardon that never came through, and "at least $335,000 in unexplained travelers checks, many of which were purchased overseas and likely imported illegally."[27] Finally, though Roger was not very helpful in gaining clemencies for others, he got one for himself for his cocaine conviction (see Appendix II) in the mid-1980s, a time when, according to former Arkansas state trooper L.D. Brown, the Clinton brothers frequented parties where cocaine was served as "hors d'oeuvres."[28]

Hillary's other brother, Tony, operated on a smaller scale than Hugh or Roger. Investigators found that he received $244,769 in salary and a $79,000 loan from Edgar and Vonna Gregory, presumably to arrange their pardons. They were not included among Clinton's last-minute pardons, having received their pardons in March 2000, probably in reciprocation for the Gregorys' large donations to the Democratic Party. Congressional investigators report that they met with President Clinton ten times. They claimed that they had employed Tony Rodham for work independent of their pardons. Investigators, however, found no evidence of such work. Two months after being pardoned by Clinton, the

Gregorys, through their company United Shows of America, Inc., began making a series of loans to Rodham that eventually amounted to $107,000 between May and February 2002, none of which was ever repaid before the company went bankrupt later in 2002. Four years later Rodham was refusing to repay the debt to United Shows' court-appointed trustee.[29]

If Rich was the most infamous of the pardoned, there was one who had committed graver crimes and would have become more notorious had the press been attentive. That would be Harvey Weinig, a Clinton fundraiser in 1992 eventually convicted as a money launderer for the Cali cartel in Colombia. Though convicted and sentenced for laundering $19 million in drug money—along with concealing a kidnapping—Weinig was granted clemency after his wife made large political donations to Democrats. She also exerted extensive political influence through the good offices of three Clintonistas. Reid Weingarten (Weinig's lawyer), David Dreyer, and Harold Ickes (both former Clinton administration officials) all brought Weinig's case to the president. Prosecutors were furious, and remain suspicious that Weinig was only prosecuted for laundering $19 million. According to investigators whom I have talked with, Weinig could have laundered as much as $120 million in drug money. He is another of the pardoned who never cooperated with authorities or showed remorse.

Weinig was not the only Cali cartel figure whose funds benefited Clinton. Another associate of the cartel was Jorge Cabrera, who, after donating $20,000 to the Democratic National Committee, was invited to a White House Christmas party in 1995 where he was photographed with Vice President Al Gore and the First Lady. Within six months he was serving a nineteen-year term for trafficking in huge amounts of cocaine. To this day, no one can explain how he made it through the White House screening process. As for the pardon of Weinig, it was publicly protested by Colombian and U. S. drug enforcers. Columbia's most famous enforcer, General Rosso Jose Serrano, told his country's *El Tiempo* newspaper, "It's very frustrating. They [Colombian drug traffickers] must be laughing at us who have openly fought this scourge."[30] The general lost over 5,000 police while dismantling the Medellin and Cali cartels. Ten of our own Drug Enforcement Administration special agents were killed in South America between 1993 and 2000.[31]

Friends and ex-friends of Clinton have speculated as to why such a clever fellow as he would blot his record all over again just after surviving the long grueling trial of impeachment. Dick Morris, once his intimate adviser, concluded that he ran this risk out of anger over his own treatment by prosecutors whom he deemed overzealous. The *New York Times* arrived at a similar conclusion weeks after the pardons, reporting that Quinn and Ickes anticipated an accommodating mood from the departing president. "The word spread through this network," the *Times* reported, "that the President would favorably consider anyone who could show that he or she had been mistreated by overzealous or unfair prosecutors, just as Mr. Clinton felt he had been victimized by the independent counsel, Kenneth W. Starr."[32] As we have seen, a year later in his *Newsweek* interview Clinton admitted, "I was very sensitive to prosecutorial abuse because I had seen it."[33]

Yet there is a deeper explanation. Throughout their public lives, both Clintons have manifested a steady insouciance for ethics and the law. Perhaps this is simply a carryover from their 1960s radicalism, but it explains their continual run-ins with prosecutors, legislative inquiries, police, in sum what many Americans call "the authorities." As we saw in chapter two, every transgression committed in Washington was a repetition of transgressions committed in Little Rock. Every gubernatorial race was marked by financial irregularities similar to those uncovered in Clinton's presidential campaigns. Even the notorious pardons of 2001 had an Arkansas precedent, to wit, when Clinton left the governor's mansion in 1981. What political observers have been witnessing for over two decades is the unprecedented phenomenon of a growing number of loyal Democrats, first in Arkansas then nationwide, electing and reelecting what law enforcement officials call "repeat offenders." Psychiatrists diagnose most repeat offenders as sociopaths. Democrats contemplating a presidential campaign for Hillary will spare themselves a reenactment of needless grief if they bear in mind that the sociopath's chances of recovery are bleak.

Despite the angry denunciations against Clinton's pardons within the *Kultursmog,* I have found no recognition there that he made similar pardons back in Arkansas causing similar obloquy. In fact, in Arkansas his pardons had been so controversial that they almost doomed his 1982 bid to return to office. Leaving the governor's mansion in 1981, Clinton even pardoned first-degree murderers, one of whom murdered again. Moreover, as with the Rich pardon, the 1981 pardons were granted despite staff members' protests. "I don't know why he commuted them," Betsey Wright, Clinton's long-suffering Arkansas aide and the source of these revelations, told biographer Nigel Hamilton, "because all of his staff was arguing against that too."[34] Some of the brazen pardons that the forty-second president gave during his presidency were for political purposes. Certainly the pardons he granted in 1999 to Puerto Rican terrorists were widely suspected as an attempt to assist his wife's senatorial candidacy with New York's Puerto Rican electorate. Others were the president's response to the generosity of financial supporters; for instance, the Gregorys. Certainly the pardoning of Rich appears to be in reciprocation for Denise's donations. But all his pardons, whether given in Arkansas in 1981 or in Washington in 2001, reflect not a generous spirit so much as an impulsive disregard for the law.

In retirement Clinton has repeatedly given himself over to mawkish plaints over the damage he insists that independent counsels did to the "innocent." As he whined in 2005 to NBC's Brian Williams, journalists "didn't do a very good job of reporting for years all the innocent people he [Independent Counsel Starr] persecuted and indicted because they wouldn't lie."[35] Actually no one was asked to lie about anything, and any independent counsel who made such a felonious request would have by now been severely penalized by the Justice Department's Office of

Professional Responsibility. Some of Starr's witnesses did indeed incur heavy penalties; for instance, Webb Hubbell and Susan McDougal. Yet all they were asked to do was tell what they knew.

As we have seen, many bystanders in the Clintons' lives have suffered misfortune, many without breaking any laws whatsoever. All they had to do was be in the neighborhood when the Clinton death wagon lumbered by. Hubbell and McDougal broke the law, but they have probably also been a part of this mysterious phenomenon, the Clinton Curse. Its carnage has been awful, not just among Clinton's lackeys but even among the rich and powerful.

Return to Marc Rich: one minute comfortable and well-fed in his Swiss estate and then on January 21, 2001, the news of his pardon hit the headlines and his life went to hell. The Clinton pardon damaged Clinton, but it probably damaged Rich more. It transformed him from being a relatively obscure international fugitive to being instantaneously recognized worldwide as one of America's most notorious felons. The victims of the Clinton Curse span the globe from Little Rock to faraway Zug, Switzerland, Rich's business address. One does not even have to come into physical contact with a Clinton to suffer the Curse. Rich made no contact with Clinton, though Denise's musky interludes perhaps substituted. At any rate, there was Rich, thousands of miles away, in alpine Zug. The Curse got to him, too.

Back in Little Rock, there were the Clintons' fated friends. In chapter three I mentioned the McDougals, Hubbell, and Vince Foster. I could have mentioned one David Watkins, an Arkansas businessman ensnared in Travelgate and fired from his White House post for allegedly taking the presidential helicopter on golf outings. Rumors persist that he took a fall for the golfingest president since Ike. Likewise, I could have thrown in the entire Rose law firm. Once respected as the oldest law firm west of the Mississippi, Hillary's old firm was so freighted with debt from defending itself from the Clintons' presidential scandals that by the time she entered the Senate it was almost extinct.

No, Clinton cannot blame all this carnage on an independent counsel. Something larger, more mysterious, is going on. Many of the Clintons' Arkansas enemies suffered almost as terribly as their Arkansas friends. To list them would take more pages than could comfortably be bound into a one-volume work. Doubtless some were as worthy of diabolical retribution as Hillary would have us think, but what of the unsuspecting women who caught Bill's eye? Some, of course, were sluts; but many were true ladies, totally innocent of unchaste thoughts. Nonetheless, sluts and virgins alike often suffered dreadful misfortune. Paula Corbin Jones temporarily became a female pugilist before suffering defeat at the paws of the disgraced figure skater, Tonya Harding. Miss Lewinsky saw her family name transformed into a synonym for sexual acts once held illegal in practically every state in the Union, including Massachusetts.

The Clinton Curse also afflicted the Clintons' White House staff. It destroyed senior adviser Sidney Blumenthal's austere claim to being a journalist. White House lawyer Bernard Nussbaum also saw his reputation go into a tailspin. It took him years to recover. Think of the painful thrashings of former Attorney General Janet Reno once out of office. In fact, almost all the administration's political hopefuls have gone down in defeat. Less ambitious members of the administration have just gone no place. Remember how former Surgeon General Joycelyn Elders was unceremoniously dumped when the public became cognizant of her campaign for a national masturbation policy? Now she resides in bemused obscurity. Other former Clinton officials would be better off in obscurity. I have in mind former Secretary of the Treasury Larry Summers and his repeated public humiliations as president of Harvard State University.

The Clinton Curse has not spared the Clintons' powerful opponents in Washington either. Even former independent counsel Starr was hexed, and he is a practicing Christian. House Speaker Newt Gingrich tumbled into disgrace even before Clinton was impeached, as did his would-be successor, Congressman Bob Livingston. During the Lewinsky sex scandal, both were exposed as adulterers by one of the president's most enthusiastic supporters, Larry Flynt. Though considered a pornographer by the general public, Flynt became so influential on Clinton's behalf that wags referred to him as the president's Minister of Culture, a Clintonista equivalent of Charles de Gaulle's André Malraux. Come to think of it, how long can Flynt remain exempt from the Curse?

My own staff at the *American Spectator* was decimated by this mysterious tribulation. David Brock, author of the first Troopergate story, fled to the Clinton camp where he sought forgiveness and publicly apologized for the "bad taste" of his interviews with Governor Clinton's state troopers—the accuracy of the troopers' stories of infidelity and squalor he did not dispute. His journalistic reputation is now worse than Blumenthal's. Other *AmSpec* writers (for instance, Byron York) came down with amnesia, either denying they had ever worked for the magazine or denying that they had worked on its Clinton investigations. York did both, whether consciously or unconsciously. As Blumenthal has written in his memoir, *The Clinton Wars,* even the magazine's financial adviser, Bud Lemley, my Chicago stockbroker, along with our troubled ex-publisher, Ron Burr (Lemley's business partner), were afflicted. Lemley betrayed the magazine's spreadsheets to Blumenthal at the White House, thus establishing early documentary support for the Clintons' delusion of a "Vast Right-Wing Conspiracy."[36] Unfortunately for Lemley, Blumenthal could not resist revealing his name in his book, *The Clinton Wars.* Lemley's betrayal is chronicled on pages 399, 400, 401, and 441.

Amazingly, I escaped with nothing more painful than the full exoneration of the grand jury that the Clinton Justice Department brought down on the *American Spectator*. Admittedly, it cost me heavily, and I almost lost the magazine but what the hell. Investigative journalism has to have some hazards. Incidentally, I might be the only editor in America's literary history who, during government harassment, found the experience thoroughly enjoyable—no public bawling from me, not even a curse word. Apparently the Clintons even set Bruno's private investigators on us. Twice the *Spectator*'s offices were burgled, and once my New York apartment was broken into. The manuscript to my biography of Clinton, *Boy Clinton: The Political Biography*, was stolen while being couriered to syndicated columnist Robert Novak for a blurb. No one killed my cat or slit my car's tires, that being Kathleen Willey's experience. Yet unidentified brutes did try to intimidate two of my employees working on a story in Little Rock. Still, I have no complaints. "Nothing in life is so exhilarating," said Churchill, "as to be shot at without result." The great man is in error. To be shot at *with* result, and survive sufficiently to sneer at the would-be assassins—that is most exhilarating of all. What is more, I remain editor in chief and in perfect health.

Of all the victims of the Clinton Curse, certainly the most unlikely is Rich. As mentioned, his contact with the president was minimal. He spent millions pursuing a pardon but always through others, and the money was a pittance. He has become stupendously wealthy. Life was good in old Zug then—*whamo*! In the chaos of his receding presidency, the impulsive Boy President heaved Rich's name in with rogues and scoundrels about to be pardoned. Rich's plans for a halcyon future blew up. He got his pardon, but it is doubtful he will ever reenter the country. Sources believe that there is a sealed federal indictment awaiting him in the Southern District of New York. Irregularities suspected in his pursuit of his pardon are likely the reason. Rich is still on the lam, and Clinton has gone scot-free. Years ago, Jim McDougal, on the day he was sentenced to prison for his Whitewater offenses, told NBC's Stone Phillips that the Clintons are "like tornadoes moving through peoples' lives." Rich lived to be Exhibit A.

What did Clinton do wrong in granting his pardons, aside from his generosity towards scoundrels and his insularity from staff critics of the pardons? There are Justice Department guidelines for reviewing clemency petitions that he utterly ignored. For instance, a pardon petition should not be made until the petitioner is out of prison for five years or until five years have elapsed since his conviction. Then too, petitions should not be made while other appeals are available. Moreover, according to the Justice Department's standards, the petitioner should have led a reformed life, have no recent serious offenses on his record, and have accepted responsibility for prior wrongdoing. None of the pardoned felons mentioned above showed remorse or acknowledged wrongdoing, and this was also the case in many of the other pardons. Finally, the Justice Department guidelines call for a demonstrated need for the pardon.

Quite aside from the Justice Department guidelines, most presidents have sought the guidance of their staffs. No president, moreover, has ever contradicted his own stated procedures for granting pardons. Clinton did. At the height of the controversy over Susan McDougal's incarceration for contempt of court in September 1996, Clinton disclosed the procedures he intended to follow for granting pardons. Asked if he would pardon her and the other convicted Whitewater figures, the president told his questioner, Jim Lehrer, "Their cases should be handled like others . . . there's a regular process for that, and I have regular meetings on that. And I review those cases as they come up and after there's an evaluation done by the Justice Department, and that's how I think it should be handled."[37]

Clinton followed none of these guidelines with any consistency. As congressional investigators reported, Clinton "granted clemency to thirty individuals who had not even filed clemency petitions with the Justice Department, and some who had not filed any petition at all, not even with the White House. The President also granted clemency to fourteen individuals who had their petitions previously denied and thus were not pending with the Justice Department." In a number of instances Clinton did not even seek the Justice Department's input. The investigators go on to state that the pardons for Rich and his partner Green "violated all these standards."[38]

Out of office, Clinton's disregard for the law has continued. Two years after the Pardongate fiasco, sources report that Clinton actually had a brief meeting with Rich. On December 14, 2002, Clinton was speaking in Geneva, at a meeting of the United Israel Appeal, for years the recipient of Rich's largesse. The log of the Secret Service shows a brief private meeting took place prior to Clinton's joining the general reception. The log does not indicate with whom Clinton met, but sources close to the Secret Service say it was Rich. A retired senior bodyguard to Rich confirms the meeting.[39] Once again, the Boy ex-President played with fire. Brief years later, on or about January 22, 2004, Rich attempted to set up another meeting with Clinton during the World Economic Forum in Davos, Switzerland. Sources close to Rich say the former president rebuffed him. By then his political recovery looked promising, and there was Hillary's political career to think about. She had ordered him to avoid damaging headlines and even a brief meeting with Rich threatened exactly that.

FIVE

THE "CHOP SUEY CONNECTION"

The recently retired president who fattened up his portfolio by appearances hither and yon worldwide was especially active at venues along the Pacific Rim. In 2001 he appeared there eight times for a grand total of $1,400,000. In 2002 he appeared 13 times for $2,462,000. In 2003 he wound down to seven appearances for $1,730,000. He did not travel to the exotic Orient in 2004 but in 2005 returned twice for $225,000. This is but the most recent use Bill Clinton has made of a political arrangement that goes back three decades. We call it his "Chop Suey Connection."

The Connection began when he was governor with a Beijing-Jakarta-Little Rock itinerary, which is a pretty awkward itinerary to those of us who know our geography. After Clinton moved to the White House, Washington, D.C. was added to the itinerary, which to the geographically minded is not only awkward but also curious. Certainly once Indonesian Chinese began showing up in the White House and after Asian money was found mixed in with the Clintons' campaign contributions, federal campaign-finance monitors became curious. As controlled technologies began leaving the United States for China, even people at the Justice Department became curious. A half dozen years after Clinton's retirement, even American intelligence agencies are taking an interest in the 1996 transactions between the Clinton administration and Chinese donors to the 1996 campaign, for some of the technology shipped to China has found its way into Iran, a rogue nation intent on becoming a nuclear power.[1]

At any rate, in the aftermath of the 1996 campaign Clinton had another scandal on his hands, this time involving campaign finance violations with foreign contributors and technology transfers. A congressional investigation was convened and the media's Episodic Apologists were again in high dudgeon. Clearly money from Beijing and Jakarta had illegally made it into Clinton's campaign purse, some apparently from the Chinese military. Yet, as with earlier Clinton scandals, this was to be but a squall that gave way to sunshine. Congressional investigations petered out. The journalists lost interest. Soon they were focused on Monica and impeachment. The Chop Suey Connection would survive.

Unnoticed at the end of the Clinton presidency was the fact that the beneficiary of Chinese campaign contributions had tilted America away from an old friend, Taiwan, in favor of China. Equally significant, the Clinton administration's relaxed technology restraints allowed China to purchase American technology. Those purchases enhanced China's strategic capacity and assisted China in supplying WMD technology to rogue states. Iran was only one of several. Clinton, who in his 1992 race had chastised President George H. W. Bush for having "coddled" Beijing, became one of China's major benefactors. Moreover, the Chop Suey Connection that had helped fund Clinton's campaigns would enrich him personally once his retirement began. It was not, however, beneficial to American national security. It has left China's military markedly more dangerous. It has bequeathed us a ticking time bomb that may one day explode.

In its annual report on Chinese military power, released in July 2005, the Pentagon warned that China was both modernizing and expanding its arsenal of nuclear weapons capable of reaching the United States. It also noted that China was emphasizing preparations "to fight and win short-duration, high-intensity conflicts over Taiwan." Just before this report was released a Pentagon official observed, "There's a growing consensus that at some point in the mid- to late-1990s, there was a fundamental shift in the sophistication, breadth and re-sorting of Chinese defense planning. And what we're seeing now is a manifestation of that change in the number of new systems that are being deployed, the sophistication of those systems, and the interoperability of the systems."[2]

All this happened on Clinton's watch. His administration relaxed its technology transfer policies, and the Chinese took advantage. America is facing a growing military threat from what turns out to be Clinton campaign contributors.

Meanwhile, in retirement Clinton has popped into places such as Sydney, Australia, where he earned $10,000 a minute—$300,000 total—for addressing the World Conference on the Peaceful Reunification of China and World Peace, a group heavily subsidized by Beijing. According to the chairman of the conference, William Chiu, the people on "both sides of the Taiwan Strait" are ardent for a single, unified China. That is thumpingly inaccurate. The majority of Taiwanese have repeatedly made it clear that they want Taiwan to retain its independence. Mr. Chiu's conference was predicated on a falsehood. Its main purpose was to further a major foreign policy goal of China, to wit: annexation of Taiwan.

The Chop Suey Connection began years before in Jakarta. There, one Mochtar Riady had risen from being proprietor of a bicycle repair shop in the 1940s to become, by the 1980s, one of the richest of the rich Chinese minority whose elite controls the Indonesian economy. His son, James, came to Little Rock at about the time that young Bill Clinton was becoming a force in Arkansas politics. James probably met Clinton sometime in 1977. Most likely Little Rock investment banker Jackson Stephens introduced them. Clinton had been elected attorney general the year before. Already he was looking ahead to the governor's mansion and beyond. His ambition was conspicuous. James, then twenty, had been dispatched to Little Rock by his father to work under Stephens, and to look for investment possibilities. Clinton proved to be the Riadys' most famous investment.

In 1984 the Riadys' Lippo Holding Company purchased $20 million worth of stock in the Worthen Bank and Trust of Little Rock. James Riady was named president of the bank, and as James Ring Adams would report in the *American Spectator*, "A whole team of ethnic Chinese from Indonesia and elsewhere came to Little Rock to work at Worthen." Over the next year, Worthen engaged in some reckless ventures, and in April 1985 it managed to lose $52 million virtually overnight by investing in high-interest, short-term loans known as repos. Actually, Worthen was not investing its own reserves or the deposits of private customers. It was investing Arkansas state pension funds, and as Arkansas' deputy treasurer told Adams, "every penny of it was gone."[3] Of a sudden, young Governor Clinton's political life was heading off the cliff.

Worthen came to his rescue. Rather than mounting a lengthy court case to make up the loss, it made it up with private funds and a new issue of common stock, removing the storm clouds from the governor's impending reelection bid. A former Worthen employee told the *Spectator* that when he suggested to the bank's new management that Worthen could make a strong case in court, "They said, 'it's politics now.'" In other words, a messy, protracted court case would expose shabby practices in Clinton's state government, jeopardizing his political future. The Riadys were looking ahead.

The Chop Suey Connection was expanding. In 1985, the same year as the pension fund debacle, Clinton visited Hong Kong. There he met John Huang, who a few years later would become a player in the Clinton administration and a figure in the subsequent campaign finance scandal. In 1985 Huang, a naturalized American citizen, was merely a Riady retainer. Serving as a tour guide, he showed the governor the sights. In 1989 he would do same for Al Gore. By 1992 this Hong Kong tour guide was raising hundreds of thousands of dollars for the Democrats' presidential campaign. Eventually Huang would be rewarded with access to top secret intelligence data that he could then pass on to the Riadys and to their connections in Beijing, as we shall see.

Eventually, federal regulators forced the Riadys out of the banking business in Arkansas after finding, among other things, that Worthen was making sweetheart loans to Riady associates for office buildings in Indonesia. Still, the family hung around and found ways to please Governor Clinton. Mochtar Riady once contributed $50,000 so the Arkansas March of Dimes would name Mrs. Clinton "Arkansan of the Year." Gestures like that were mere holding actions, however, and the best was yet to come. When Clinton needed money for the critical New York presidential primary in the spring of 1992, James Riady persuaded Worthen to extend $3.5 million worth of letters of credit to the campaign. Riady, by then a United States resident, and his wife went on to contribute $450,000 to the Clinton-Gore campaign, making them the campaign's biggest contributors that year. In the final weeks of the campaign Riady family members and their associates donated some $600,000 to the Democratic National Committee and to various Democratic state parties. In a further display of munificence, Riady and Huang each gave $100,000 for the inaugural activities in Washington. The Chop Suey Connection is no joke! These Indonesian Chinese think big . . . and strategically.

Indeed, without the aid and comfort that the Riadys extended over the years it is unlikely Clinton would have made it to the White House. So he owed them in a very big way, and when he was elected president their investment came due. They could shape American foreign policy, while doing well financially themselves. That was their hunch and Beijing's, too. On November 7, 1992, just two days after the election, the Riadys solidified their ties to the Chinese military. They entered jointly into a partnership with China Resources Ltd. to own and operate the Hong Kong Chinese Bank. China Resources is a vehicle for Chinese military intelligence. According to congressional investigators, China Resources funneled money from the People's Liberation Army military intelligence department to intermediaries in the United States for campaign donations.[4]

The Chinese have a word, *guan-xi*. If one has *guan-xi* it means he has access to someone in authority who can be helpful. A related expression, *zou-hou-men*, means going through the back door. The Riadys spent more money than anyone else acquiring *guan-xi* and going through the back door at the Clinton White House, but there were others. The menagerie that was revealed by an indignant media and congressional investigators surpassed any aggregation ever seen on government property anywhere in the United States including the Mayor's office of New York City in the great days of Tammany. It included arms dealers, spies, drug traffickers, con men, and lowlifes of every kind. Even accomplices to the slaughter that took place in Tiananmen Square were welcomed to Washington as long as they brought campaign contributions. No other White House has ever played host to so much international riffraff.

Consider Ng Lapseng, who ran a prostitution ring in Macau. He arrived in San Francisco one day with $175,000 in cash. Two days later he had lunch at the White House and in the evening attended a Presidential Gala with his pal Charlie Trie. Over a period of time, Trie, once a fry cook at a Little Rock restaurant, received more than $1 million from Ng, and he gave at least $645,000 of this to the Democratic National Committee. On one particularly busy day, March 21, 1996, the retired fry cook handed over $460,000 in checks and money orders to the Presidential Legal Defense Trust. Then, at lunch with a White House aide, he passed on a "Dear President" letter, admonishing Clinton not to project American force into the Taiwan Straits because "it is highly possible for China to launch real war."[5]

The Boy President actually replied, and in a "Dear Charlie" letter he assured Trie that Washington's actions were "not intended as a threat" to China. The letter, in effect, was an outright apology to Beijing by the United States for having deployed two aircraft carriers near the Straits. The presence of shady figures such as Trie and Ng did not go unnoticed. Writes former FBI special agent I. C. Smith, "It is astounding that a person of modest means such as Trie could contribute over $100,000 to dine with the president of the United States [Smith is referring to Trie's attendance at a Democratic National Committee dinner held at the Washington Hilton.] along with a foreign individual [Ng] who, if not directly aligned with the Chinese Communist government, was certainly indirectly aligned with it." Smith also notes that the FBI caught Trie's secretary shredding documents in his modest Little Rock home, many of which linked him to White House fundraisers.[6] Roused by the evidence of foreign campaign contributions coming from Asian sources—and Asian sources linked to the Chinese military at that—both law enforcement and congressional investigators sought to close in. Unfortunately, they got little cooperation from the Justice Department.

And so it went. Undesirables of one kind or another were wined and dined by the Clintons—Ng, the whoremonger from Macau, was at the White House twelve times! The buying and selling went on unabated. California businessman Johnny Chung, though characterized as a "hustler" by Clinton's own National Security Council, was allowed into the White House fifty-one times! Chung specialized in arranging photo ops and meetings with the Clintons and his Beijing clients, one of whom, Lt. Col. Liu Chaoying, gave him $366,000 to pass on to the Democratic National Committee. Colonel Liu, the daughter of the most senior general in the PLA, was a high-tech spy and arms dealer in her own right. She met with Clinton at least twice.

There is little chance that we will ever get a full accounting on these and other improprieties. Key documents have disappeared, and many of the important players—Ng, James Riady, members of his family, and other Lippo employees—have fled the country. Others, when questioned, have pleaded the Fifth Amendment. China's government, or the part of it charged with suborning, cajoling, or otherwise influencing American politicians, could tell us who did what for whom, but under the present regime it is unlikely to do so. One day this may change. After all, once the Soviet Union collapsed, the KGB opened some of its archives. For now, however, we do know that during the 1990s Clinton moved from being a critic of Beijing to being a benefactor. As a consequence, five years into Clinton's retirement Secretary of Defense Donald Rumsfeld was warning Congress of the growth of the Chinese navy; and Central Intelligence Director Porter Goss was warning that China's military modernization "could tilt the balance of power in the Taiwan Strait."[7]

Clinton's tortuous route from China critic to well-paid lecturer along the Pacific Rim is worth reviewing, for it shows him at his most pliable, opportunistic, and short-sighted moments. Unfortunately, along the way we shall see a worrisome array of strategic hardware transferred to Beijing and Taiwan betrayed.

As a candidate in 1992, Clinton accused President Bush of ignoring China's human rights abuses and placating its regime. "Instead of leading an international effort to pressure the Chinese government to reform," Clinton declared, "the Bush administration has coddled the dictators and pleaded for progress, but refused to impose penalties for intransigence." Then, in March 1993, Clinton issued a formal executive order, warning the Chinese leaders that he was giving them only one year to improve their record on human rights. If by then there was no "overall significant progress" in several areas (including the treatment of political prisoners and the families of dissidents), the executive order said, China would be removed from the list of trading partners with Most Favored Nation status.[8]

Clinton was merely posturing. He might have liked to see China improve its record on human rights, but it is doubtful that he ever felt it to be a serious concern. The executive order, though forcefully stated, was an empty threat. The same month in which Clinton issued the order he received a letter from the Chop Suey Connection's Mochtar Riady. Marked "Personal & Confidential," the letter urged Clinton not to withdraw China's Most Favored Nation status. "The best way of achieving political reform in China," Riady asseverated, "is through capitalist interaction."[9] A month later, on April 27, 1993, Secretary of Commerce Ron Brown echoed Riady's sentiments, telling Asian-American business leaders in Los Angeles that he "would be surprised if China's Most Favored Nation Status is not renewed."[10]

It was, indeed, renewed. Notwithstanding Clinton's tough talk, China's failure to improve its human rights record proved to be irrelevant. Still, Clinton had to keep up appearances. Beijing knew by early 1994 how easily the passive Clinton could be compromised, but he would still make the obligatory gestures. In his State of the Union speech in January he said, to great applause: "As we build a more constructive relationship with China, we must continue to insist on clear signs of improvement in that country's human rights record."

It may be that he saw no contradiction between what he was saying and what he was actually doing. But the same month in which he promised to monitor China's "human rights record" Huang was granted an interim Top Security clearance, ostensibly because Commerce Secretary Brown was in urgent need of his help. In other words, the representative of a foreign bank with close connections to the repressive Chinese government and its intelligence agencies could see classified information that was withheld from most American officials. Brown, who died in a plane crash on April 3, 1996, never offered any public explanation about this, but perhaps none was needed. Clinton's Chop Suey Connection went back a long way.

In 1996, Judicial Watch, a conservative legal foundation, took the only deposition Huang ever gave. When he was asked if he had had any relationship with Clinton before he joined the Commerce Department, he swore he had none. He said he had met Clinton once in Hong Kong and once in Atlanta, both times only briefly. He was lying. Secret Service records show that between March 15, 1993, and July 18, 1994, the day Huang began at the Commerce Department as a full-time official, he entered the White House at least forty-seven times; nine of his visits were with the president, most of them in the family quarters in the White House.[11] Why did Huang feel he had to lie?

Huang also insisted that he had severed all connections with the Riadys and Lippo when he joined the Commerce Department, and that was a lie, too. In *Year of the Rat*, Edward Timperlake and William C. Triplett II, who tracked the flow of Chinese money into the Clinton White House, write:

"The Riadys themselves never took their American business interests too seriously. They were mostly vanities designed to promote the Riadys' personal and political agendas. . . . All indicators force the conclusion that Huang's real job in the three or four years before he went to Commerce was overseeing the Riadys' political and financial investment in the Democratic Party in general, and Governor Bill Clinton in particular."[12]

And when Huang received his Top Secret security clearance:

"The Riadys got value for their money in the form of economic intelligence forwarded to them—and, in all likelihood, through them to their associates in Chinese intelligence. Huang truly lived up to the label James Riady gave him: 'My man in the American government.'"[13]

But the top secret clearance that Huang got in January 1994 was only on an interim basis, and it was without some of the perks that go with a clearance on a regular basis. So something had to be done, and it was. Huang and the Riadys saw an opportunity in the shabby moral atmosphere that enveloped the White House, and with Hillary Clinton's help, they seized it.

Webb Hubbell, once a close friend of Hillary and her law partner, thence an associate attorney general in the Clinton administration, and finally a casualty of the Clinton Curse, was a troubled man in the summer of 1994. He had many debts, legal and otherwise, and as the *Washington Post* would later report, he was down to $6,780 in his checking account. Meanwhile independent counsel Kenneth Starr was asking him about various criminal acts in Arkansas, which meant that there was a very good chance that Hubbell, if not handled properly, would implicate Mrs. Clinton in illegal acts of her own. This was a grave matter for an already beleaguered White House, and it had to be headed off. It would not do to have the president's wife indicted. Considering the high stakes, it was always understood that Clinton could be bought quite cheaply. It turned out that Mrs. Clinton came cheaply, too. The word went out, and the riffraff gathered. Here is what happened in a single week.

On Monday, June 20, Hubbell met with Mrs. Clinton. This was the same day that Ng, the Macau peddler of delights, arrived in San Francisco with $175,000 in cash. The next day, Tuesday, Riady and Huang visited the White House, and that night Huang attended a reception on the South Lawn. On Wednesday, Ng and Trie, the old fry cook, had lunch at the White House. Also on Wednesday, Huang and Riady dropped by again. That night Ng and Trie sat with Clinton at the head table during the aforementioned Presidential Gala at the Washington Hilton. (As the FBI's Smith later wrote, "Wasn't anyone curious at the presence of these foreign nationals at a DNC political fundraising event? They could not have gone unnoticed sitting at the head table with the President of the United States."[14]) On Thursday, Riady met Hubbell for breakfast and lunch, and then returned to the White House. Huang, meanwhile, stopped in at the White House twice that day. And on Friday Riady and Huang were back there again.

On Friday, Riady and Huang were on hand when Clinton taped his weekly radio address from the Oval Office. White House photographers videotaped the event; according to the *Los Angeles Times*, Riady and Huang are seen in a corner of the Oval Office as the tape begins.[15] After Clinton's address they are seen again, although Riady is dressed differently than before. Presumably he was an overnight guest, and had a change of clothes. The tape also shows Clinton saying good-bye to the other guests, while Riady and Huang stay behind.

Mind you, that was on a Saturday. On Monday, June 27, the first business day after that, the Hong Kong Chinese Bank wired Webb Hubbell

$100,000 from a Riady account.[16]* And on the same day of that initial $100,000 payment the Lippo Group in Jakarta sent a memo to Huang, congratulating him on his appointment to the Commerce Department.[17] Apparently Lippo knew about the appointment before Commerce did. Huang was also told his severance pay from Lippo would be $468,125.

Three weeks later, Huang started work at Commerce as a principal deputy assistant secretary. The *Washington Times*, quoting Commerce officials, reported later that it was "common knowledge" that Mrs. Clinton had arranged the appointment herself.[18] Apparently this upset some of the officials at Commerce, although for Huang and Lippo it was ideal. Huang would not have to answer any awkward questions at a committee hearing because an appointment as deputy assistant secretary did not require Senate confirmation. And he and his masters no longer had to be content with only an interim top secret security clearance. A full top secret clearance came with his new position.

The CIA would later tell a Senate committee that it gave Huang thirty-seven individual briefings while he was at Commerce; it also gave him hundreds of classified documents to read. In addition, Huang attended many meetings where classified information was discussed, including some at the White House.

Meanwhile Huang operated quite openly. It seemed he had nothing to fear. He would leave the Commerce Department with a folder or briefcase, and cross the street to the Willard Hotel, where Stephens Inc. of Little Rock had an office. As we have seen, Stephens, the longtime Riady-Lippo partner, was also a longtime Clinton benefactor. For Huang the Stephens office must have been a home away from home. He could

*Eventually Hubbell would receive a good deal more Riady money. In August, 1997 an *American Spectator* investigator telephoned a startled Hubbell, who was then hidden away at the Clintons' vacation retreat in Martha's Vineyard. Hubbell refused to divulge any details of his relations with his hosts because he said the Riadys were going to make him and former Arkansas governor Jim Guy Tucker, a Whitewater felon, "millionaires." Tucker did indeed wind up with a lucrative job with the Riadys. Hubbell's seems to have fared less well. Late in 2005 he was still shambling along the streets of Washington, working at a low-level job in a teachers' union.

send faxes, make calls, and receive packages. No one in the Commerce Department would know. Huang's secretary at Commerce told a Senate committee in 1998 that she had "never heard of Stephens Inc."[19] Others at Commerce said the same. And while Huang's daybook at Commerce noted many of his activities, including visits to the White House, Stephens Inc. was never mentioned, even though Huang visited the Stephens office two or three times a week.

The Senate committee that looked into Huang's activities found that he had access to ten types of intelligence reports—all of them of interest, one way or another, to Beijing, Lippo, or Stephens. Among other things, the reports dealt with technology transfers to China, the power struggle in Beijing, the nuclear power industry in Asia, North Korean food shortages, and investment opportunities in China.

Obviously international investors such as Lippo or Stephens would like to know what the CIA knew about places they might invest in; it would have enormous financial value. But the intelligence reports could be used for darker purposes. As Timperlake and Triplett, both of whom are recognized security experts, note:

"Without question, at the top of the PRC's list would have been the issue of American military-related technology transfers to China. The Chinese military is using American high technology for its military modernization program. Chinese intelligence . . . would simply love to know what and whom the CIA was watching. For example, if [Chinese intelligence] found out that the CIA knew of China's interest in certain kinds of lasers with military applications, it could put that acquisition effort into deep freeze for a while. And if the CIA did not know of a Chinese effort to acquire another kind of American high technology—encryption gear, for example—it would be full speed ahead. Anything with a nuclear application, such as nuclear power projects in Asia, would be another high priority target. . . ."[20]

We do not know all the uses Beijing made of the intelligence reports, but certainly China made significant military and technological advances in the 1990s, and that is the most enduring part of Clinton's presidential legacy. When Clinton and Gore took office China had a very limited military reach. Its strategic missiles had technical problems, and its theater missiles were unreliable. It had no command-and-control systems, no modern air-defense systems, and no effective military communications system. It had no antisatellite weapons that could blind our early-warning systems, and it had no imaging or electronic eavesdropping satellites of its own. Meanwhile its air force and navy were sliding into obsolescence. China, in fact, was ill-equipped to fight a modern war, or to threaten anyone other than its closest neighbors.

All the military weaknesses and shortcomings I have just cited were either improved upon or overcome during the Clinton presidency after the Chinese became prominent among the Boy President's campaign donors. It would be incorrect to say that Clinton alone was responsible for the Chinese ascendancy. Corporate America and its K Street representatives, as well as former officials from both Republican and Democratic administrations who now lobbied for Beijing, played major roles. But, as president, Clinton had the final word on United States policy; he abdicated responsibility. Export controls were loosened, and China went from bit player in world affairs to global power. When it could not steal a particular technology, it was allowed to buy it. When Clinton took office in January 1993, for example, only the United States and Japan possessed any so-called supercomputers, the distribution of which was tightly controlled. The United States and Japan even had a bilateral agreement under which they would review any supercomputer exports before they took place. Supercomputers were not supposed to fall into the wrong hands.

But the Clinton administration had a different view, and while Congress slept, the export controls that governed supercomputer sales were rendered meaningless. In 1998, a bipartisan House investigation found that China had been allowed to buy more than 600 supercomputers, and that it had made little attempt to disguise what they were to be used for. Many had been shipped directly to weapons-design facilities or PLA-controlled enterprises.

And so it went in those reckless Clinton years. China obtained from the United States sophisticated microbathymetry equipment that can be used to advance its anti-submarine capability. It got the technology that allowed it to develop an encrypted military-communications system joined to a national command-and-control system that is virtually impervious to electronic eavesdropping. It acquired the technology for a new generation of road-mobile, solid-fuel strategic missiles, including the DF-31, which can reach the American heartland.

The way that China acquired a so-called fly-by-wire technology is an example of how these technology transfers took place to the detriment of American national security. The technology was originally listed on the Department of State Munitions Control List. At the Clinton administration's request it was transferred to the Commerce Department's Control List, whereupon it was allowed to be licensed for production outside the United States. China licensed it supposedly for use solely on civil airliners. By 2004 it was discovered on advanced Chinese and Pakistani combat aircraft as was the single-crystal jet engine fan-blade technology, which had either been illegally or accidentally transferred to China. The consequence has been that the Chinese and Pakistani fighters both are achieving performance capabilities comparable to our F-16A Block 15. America's security has rested in part on the technological advantages it enjoyed for decades over potential adversaries. During the Clinton administration, those advantages were greatly diminished.

A spectacular example of the Clinton administration's inability to maintain control of American technology came in 1993. In that year an entity named CATIC, the procurement arm of the Chinese military aviation ministry, acquired the McDonnell-Douglas aerospace plant in Columbus, Ohio, took it apart, and shipped it home. Some 90 to 95 percent of the plant was defense-related—its sophisticated machine tools were needed in the production of missiles and military aircraft—and, as a

Pentagon report found later, at least 275 semitrailers were used to haul the plant's equipment from Columbus to the West Coast, where it was shipped to China.[21] According to the *New York Times*, military experts affirmed that "the machines would enable the Chinese military to improve significantly the performance abilities—speed, range and maneuverability—of their aircraft. And if diverted, they could do the same for missiles and bombers."[22]

Beijing said the equipment would not be used for military purposes, the same thing it had said about supercomputers and fly-by-wire technology. Knowledgeable critics had warned that Beijing would not keep its word, and in each instance they were right. The pattern repeated itself on other occasions. Experts who pointed out China's untrustworthiness during the Clinton years were either ignored or disputed. In the case of government employees, they were shunted aside. Some were dismissed. In the summer of 1997, Gordon Oehler, the CIA's top proliferation expert, delivered a report to Congress that said: "During the last half of 1996, China was the most significant supplier of weapons of mass destruction-related goods and technology to foreign countries."[23]

Oehler was right. It would be disclosed later that China was exporting WMD technology to Iran, Syria, Libya, Pakistan, and North Korea. The White House, however, had other priorities, and it objected to Oehler's candor. When he returned from vacation in the fall, Oehler found his authority at the CIA curtailed. He retired soon after.

As Timperlake and Triplett also note: "The timing of Dr. Oehler's problems at the CIA is quite interesting. He departed just as Chinese President Jiang Zemin arrived for the first-ever visit by a Chinese Communist leader. Highlighting the Jiang visit was the announcement that the United States planned to transfer American nuclear technology to China. CIA reports of continuing nuclear sales to terrorist countries would have spoiled that little garden party for sure."[24]

Indeed it would have, and Jiang's visit was treated in official circles as a triumph of American diplomacy. Most of the press went along with this, as if it would be bad manners to remind Americans that Jiang presided over a country that condoned extrajudicial killings, the torture and mistreatment of prisoners, slave labor, forced confessions, arbitrary arrests and detentions, mandatory abortion and sterilization, along with the oppression of minorities.

Meanwhile, in the months after Jiang's Washington visit, in October 1997, it became clear the White House was making concessions to China. The principal concession would involve Taiwan, and within a year the Boy President would sell Taiwan out. When he and Jiang held a joint press conference in Washington in October 1997, Clinton had been firm about Taiwan's status. United States policy, he said, "has allowed democracy to flourish in Taiwan and provides a framework in which all three relationships can flourish—between the United States and the PRC, the United States and Taiwan, and Taiwan and the People's Republic of China."[25]

That was consistent with established policy. In February 1972, toward the end of President Nixon's historic visit to China, national security adviser Henry Kissinger and Qiao Guanhua, the Chinese foreign minister, drafted the so-called Shanghai Communiqué, a masterpiece of obfuscation that allowed the United States and China to reach a diplomatic rapprochement over Taiwan. The key part said: "The United States acknowledges that all Chinese on either side of the Taiwan Strait maintain there is but one China and that Taiwan is a part of China. The United States Government does not challenge that position. It reaffirms its interest in a peaceful settlement of the Taiwan question by the Chinese themselves."[26]

It was not true that "all Chinese on either side of the Taiwan Strait" believed that Taiwan was a part of China. Many of Taiwan's Chinese did not believe it then; many more resist the idea now. Taiwan, then as now, enjoyed de facto independence. But in acknowledging that the Taiwan Chinese and the mainland Chinese both claimed to be the legitimate rulers of China, the United States took the position that, while it recognized there was a dispute, it was not taking sides.

In his memoir, Kissinger, surely one of the century's most adroit diplomats, said of his negotiations over Taiwan with Beijing as formulated in the 1972 Shanghai Communiqué, "We recognized that on some issues the only thing negotiators can achieve is to gain time and dignity. On Taiwan it was to leave the ultimate outcome to a future . . . to be worked out over time."[27] A year later when he was back in China after the drafting of the Shanghai Communiqué, Kissinger says Chairman Mao told him, with at least the appearance of sincerity, "I say that we can do without Taiwan for the time being, and let it come after 100 years."[28]

The carefully crafted resolution more or less determined the boundaries of United States policy. Even during the Carter administration, when we switched diplomatic recognition from Taipei to Beijing, the resolution held. Following Carter, President Ronald Reagan would reassure Taiwan that the United States still recognized it as a sovereign state.

But then came the Boy President, still working his Chop Suey Connection. He owed so many people, and had so few scruples about how they should be paid off. In the months after Jiang's Washington visit, it became apparent the White House was ready to accommodate Beijing in matters large and small. When American and Chinese diplomats met to plan a reciprocal visit to China by Clinton, the Chinese insisted that Clinton stay nine days, the same amount of time Jiang had spent in America. This would show that Clinton regarded China as the United States' equal. Earlier presidents would have objected, but the passive Clinton acquiesced readily.

Clinton would make it a nine-day visit to China, even though no one could remember an American president ever staying in any foreign country that long. Then, when the Americans said Clinton would stop off in Japan on his way home, the Chinese objected. Jiang had returned directly to China after he left Washington. Clinton must return home directly, too. That Japan was our closest Asian ally did not matter. Even though he was in the neighborhood, Clinton would pass on the anticipated visit.

The limits of Clinton's passivity had not been reached. There was a disagreement over the dates of his trip. At first the White House said the president would not travel until after the November elections. Beijing, however, wanted him to visit in June, the month marking the ninth anniversary of the 1989 Tiananmen atrocity. Hundreds of dissidents, perhaps thousands—we still do not have an accurate count—had been killed by the military for demonstrating against the totalitarian Communist regime. If, however, this American president were to visit in June—China takes anniversaries seriously—it would help Beijing to put memories of the unpleasant episode behind it.

Clinton agreed to a June visit. After all, it met his needs, too. Once again, expedience triumphed. At this point in 1998 the White House was plagued by scandal. By traveling abroad, Monica Lewinsky's lover might look statesmanlike. That year he would be in Africa in March, South America in April, Europe in May, and China in June. The symbolism of Tiananmen, and the support his visit would give the repressive regime, could be ignored.

Jiang was explicit about what else he wanted when he and Clinton held a joint press conference on the day of Clinton's arrival in Beijing. "The Taiwan issue," he said, "is the most important and the most sensitive issue at the core of China-United States relations." Jiang knew his man. Clinton was ready to fold. When asked at the press conference what he had told Jiang, the president responded: "I reaffirmed our longstanding one-China policy." That answer could mean almost anything. Later that day, when he briefed the press, and presumably amplified Clinton's remark, Sandy Berger, Clinton's national security adviser, who, as a Washington lawyer had represented China in the 1980s, said, "We don't support independence for Taiwan, or one China, one Taiwan, or Taiwan's membership in organizations that require statehood."[29]

The statement was remarkable, and not only because it was made in Beijing, where it would reverberate throughout Asia. It was also out of sync with Washington. Just before Clinton left for China, the House of Representatives voted, 411 to 0, for a resolution praising Taiwan for having moved toward democracy and for its economic progress. The resolution also urged a bellicose China to renounce any military threats against Taiwan. Two years before, on the eve of Taiwan's first democratic election, China had conducted missile and air and naval tests in and around the Taiwan Straits. The exercises were intended to influence the election, and perhaps even lead to its cancellation.

Berger's interpretation, however, suggested that neither longstanding United States policy nor progress in Taiwan mattered. Despite Taiwan's move toward democracy and its economic progress, it did not merit independence, or even membership in international organizations. Berger, an undistinguished choice for national security adviser, eventually revealed himself as typical of the Clinton White House in terms of mendacity and laxness. In 2003, as the 9/11 Commission was investigating the terrorist attacks on New York and Washington, D.C., Berger, then a witness before the commission, filched copies of classified documents from the National Archives. When Archives staffers later confronted him about the missing copies, he said that he had inadvertently mixed the classified documents in with his personal papers. Actually the 9/11 Commissioners concluded that Berger, out of laziness, simply wanted to take them away to read in the greater comfort of his personal study.[30]

When the reporters in Beijing asked Berger if Clinton had told Jiang that the United States did not support independence for Taiwan, Berger waffled. He may have been an undistinguished choice for national security adviser, but at least he knew his place. It would not do for him to get out in front of the president, or to speak for him. At Beijing University the next day, however, Clinton did speak for himself, and when he did he moved a step closer toward acceding to Beijing's wishes. "United States policy," he said, "is not an obstacle toward the peaceful reunification of China and Taiwan."[31] But in the past, the United States had said only that China and Taiwan should settle their differences peacefully; reunification had never been mentioned.

Clinton went the final distance in Shanghai two days later. He completely repudiated the position he had taken in Washington the year before, when he said United States policy had allowed democracy to flourish in Taiwan, and that the United States could maintain separate relationships with both Taiwan and China. Echoing Berger word for word he said he had told Jiang: "We don't support independence for Taiwan, or two Chinas, or one Taiwan, one China. And we don't believe that Taiwan should be a member in any organization for which statehood is a requirement."[32]

Predictably, administration flacks claimed that there was nothing new in what Clinton had said. But no matter how offhandedly or casually his remarks were delivered, Clinton had changed America's diplomatic posture. Richard Halloran, a former *New York Times* reporter, was perhaps the first to note that, "Fundamentally, Mr. Clinton was the first United States president to accept Beijing's concept on the issue of sovereignty over Taiwan, the island nation of 21 million people who consider themselves independent, but that Beijing claims is a province of China."[33]

The *People's Daily* agreed. "Clinton's remarks indicate that the United States government has clearly realized the importance of the settlement of the Taiwan issue," it solemnly declared, and the Chinese Foreign Ministry called on Taiwan to face "realities," and agree that there was only one China.[34] It also called for the resumption of negotiations, neglecting to mention that three years earlier Beijing itself, in a high-handed show of pique, had broken off negotiations because President Lee Teng-hui was allowed to visit Cornell University.[35]

In fact, the Boy President had made the possibility of successful negotiations between China and Taiwan even less likely than before. Beijing, confident that it had American backing, would see no reason to make concessions. Meanwhile the dismayed President Lee said the United States should not have held talks with China on the future of Taiwan. He warned that the Taiwanese people would not give way easily on the independence issue. There was also dismay in Japan and India. Japan, traditionally nervous about China, had been considered America's main ally in

Asia, but Clinton had called that relationship into question. India was even more unhappy than Japan. Clinton had said he was seeking China's help to end the arms race—a bad joke in itself as China was the world's leading proliferator. India had just conducted a nuclear test, claiming it felt threatened by China.

So despite his professed liberal democratic beliefs, Clinton had managed to alienate democratic governments in Taipei, Tokyo, and New Delhi. He had also broken faith with Chinese dissidents who braved beatings and jail terms when they called for reform. Even by his own laissez faire ethical standards, Clinton's conduct in China was appalling. Recall that in 1992 he had criticized President Bush for his supposed leniency toward the "aging leaders in China" after the Tiananmen Square massacre. But Bush had not visited China after the massacre, as Clinton would. Nor did he invite Jiang to visit Washington. Bush maintained controls on technology exports, and American military officers were forbidden from having contact with high-ranking PLA officers. ("And just to make sure he had the PRC's attention," Timperlake and Triplett point out, "Bush sold Taiwan 150 F-16 fighter planes.")

Shortly after Clinton returned to Washington, the Senate, properly alarmed, and for once putting aside partisanship, repudiated his new policy by voting 92 to 0 for a resolution reaffirming support for Taiwan—a clear slap at the President.

Probably the most notorious technology case involved Loral and its chairman, Bernard Schwartz, and Loral's partner, Hughes Electronics. Schwartz donated a modest $12,500 to the Clinton-Gore campaign in 1992. In 1994 he gave the Democrats $100,000. Shortly afterwards he joined Ron Brown's trade mission to China, where he met with Chinese officials. Schwartz, of course, denied (as did everyone else on the trip) that the $100,000 had anything to do with this.

In 1994, meanwhile, things were going badly for the Boy President. His approval ratings were in decline, and he was in another Clintonian funk. The Republicans had snatched control of the House from him by capturing a stunning fifty-four seats in the mid-term election, and as Dick Morris, Clinton's erstwhile political strategist, noted, this left Clinton "devastated. . . . He would talk about the defeat endlessly, ruminating on what had gone wrong."[36] He wondered what would happen to him. He even "concluded," according to Morris, "that he faced permanent defeat."[37]

We have seen him in such despair before, and the turbulent Boy President would face such glum times again—recall his post-Pardongate despair—but for now he had the resourceful Morris at his side. His impending political comeback can be credited to the television ads that they ran from the summer of 1995 until the November 1996 election. The ads ran nationwide, except in New York and Washington, and, according to Morris, they were seen three times a week by some 125 million people. It was a brilliant example of stealth politics. By keeping them out of New York and Washington, and, to some degree, Los Angeles, the ads did not attract the attention of the *New York Times*, the *Washington Post*, *Time* and *Newsweek*, or even the TV network news organizations. When the cunning Clinton, early in 1996, complained that the Republicans had begun the presidential campaign prematurely, the media were hoodwinked once again.

But the ads cost money, and once again expedience triumphed. The modest $12,500 that Schwartz contributed in 1992 grew to $632,000 in 1995 and 1996. By 1998, with the help of family members and business colleagues, Schwartz had given more than $2.2 million to Clinton-Gore and other Democratic causes. It hardly seems an accident, then, that Loral and Hughes were allowed to circumvent established security procedures and help China develop its Long March booster rocket. (Unbelievably, Berger strenuously denied any connection between the campaign contributions and the favoritism shown to Loral and Hughes.) In February 1996, a Long March rocket launching a satellite exploded, killing an unknown number of Chinese villagers. Loral and Hughes engineers then helped the Chinese to remedy the cause of the explosion and make the

Long March reliable. The Long March technology, though, is similar to that found in China's intercontinental ballistic missiles. So when Loral and Hughes made the Long March reliable, they were also making it easier for China's ICBMs to reach the United States.

Someone ought to have gone to jail for that, but this was the Boy President's America, and no one did. Nonetheless, while one does not want to minimize the seriousness of the offense, given the Clinton administration's obliviousness to national security, this technology transfer was perfectly understandable. Sandy Berger and other party hacks notwithstanding, this was a straight out financial transaction. Schwartz was giving a lot of money, and Clinton, as always indifferent to the consequences, intervened on his behalf. When it appeared that the Justice Department might actually prosecute Loral for helping China acquire an illegal technology, the White House simply changed the rules on technology transfers, undermining the Justice Department's case.

This was not done openly, and Clinton stayed out of sight. The financial arrangements were handled by others, and despite his generosity it may be that Schwartz never met Clinton. "I have never spoken to the president of the United States about my business," he said on ABC's *This Week*, and perhaps he never did. In 1998, a Loral vice-president, in a letter to Berger, said Schwartz had been at a White House dinner, but had been unable to talk to the president. The Loral vice-president, incidentally, had worked for Berger at the National Security Council before Loral hired him as its chief Washington lobbyist.

Clinton stayed in the background on this and on similar activities. Aides and assistants handled things for him. Taiwan he handled himself and in the open. Congressional opposition and the unhappiness it caused our allies made absolutely no difference. It made no difference, either, that Taiwan, centered in the chain of islands that reach from Indonesia and The Philippines in the south to Japan and the Russian Kamchatka peninsula in the north, would be an ideal base for China's new blue water navy. Taiwanese independence, of course, stands in the way.

But Clinton did not care. He supinely sided in public with China at the expense of Taiwan, and then, I suspect, forgot about it. His passivity in dealing with assertive foreign powers is a matter of record. His principles come and go, and there is no reason to think this has changed in retirement. His *Ghost Ship* drifts around the world now, and occasionally washes up in China, where he will give a speech, and perhaps catch up with old friends from the Chop Suey Connection, many of whom would find it awkward to return to America. They might be served with subpoenas. Clinton is doing fine financially this way, once again selling himself, just as he did in the White House. Not long after he spoke at the pro-Beijing, anti-Taiwan conference in Sydney, Australia, he turned up in Hong Kong. A French financial house there paid $250,000 to hear him speak. The next day he was in Shenzhen, a boomtown on the Chinese mainland, and a favorite place for the riffraff. Real estate developers there also put up $250,000. They said he would talk about the World Trade Organization, but that was only a cover, intended to dignify an otherwise cheesy occasion. Bill Clinton, the forty-second president of the United States, was there to help the developers sell condos.

SIX

THE FIRST COMEBACK OF THE TWENTY-FIRST CENTURY

It is Saturday morning in mid-September, 2003, in Iowa. Nearly 7,500 Democratic stalwarts have paid $25 each to assemble twenty miles south of Des Moines for Senator Tom Harkin's 26th Annual Steak Fry, a grand political event in these parts and this year grander than usual. The Democratic primaries are drawing nigh, and so most of the Democrats' presidential aspirants are in attendance, hoping to leave an imperishable mark on each Iowan there. A few months from now the Iowa caucus will put their candidacies to the test. The fate of the Republic could be decided by a few thousand Iowans in caucus assembled. That the steak fry takes place on a grassy, undulating field outside of the rural town of Indianola is appropriate. It is also the locus for one of the nation's major hot-air balloon competitions.

The date is September 13. Everything is in place for Tom Harkin's Steak Fry: the greasy grills, the dining tents, the outdoor comfort stations, the hundreds of campaign signs planted by the candidates' admirers. A stage beckons. It has been decorated in red, white, and blue; and there are bales of hay set around it to remind the participants of their folksy roots—hay, not straw, for straw is "too yellow." Atop the hay, dried ears of corn and apples are strewn. It is harvest time. Along with the bounty of the field there are votes to be harvested. In anticipation of photo ops that might stir Democrats everywhere, a huge Iowa farm tractor is parked behind the stage and behind that a large mural depicting the sun setting on a corn field under the proclamation: "Tom Harkin's Steak Fry." These words have been painted in what an organizer of the event calls "John Deere green." This aesthete knows his stuff. He once served as an advance man for Bill Clinton.

Seven of the nine announced candidates have gathered for this grand opener of the presidential election season. (The Rev. Al Sharpton of New York was not on hand nor was Senator Joe Lieberman of Connecticut, he being a devout Jew who would not campaign on the Saturday Sabbath.) More than 5,000 ticket holders from a dozen states have shown up in hundreds of vehicles and tour buses, causing a miles-long traffic jam through Indianola but no delay in the oratory. The candidates began on time, each having been allotted five minutes. As each alternately blubbered and roared before the painted sun, cheers and applause went up from their small pockets of volunteers in the audience. Those in the audience not already favoring one candidate or the other listened in stony silence during the short talks, their reticence perhaps being caused by the steady drizzle that continued throughout most of the four-hour event, transforming the field into a hinterland mud-pit. Finally the main event arrived.

Even the rain seemed to stop when the event's rock star was driven up to the stage in a black SUV to the sound of his favorite 1992 campaign song blaring from the loudspeakers, Fleetwood Mac's "Don't Stop Thinking About Tomorrow." From the SUV the star emerged: the familiar bonnet of gray hair first, the large forehead, the famous ruddy face with the tiny blue eyes, *twinkling*. He stands there. Then comes the *aw shucks* smile. The Democratic crowd went wild. They cheered and chanted, hundreds of them waving pre-printed red-and-white signs with "WELCOME BACK BILL" on one side, and "WE MISS YOU" on the other. "Let's be honest," host Harkin had said in advance of the event, "no one can excite Democrats like Bill Clinton."[1]

After all the disappointment of the Clintons' last-minute scandals, the Comeback Kid had done it again. All was forgiven and forgotten. The cheering seemed endless even as Harkin tried to quiet the throng for his introduction, during which he credited the former president with bringing rain to drought-stricken Iowa. Clinton accepted it with a grin. Tom Harkin's Steak Fry, now immortalized by the presence of the Democrats' political Elvis, had, with the sogginess and sloshing mud, become a political Woodstock. "He was my first vote," enthused a 24-year-old young lady from Omaha, as if she were talking of a former boyfriend. "Oh, my God," gushed another lady to CNN. "He is one of a kind—like Elvis." And the rapture was not contained to the fair sex. "He's a god," agreed a 51-year-old painting contractor from Cedar Rapids to a reporter. "He floats around and drops in for a while and then he's gone. Unfortunately, he can't run again."

Alternately funny, folksy, and fulminating, Clinton offered a rambling twenty-two-minute speech that began by abandoning the unwritten rule that former presidents do not criticize the current office-holder. "The last election [in 2000] was tight as a tick," Clinton began. "That election was not a mandate for radical change, but that was what we got." Under Bush, whom Clinton never named, "we went from surplus to deficit, from job gain to job loss," and so on. He lambasted Bush for squandering the Clinton-era economy, and the international goodwill that followed 9/11. "Instead of uniting the world, we alienated it. And instead of uniting America, we divided it by trying to push it too far to the right." The Democratic partisans loved it.

Then Clinton turned to the matter at hand: the 2004 election. He urged unity among Democrats. While it was okay to "fall in love (and) be for somebody" now, during primary season, "when the primary's over, let's fall in line and bring the White House back to our party." As for the eight men and one woman who were vying for the party nomination, Clinton said he was tired of pundits denigrating them as political dwarves. "If people are telling you they're not big, they don't know what they're talking about. They're just not famous yet. I like this field, and I'm tired of people saying that this field can't beat an incumbent president. I know all these people and *this is the best field of candidates we've put forward in decades*." (Emphasis added.) At that signal, the five candidates in the audience clambered up to join the former president on stage for hugs, jubilant grins, and arms lifted—all to the sound of Sister Sledge's "We Are Family."[2]

What was most significant about the event, in retrospect, was not the oratory, nor the four-hour ban on Democratic primary candidates' sniping at each other. September 13, 2003 was the day on which Clinton returned as party leader. It was almost five years to the day—September 11, 1998—that independent counsel Kenneth Starr released his report detailing Clinton's affair with intern Monica Lewinsky. Then came impeachment, then Pardongate, and forget not the Pilfering and Trashing of the White House. After that the Democrats' presidential aspirants shied away from Clinton, at least in public. There probably was some truth in Terry McAuliffe's assertion, quoted earlier in this book: "The guy was still a huge star in the party." But that probably was because, as McAuliffe went on to say, "He did a lot of events for us in 2001 and 2002," which were mainly fundraising events.[3] Otherwise many Democrats, certainly those in the rank and file, felt uneasy about the Clintons. But now at the site of Indianola's famed hot-air balloon race, Clinton stepped on stage and was openly welcomed by the party's presidential contenders. It was acceptable again to be seen with him, to quote him, to cite his record—at least those parts of his record that the Clintons acknowledged. Once again the Comeback Kid had come back, and along with the Episodic Apologists in the media he had his Episodic Apologists in the party. As the 2004 Democratic National Convention approached they would cheer his growing power.

Vice President Al Gore was the Salieri of the 1990s; Salieri's boss was Wolfgang Amadeus Mozart. Both Gore and Clinton took pride in the era's balanced budgets and surpluses, ignoring the role the Republican-controlled House played in the healthy economy. Ignored, too, was the fact that Clinton's balanced-budget plan for economic growth through lower interest rates had failed. Interest rates actually went up until the election of the Republican Congress in 1994. Nonetheless, Gore had an inviting economic record to run on. Yet Gore, who might have once genuinely liked Clinton, had been personally sickened by Clinton's affair with Lewinsky, his other suspected assignations, and all the lies needed to cover up Clinton's slipups. Sure, a pol will exaggerate every now and then and even resort to an occasional petite white lie. But the Clintons' propensity for big lies when little ones would do and a little lie when no lie was needed finally got to Gore. Thus, Gore and his staff decided that it was both proper and prudent to distance the veep from Clinton, even if it meant putting distance between him and Clinton's economy. Gore would run as his own man, leaving Clinton and the trailer park stuff off limits.

While some Democrats believe the distancing of Clinton was a fatal campaign mistake, the greater error was that Gore decided to lurch left and run a populist campaign. It did not work with the electorate of 2000. Perhaps Clinton had been right when he said "the era of big government is over." Certainly after nearly two decades of unsurpassed prosperity the electorate was insufficiently sullen for the populist harangue. Ignoring the Clinton-Gore economic success, the man who grew up in Washington's posh Fairfax Hotel declared it time to soak the rich corporations with taxes. His campaign was framed as a new class war of us-versus-them. Gore called it "the people versus the powerful." The more he plied the line, the more the election that was his to lose was lost. Bush ran as a more centrist candidate, a "compassionate conservative," and the voters responded to his message.

At the time, Clinton, now lost in another Clintonian funk, was dismayed by his vice president. Clinton is a man who hates rejection, as a long line of startled women can attest. During the last several months of the presidency, Clinton and Gore were not even talking to each other. The president found that Gore preferred to communicate through his campaign chairman, William Daley, the former commerce secretary. It was an awkward distancing between the administration's two highest officials, and a painful rejection for Clinton. Yet it was understandable, given the repugnance Gore had for Clinton's self-destructive personal activities. Clinton had brought scandal to what should have been a presidency that in its immediate aftermath seemed successful.

"He just wouldn't listen to me!" Clinton complained in frustration two weeks before the election at a small gathering in the home of a Washington, D.C. supporter, and the fellow whose ear he was bending was no one he knew well. But by now Clinton's frustration was such that he would bend even the ear of a stranger. Such outbursts had become common. His self-absorption on display, he continued in his monologue to portray himself as the only one who could save Gore, and now maybe Gore had seen the light. "He's [Gore] gone back to the theme that I've been advocating all this time. He is saying, 'Don't put the prosperity at risk.' 'Let's keep it going.' 'Don't reverse it.' And now he's gained four points in four days. This thing is going to be all right! All we've got to do is say the right thing, and we'll win."[4] One lovely young lady in her late twenties who had overheard these remarks took the listener aside and observed that Gore's message was not as great a problem as the messenger. Clearly overwhelmed by Clinton's presence, as if he were the love of her young life, the lady said the problem was that, compared to Clinton, Gore had about as much charisma as—knocking on a wooden end table—"this piece of furniture." She was an ardent Democrat, she added, but George W. Bush had twice the presence of Gore.

Actually along with the taint of Clinton's scandals there was another factor prompting the Gore campaigners to distance themselves from the Boy President: his "overshadowing effect." It was not just the charisma gap. Prior to Pardongate the magnitude of Clinton's popularity among Democrats, his previous scandals notwithstanding, was prodigious, leaving Gore puny by comparison. After one popular black radio personality, Tom Joyner, listened to Clinton pump up Gore's candidacy on-air, the host sighed, wishing that Clinton were again the presidential candidate rather than Gore. Ever the egotist, Clinton responded by damning Gore with faint praise, saying that, after all, the Vice President was "*the next best thing.*" (Emphasis added.) There had to be a more favorable choice of words available. About this time *U.S. News & World Report* observed that any Clinton involvement in the campaign appeared to be a "double-edged sword. . . . Every move he [Clinton] makes seems to somehow suck the air out of the veep's bubble, step on his message, or otherwise get in his way or mess up his day." A Gore staffer was quoted as saying, "The president takes up, as you know, a lot of space; any president, but especially this one. And it's been hard for Gore to break through that."[5]

Could better use have been made of Clinton's advice? Could his appearances have been better chosen? Democratic advisers such as California Democratic operative Bob Mulholland think so. "I was an advocate and arguing on the phone to anybody that would listen, 'Get Bill Clinton out there in those states. Get him out there,'" recalled Mulholland. "I think it was foolish of the Gore campaign to act like, 'OK, I'm Al Gore, I'm the nominee, and I have to do it on my own.' Baloney! You got Bill Clinton. Greatest economy in the history of the world. Get him out there!"[6]

Mulholland and other Democratic sages say that Gore could have distanced himself from Clinton's scandal-related negatives, while successfully embracing the policy achievements. With hindsight they opine that if Clinton had gone to Florida several times to energize the Democratic base there, then Gore would not have lost the state by 537 votes—which cost him, after a Supreme Court ruling, the state's twenty-five electoral votes, and the election. Some say Clinton should have been dispatched repeatedly to his home state of Arkansas, where he was still highly popular. It is likely that he could have swayed 25,087 voters there to back Gore, which would have then won him the state's six electoral votes. Assuming Florida still went for Bush, winning Arkansas would have been enough to put Gore on top. His electoral victory would have been 272 to Bush's 265—instead of what was the actual electoral Bush victory of 271 to Gore's 266.

During the following year, Gore and Clinton rarely talked. The former vice president was smarting not only from his loss, but also from a stormy post-election meeting with Clinton, in which Clinton criticized Gore for the way he ran his failed campaign. At the time, Clinton did not say that he could have won it for Gore if he had been allowed more involvement in the campaign. Instead, he criticized Gore for abandoning their shared base in the Democratic Leadership Council, the organization founded to move the Democratic Party from the McGovernite left to the center. If Gore had not gone left, he could have won, Clinton scolded.

The first sign of a slight thaw came with the national unifying effect of the terrorist attacks on the World Trade Center and the Pentagon. At the time of the event, Gore was on his way to a rare visit with Clinton in Chappaqua. When all flights were grounded, Gore got stuck in Buffalo, New York. He decided to drive the length of the state to see his old comrade, and Clinton—ever the night owl—waited up until 3:00 a.m. for Gore. Thus began another of these 1960s kids' nocturnal bull sessions. They talked until dawn about the new America that would emerge from this contemporary Pearl Harbor. They pondered what their roles might be. Occasional calls were exchanged afterwards, though both knew that they could never be good friends again. Finally, in early 2002 Gore publicly invoked the famous name that had not passed his lips throughout Campaign 2000. In a fiery anti-Bush speech on April 13 at the Florida Democratic Convention, a pulpit-pounding Gore pronounced: "*Bill Clinton and I* did a damn good job!"

The signal had been given. If Al Gore had begun to forgive Bill Clinton, others in the party could as well. Almost as if the former president was being let out on political training wheels, various Democrats asked for his help during the 2002 midterm elections. Clinton himself reckoned he made more than one hundred appearances in 2002 on behalf of Democratic candidates (including fundraisers for the

Democratic Party as a whole). As the campaign progressed, the question at hand regarding the ex-prez was pithily put by *New York Times* columnist William Safire: "Is a Clinton connection a political plus or the mark of Cain?"[7]

Well, "mark of Cain" might be a little strong, but Clinton's support was not all that helpful to candidates in 2002. Yet has it ever been? As noted earlier, the Democrats have been good to Clinton, but the Clintons have never been particularly good for the Democratic Party. The party's contingent of fifty-eight United States senators declined to forty-four between 1992 and 2005. Its 258 House members declined during those years to 202. From the forty-second president's first election to 2005, the Democrats lost nine governorships, leaving them with only twenty-two in 2005. In 1992 the Democrats controlled the majority of state legislatures. By 2005 the Republicans had the majority. I have tracked thirteen specific candidates who ran with Clinton's help during the 2002 midterm elections. Ten lost; three won. Of those three, only one victory—a minor House race in Maine—may be attributable to Clinton's assistance. Because Clinton showed up at an Augusta rally with Michael Michaud, the Democratic challenger in that race, 5,000 people turned out. "It was great," Michaud reflected. "I never could have attracted that many people myself."[8] Clinton's infusion of national political energy helped Michaud win 52 percent of the vote to become a freshman congressman, or so Michaud thinks.

As for the other races where Clinton participated, behold the dismal outcomes.

Janet Reno, Clinton's attorney general, ran for governor of Florida and was beaten in the Democratic primary by Tampa lawyer Bill McBride. Clinton then supported McBride energetically in a race against Governor Jeb Bush that was intensely personal, despite all the former Boy President's admonitions in the 1990s against the "politics of personal destruction." I cannot find any former president in modern times campaigning as partisanly as this one did on behalf of McBride against Governor Bush. He even took up the irrational party mantra that Bush had helped his brother George "steal" the 2000 presidential election; this despite the fact that every credible study of the election refutes the claim. Late in the gubernatorial race, Clinton's pal, McAuliffe, then chairman of the Democratic National Committee, announced that unseating Governor Bush was his party's *primary* election goal. A Democratic victory would be "devastating to President Bush." Possibly so; President Bush was so committed to his brother's reelection that he made repeated visits to the state on Jeb's behalf. His last campaign appearance was November 2, three days before the election and the same day that ex-president Clinton also toured the state whipping up support for McBride among blacks and seniors. What had appeared to be a close race when it began ended with Clinton's candidate being trounced by thirteen points. The outcomes were not much better elsewhere.

In Massachusetts, Clinton's former secretary of labor, Robert Reich, ran for governor. As with Clinton's attorney general, Reich did not survive the Democratic primary. The victor, Shannon O'Brien, appeared to be a sure winner in this rock-solid Democratic northeastern state. She was Irish, had the support of the unions, the *Boston Globe*, the Kennedys, and most liberal-front groups. What is more, Clinton went out and stumped for her. Or was it for himself? P.J. O'Rourke attended a Boston Teachers Union rally for O'Brien in October at which Clinton was O'Brien's chief tub-thumper. After a succession of dull speeches, including O'Brien's, Clinton was introduced. "He was a mammoth thawing in its Siberian exile from the center of attention, a nameless creature of Mary Shelley's sparked to animation by the lightning of handclaps," O'Rourke wrote.[9] His speech was so dramatic that O'Brien and others "were idiots to share the stage with him." But Clinton mostly spoke about himself and what he had done as president, or at least what he wanted the citizenry to think he had done. "It was a long and fulsome brag," O'Rourke continued. "And just as the brag was reaching Mike Fink-keelboat limits of good taste, Clinton opened his arms to the crowd. 'But that's nothing!' he said. 'You would have done the same thing! Because you're Democrats!'" He had encouraged adulation for himself; and not much was left for O'Brien, who lost to Mitt Romney, the head of the Salt Lake City Winter Olympics and son of Nixon cabinet member George Romney. Romney *fils* netted 50 percent of the vote to O'Brien's 45 percent.

In the Ohio gubernatorial race, we cannot fault Clinton greatly for his candidate's almost twenty-point loss to incumbent Republican Governor Bob Taft. From the start, the challenger, Tim Hagan, ran well behind the better-funded, better-known and more popular Taft. Nevertheless, Clinton gamely campaigned for him, including an appearance at a Cleveland fundraiser where he helped raise about $200,000 for the campaign. Hagan joked at the event that he had called a particular United States senator for an appearance at the fundraiser to bring out as many people as possible. "Senator Hillary Clinton is busy," he was told. So she sent her husband.

In Connecticut, Clinton's help for another of his administration's fledgling candidates, former White House policy adviser William Curry, Jr., was not enough to produce a gubernatorial win. Curry was outspent four-to-one by the incumbent Republican governor John Rowland. Despite an election-eve campaign appearance by Clinton for Curry, Rowland's lead could not be overcome. He won reelection with a twelve-point victory, becoming the first Connecticut governor to win a third consecutive term in almost two centuries.

Clinton's assistance could not even make up the difference for a Kennedy family member running in Democratic Maryland, but at least that gubernatorial race was close. Republican Robert Ehrlich, Jr. managed to edge out Kathleen Kennedy Townsend by four points to win the governorship.

One of Clinton's former presidential advisers, Rahm Emanuel, ran for the Illinois congressional seat of former Democratic Ways and Means chairman Dan Rostenkowski, a convicted felon. The district is so densely Democratic that Emanuel coasted to victory against the Republican challenger—67 to 29 percent—with no need for Clinton to intervene. Meanwhile, in North Carolina, Clinton's former chief of staff Erskine Bowles asked his old boss *not to come to the state or say anything on Bowles's behalf.* North Carolina's voters were not fond of Clinton, and, anyway, Bowles stood little chance in the Senate race against the popular Elizabeth Dole, a Reagan cabinet member and wife of Clinton's 1996 opponent, Senator Robert Dole. She won handily, 53.6 to 45 percent.

New Mexico was a singular bright spot for Bill Clinton in 2002. He had previously won the state twice, and Gore narrowly won it in 2000. So Bill Richardson decided his own Clinton connection would not hurt in an open race for governor. Before he had been Clinton's energy secretary and served as U.N. ambassador, Richardson had been a popular seven-term congressman from New Mexico and thus had an independent base of support. His opponent, John Sanchez, tried in different ways to "smear" him with the Clinton connection, but the voters were not listening. Richardson's victory was such a blowout—55.5 to 39.1 percent—that the candidate himself obviously won the election on his own, without any *pro forma* assistance.

The New Mexico victory, however, could not make up for the bitter pill the Clintons had to swallow in New York. First, Andrew Cuomo, the former Secretary of Housing and Urban Development in the Clinton Administration, threw his hat in the ring. There was a bit of the personal in that bid—a chance to oust two-term Governor George Pataki, who himself had booted Cuomo's father, Mario, out of the governor's chair. Married to a daughter of the late Senator Robert Kennedy, the forty-four-year-old Cuomo was a Clinton favorite. But after the sixty-six-year-old state comptroller, H. Carl McCall, began his run, hoping to become the state's first black governor, the Clintons pledged to remain neutral throughout the primary.

Hillary, the junior senator from New York, thought she had a promise from the senior senator, Charles Schumer, to do the same. But in late July, he came out for McCall, and other New York Democratic bigwigs rushed to do the same. Though described as "furious," Hillary and her husband adroitly abandoned their good friend Cuomo out of political exigency. They would support McCall, thus ingratiating themselves to New York's black voters. Cuomo struggled but finally, after a persuasive call from Bill Clinton, withdrew from the race a week before the primary was held. (Since Clinton, in a similar private telephone call, also urged the disgraced Senator Robert Torricelli to abandon his reelection bid, a Democratic strategist suggested: "If he's on the phone, you probably don't want to take the call. He's the Tony Soprano of tri-state politics."[10])

Despite active campaigning by the Clintons and other eminent Democrats, McCall was trounced by Pataki, losing by 16 points. A third major candidate, billionaire Tom Golisano, received almost half as many votes as McCall, but only after spending $70 million of his own funds on his independent campaign.

The 2002 midterm election turned into a major Democratic rout. The national campaigner who proved to be the decisive factor in many of the campaigns was not Clinton but President George W. Bush, who accomplished the rare feat of improving his hold on Congress despite being an incumbent president. Notwithstanding the demands of his office, the president campaigned almost as extensively as the former president, expanding his lead in the House while regaining control of the Senate. (It had been temporarily lost in 2001 when Senator James Jeffords, after being promised the moon by the Democrats, left the Republican Party and, as an Independent, declared he would caucus with the Democrats, giving them a slight 51-49 majority.)

Margaret Carlson, in a *Time* magazine review of the 2002 election results titled "Say Good Night, Bill," wrote that "Clinton-era values are no longer America's. Though a baby boomer, Bush rejects the instant-gratification ethic embraced by Clinton, the nation's first baby boomer president. . . . Clinton revered CEOs; they now appear regularly in televised perp walks. Clinton loved Hollywood; celebrities like Barbra Streisand had his ear and an invitation to the Lincoln Bedroom. Bush doesn't have movie stars over; he's in bed with Laura by 9:30." While Clinton had proved to be "a major presence, raising funds, campaigning for candidates and generally trying to help his party regain its *mojo*," she added, the "vote was a repudiation of his efforts." Clinton had no coattails. "Hillary Rodham Clinton is the one politician to survive the association with Bill, although at a high personal price."[11] Given Clinton's feeble track record in 2002, political prognosticators might have been forgiven for predicting that his visible help (other than fundraising) might not be sought by the Democratic presidential candidates—in the end, not at all.

A close look at the public pronouncements of those candidates in the late summer of 2003 shows a distinct turn toward Clinton, the only Democrat to be reelected president since Franklin D. Roosevelt. Perhaps the turnaround was fueled by the growing budget deficit under the Bush administration, which could be contrasted with the Clinton era. Or perhaps just enough time had passed for Clinton's inflated claims of domestic successes to overwhelm memories of his moral failures in the minds of the Democratic faithful. As we have seen, the Clintons set off cycles of hope, indignation, and hope renewed many times before.

Whatever the reason might have been, by 2003 most of the Democratic candidates were seeking Clinton's embrace. As for the former president's endorsement, that was something he had pledged *not* to give to any candidate during the primaries. He and others around Hillary had hoped she would seek the Democratic nomination in 2004, and Hillary apparently liked the idea until sometime in the spring of 2003, when she decided to sit 2004 out. Bill never fully gave up thinking she might run in 2004, and that gave him yet another reason to withhold support for others in the primaries.

So the rock star politico who arrived in the black SUV on that September day in Indianola was back on top, at least among Democrats. "Aren't we proud to have Bill Clinton as an American and as a Democrat?" Senator Bob Graham of Florida asked the crowd, to a resounding cheer. Then the Floridian went on to say that he would welcome Clinton's involvement in his own campaign. Graham proceeded to compare the "dividing presidency of George Bush to the uniting presidency of Bill Clinton." Former Illinois Senator Carol Moseley Braun agreed. "President Clinton brought us peace and prosperity, (while) the Bush crowd has brought us depression and war," she explained. Missouri Representative Richard Gephardt noted that "Bill Clinton was a great president for the economy," adding cheerfully: "When I'm the nominee, I'm going to have Bill Clinton out on the road for me, fighting to win this presidency."

Dr. Howard Dean, until recently governor of Vermont, had declared previously at an appearance in Chicago: "It's time we stop running away from Bill Clinton and say, 'This is a president who helped America when it needed it.'" At another event, this one a labor forum in Waterloo, Iowa, he had invoked Clinton's name after suggesting that the time was nigh to roll back the Bush tax cuts in a time of increasing deficits. "People would gladly pay the taxes they paid under Bill Clinton, if only they had the same economy they did under Bill Clinton."[12] At the historic steak fry, Dean postulated that Clinton *and* Al Gore are "both going to help us a lot" during the 2004 campaign. While he would welcome Clinton's side-by-side campaign help, Dean continued: "He's a larger-than-life figure, so there's always a risk that he'll diminish whoever the nominee is, but I think that he'd be a very valuable asset on the campaign trail."[13]

That "overshadowing effect" might have been the reason that Senator John Edwards of North Carolina ducked out of the steak fry before Clinton's arrival. Because of his youthfulness and Southern appeal, Edwards was styling his campaign after Clinton's 1992 race. He asserted that he was grateful Clinton had campaigned for him during his successful Senate run in 1998. He reminded the crowd that he had returned the favor by supporting the Clinton administration's initiatives in the Senate. "I stood with Clinton, and it worked," he bragged. "He led the greatest period of economic expansion in history and we ought to be proud of him."[14] In fact, he concluded with gusto, echoing Dean's line: "I'm tired of Democrats walking away from Bill Clinton."[15] Minutes later he did just that, citing a "scheduling conflict."

Massachusetts Senator John Kerry cited Clinton as frequently as Dean in the previous month's speeches, often using the tagline: "If you liked the economy under Bill Clinton, America, you're going to love it under John Kerry." At the steak fry, Kerry joined in extolling Clinton's political virtues, adding that in Clinton's upcoming speech, the Democratic faithful would hear "more common sense for the country in twenty minutes than George W. Bush has offered in two and a half years."[16] Then about fifteen minutes before Clinton arrived, he, too, vamoosed, also claiming a "scheduling conflict." (In retrospect, the absence of Kerry and Edwards from Clinton's appearance that day, though noted by only one of the journalists present, spoke volumes about their lingering unease over being seen with Clinton—Clinton "the concept" was as far as they would go. The impact on the independent vote of being pictured onstage with the Great Pardoner was still too risky.)

Of all the candidates to speak admiringly of Clinton, the most unlikely was Senator Lieberman. Though his religious beliefs kept him off the stage at the Iowa steak fry, he had acknowledged Clinton's political genius on recent occasions, which is surprising, given Lieberman's forthright denunciation of Clinton in 1998. Before 1998, Lieberman was one of the centrists who, along with Governor Clinton, established the Democratic Leadership Council to close the curtain on their party's McGovernite past. Through the years, however, Lieberman had become the leading Democratic advocate for family values. Then came 1998 and the transient fame of Monica Lewinsky. In September Lieberman stood alone among Democrats and on the Senate floor became the first Democratic senator to inveigh against Clinton for his abuse of power with a White House intern.

Clinton was in terrible trouble. Yet, once again, Clinton diagnosed his fellow Democrats' anxieties, whipped them into a frenzy against his prosecutor, and survived. Now, five years beyond the frenzy, Lieberman saw

Clinton anew. On the stump he vowed over and again to continue the Clinton political legacy. He reminisced on their ancient "friendship." It had begun, he would recall, in 1970, when in Lieberman's first campaign he met "a young Yale law student named Bill Clinton." Nineteen ninety-eight was forgotten. In a single speech Lieberman mentioned Clinton's name twenty-two times!

As the primary field filled out in 2003 and Clinton's role became more prominent, political commentators became increasingly absorbed with the question: "Who is Clinton's candidate?" Certainly it was not the discredited Senator Moseley Braun, whom some speculated served as Gore's stalking horse after he coaxed her into the race. The other black in the race, the Rev. Al Sharpton, had a personal friendship with Clinton, who surely admired the Rev's roguish charm, but Sharpton had no chance. Clinton would not stake his reputation on Sharpton. Nor, in Clinton's calculations, were Representative Dennis Kucinich or Senators Graham and Lieberman likely to win the nomination, so supporting them would be unproductive. Gephardt, the early favorite to win the Iowa caucuses, might get the nomination, but Gephardt would never be a Clinton protégé. Howard Dean's political views and campaign were too liberal for Clinton. John Kerry was too close to Kennedy, and his Boston Brahmin background clashed culturally with Clinton's down-home façade.

By all accounts, both from the dozens of interviews done for this book and from the media chatter, at the time of the Harkin steak fry the candidate then favored by Clinton and his loyalists was Edwards, Hillary having become adamant against a 2004 run. The Clintonistas envisaged Edwards as Clinton redux, a malleable fan of the forty-second president, who just might return Clintonism to 1600 Pennsylvania Avenue. Clinton had been cultivating Edwards since early 2002. He saw in Edwards many of his own political assets. As Clinton once put it, he thought Edwards looked great on TV and "could talk an owl out of a tree." But North Carolina's freshman senator was a slow learner, lacking Clinton's cunning and his photographic memory. His shallowness on the issues had not earned him respect among senatorial colleagues, and Senator Clinton publicly showed her disdain. In October 2002, after Edwards took offense when Hillary squeezed him out of a choice speaking slot during a Senate discussion of Iraq, Hillary sniped: "Just stand there and look pretty, John." The remark struck like lightning throughout the chamber. Nonetheless, thanks perhaps to Bill Clinton's tutelage, by the fall of 2003 Bill perceived signs of maturation in Edwards and the possibility that he might beat George W. Bush in the election.

Despite being favorably inclined towards Edwards, Clinton had promised to help any candidate who asked him, and this was one of the rare occasions when Clinton kept his word. He helped rewrite some of Gephardt's speeches. Lieberman boasted that he talked to Clinton "all the time" about his campaign, a relationship that was enhanced by the fact that Clinton had hired a Lieberman man, Jim Kennedy, to be his primary post-presidential spokesman. John Kerry had a key connection to Clinton through his campaign spokesman, Chris Lehane, a Clinton man. Kerry also talked directly to Clinton and took his advice. For example, Clinton had suggested in August that Kerry might be more effective with his stump speech if he quoted newspaper headlines critical of the Bush administration, which Kerry began to do. Confessing that he spoke frequently with Clinton because "I like the advice I get," Kerry told an Associated Press reporter that it was his understanding that Clinton was "available to everybody."[17]

Dean's campaign manager, Joe Trippi, recalled that Clinton had a knack for making each candidate "believe that, somewhere deep down, Bill Clinton wanted them to be president. Clinton did a really good job of that." Not since 1944, when FDR had no less than three vice presidential candidates believing he was for them, had a political prestidigitator kept so many seasoned pols in the air. As an example of Clinton's duplicity, Trippi cited a supportive call from Clinton to Dean a couple days before the steak fry. Already under fire for saying that the United States should be even-handed in the Israeli-Palestinian conflict, Dean made the mistake of calling Hamas terrorists "soldiers" in an interview with CNN's Wolf Blitzer. Ripping Dean's remarks out of context, the media feasted on that botch. Blitzer had asked Dean if he approved of the Israelis' assassinating "Hamas militants." Dean essentially said "yes" under the rationale that "there is a war going on in the Middle East, and members of Hamas are soldiers in that war, and, therefore, it seems to me, that they are going to be casualties if they are going to make war."[18]

As the media storm over the remark reached its crescendo, Dean received an unsolicited call from the former president. "Don't worry about it, Howard," Clinton laughed. "I made that same kind of mistake when I was running. We governors have good judgment but we just don't understand how those foreign policy people talk. Once you learn the lingo, it'll be fine. So don't worry about it. I screwed up—I can't even remember how many times I screwed up like that in my own campaign. You're doing great! Keep it up!"

Dean was greatly cheered by the call, which he recounted in detail to Trippi. "So, here I am inside the campaign, and I'm thinking, 'Hey we didn't call *him.* He picked up the phone and called my guy. Clinton must really like him.' Yet Clinton never said anything like that. When you're in a campaign, you read into it what you want to. And everybody in all the campaigns was probably doing that with Clinton's calls."[19] That view would change, however, once a candidate entered the field whom Clinton himself recruited. The candidate arrived enigmatically, late in the game, but with extensive help from Clinton—an occurrence that caught political watchers by surprise.

A week before the Iowa steak fry, on a cool Sunday evening in Chappaqua, Bill and Hillary Clinton hosted a thank-you party for about 150 major campaign donors from Bill's past campaigns and from Hillary's more recent Senate race. As they sipped cocktails in the backyard, Clinton made a pointed comment that astonished those gathered around him. He said that the national Democratic Party really only had "two stars."

His wife was one. The other was a retired four-star general and fellow

Arkansan, Wesley K. Clark. Clinton pointedly failed to mention as "stars" any of the nine already-announced Democratic candidates for president. Later in the evening, with an implied wink, he predicted that "we might have another candidate or two jumping into the race."[20]

By that time, Clinton was fully aware that Clark was going to join the presidential race. Once Clinton was convinced that his wife, Hillary, would not make a run, he personally recruited Clark to join the Democratic field. In fact, only the day before, on September 6, Clark had briefed him on a secret summit he had had with Howard Dean in Los Angeles. Dean, whose Internet-funded campaign had been fueled by his "outsider" status, was fretting that Clark might enter the race and challenge him on both fronts. A "Draft Clark" movement was crawling the Internet, and such Web sites could easily transform themselves, once coalesced, into the same kind of fundraising powerhouse that Dean and his campaign manager Trippi had pioneered. Adepts of the Internet seemed to favor the "outsider"; and who could be more the "outsider" than a respected general who had never held elective office?

The two met off the lobby of the Sheraton Hotel at the Los Angeles airport for the one-on-one conference. According to Clark, the essence of the conversation was this:

"Howard, I'm trying to decide whether to run or not to run," Clark said at one point.

"Don't you want to know the alternative?" Dean queried.

"Okay, what's the alternative?"

"You can be my vice president," Dean offered, "but you'd have to be vetted."

Clark turned aside the suggestion. He had finally made up his mind to run, and it was now only a matter of getting his wife's approval. "Gert doesn't want me to run," Clark confided to Dean, as Trippi joined the pair. Now that the business portion was concluded, an affable Dean remarked that his wife, Judy, "had the same type of feelings initially. But now that I'm out there running, she thinks it's great. I'll be glad to have

Judy call Gert." Dean's campaign manager was astounded. The whole purpose of the meeting had been for Dean to persuade Clark not to run, and now he seemed to be encouraging Clark to join the field.[21] When Clark recounted the meeting in a telephone conversation with Clinton, it was clear to the former president that Clark had decided to run. Clinton immediately offered practical advice on where, when, and how to make the announcement.

A week later, at the Iowa steak fry, a surprised CNN reporter noted that when interviewed after his speech, Clinton "talked up the candidacy of somebody who isn't even in the race yet, General Wesley Clark." Clinton expounded to CNN viewers: "I think he'd be quite good. He's a very smart man. I've known him since 1965. He's served our country well. He was fabulous in the Bosnian peace process and the conflict in Kosovo."[22] Four days after that, on September 17, Clark declared his candidacy, surrounded by a host of old Clinton hands who had signed onto his campaign, which would be headquartered in the only place he and Clinton considered home—Little Rock, Arkansas.

Twenty months apart in age (Clark is older), the two had strikingly similar early lives. Both are Arkansas natives who were raised by their doting mothers after their fathers died while they were young.* Both were raised Baptist, and go by the last names of their stepfathers. Both learned in adulthood about brothers they had never met. Both had dreams of stardom beyond the borders of their rural state. During the 1960s both were selected as Rhodes Scholars.

Clark first met Clinton in November 1965 when the young West Point cadet attended a conference on international affairs at Georgetown

---

*Actually, in the case of Clinton, his paternity is probably unknown. As he is the kind of modern politician who exploits for political preferment almost any personal matter heretofore considered private including his rough origins, I would be remiss in failing to note that scholars doubt Clinton's mother's claim that her first son was fathered by William Blythe, III, an ignorant, unintelligent drifter. She lived with him but two weeks before becoming pregnant. More likely, the historian Nigel Hamilton suggests, any of three other men, one of whom was a doctor in Hope, fathered Bill.

University. When the registrant noted that Clark was originally from Arkansas, she insisted he meet a fellow Arkansan in residence, the class president, Bill Clinton. About an hour later, Clinton came to meet him, with a beautiful young girl on each arm. It was a story Clark was given to repeating on the campaign trail in Iowa.[23]

The two recognized in each other a similar intellectual acumen and boundless ambition. Unsurprisingly, these two 1960s generation go-getters decided to keep occasional tabs on each other, even as their paths sharply diverged. While Clinton dodged the draft and protested the Vietnam War in London, his fellow Rhodie did the opposite. Clark gave speeches for the United States Embassy throughout England in defense of American foreign policy, despite volleys of tomatoes thrown by the peaceful protesters. Eventually he shipped off to Vietnam, where the projectiles were more dangerous. During a patrol in the field, his unit was ambushed and, though Clark was shot in the shoulder, the leg, the hip, and the hand, he directed a counterattack long enough to lead the platoon to safety. He received a Silver Star for valor.

Clark advanced in the military *pari passu* with Clinton's advance in politics. In the 1980s, Clark remembered a dinner he enjoyed with Governor Clinton in Little Rock. There both reveled in their successes. Clark did not lay eyes on Clinton again until after his 1992 presidential victory. Then a mutual friend and Arkansan, actress Mary Steenburgen, put them together. "There is this feeling of being part of a family of people that come from there," Steenburgen explained. "I think Bill and Wes and I—all three—really ferociously love where we came from."[24] Steenburgen and Clark served on a commission selecting White House Fellows, which brought Clark and Clinton together again in October 1993. After that reunion, Clinton took an intense interest in Clark's career, becoming the ambitious officer's most important patron. For his last three military posts, Clark was not the Army's choice but the president's, engendering what proved to be an ultimately deadly animosity at the Pentagon.

Clark soon distinguished himself as a military aide to Ambassador Richard Holbrooke, during the successful 1995 Dayton, Ohio peace talks over the Bosnian conflict with Slobodan Milosevic. As Clark received subsequent commands, he gained a reputation as a grandstander, though for a while his enemies could do nothing. He was Clinton's man. Eventually he was promoted to four-star general and to his final command as the Supreme Allied Commander of Europe. By now a committed interventionist, Clark joined Secretary of State Madeleine Albright in urging NATO to intercede against Milosevic's Serbs in Kosovo. Once he got the go-ahead in late March 1999, General Clark directed an air campaign that, he assured President Clinton, would bring Milosevic to his knees in short order. But in this, NATO's first and probably last European war, the various governments insisted on separate approval for each bombing target. Consequently, the air campaign dragged on well past Clark's first estimates.

As the summer approached, Clark began getting pressure from the White House to wrap it up. Political considerations in the Clinton administration were again trumping all else. As Clark recounted privately to a historian several months before he left his NATO post: "There were those in the White House who said, 'Hey, look, you gotta finish the bombing before the Fourth of July weekend. That's the start of the next presidential campaign season, so stop it. It doesn't matter what you do, just turn it off. You don't have to win this thing; let it lie.'" He never identified by name the administration official who applied the pressure, though in later remarks (during the presidential campaign), Clark exempted both Clinton and his national security adviser, Sandy Berger. As it happened, Clark concluded the war just in time for Vice President Al Gore's announcement of his candidacy a week later, on June 16.[25]

In retrospect, it was a remarkable achievement. Though it took longer than expected, the fact is that Clark ended an internecine European conflict via a seventy-eight-day air campaign that never required a soldier on the ground, and during which there was not a single American casualty. Rightly expecting to be hailed as a hero, and to have his NATO appointment extended, Clark was stunned in July when two powerful bureaucratic enemies, Chairman of the Joint Chiefs of Staff General Henry Shelton and Secretary of Defense William Cohen, engineered his removal by subterfuge. In routinely signing the order for Clark's transfer from NATO, his patron, the eternally disorganized Boy President, neglected to note that it meant Clark's early retirement. "He was hornswoggled," Clark recounted.[26] "This was a behind-the-back power play. Bill Clinton told me himself he had nothing to do with it, and I believe him."[27]

By the time he received the Presidential Medal of Freedom from Clinton at the White House, Clark was glad to be leaving his Pentagon days behind. He headed to Little Rock to make his fortune, which he did from two Clinton-connected Arkansas-based companies, Acxiom Corp. and the Stephens Group investment firm. He also went on the lecture circuit and became a popular CNN military analyst, where he voiced criticism of Bush's incursion into Iraq. Those reports and Clark's TV fame are what prompted independent admirers to begin a proliferation of "Draft Clark" Web sites, a phenomenon that, Clark maintained, finally persuaded him to join the presidential race in mid-September.

It was an immediate and serious setback for Howard Dean's front-running effort—"the first real blow to our campaign after seven months of mostly easy sailing," Trippi recalled. "Suddenly, we weren't the only Washington outsider in the field anymore. And the other Washington outsider was a goddamned Rhodes Scholar war hero, hand-picked by Bill Clinton. Instantly, Wes Clark became the one guy we most feared."[28]

The Clark campaign became abundant with veteran Clintonistas who dominated its headquarters on the fourth floor of an old railway building in Little Rock just down the street from where some of the same pols had run their upstart presidential campaign back in 1992 from the soon-to-be famous "war room." Two of the veterans from that war room were at the top of Clark's campaign—Eli Segal, the campaign manager and prodigious fundraiser, and Mickey Kantor, Clinton's former commerce secretary and U.S. trade representative. Also on hand for Clark were Clinton's long-time *consigliere*, Bruce Lindsey; Clinton's top troubleshooter on the Whitewater matter, Mark Fabiani; and Ron Klain, an attorney who was part of the 1992 campaign and then became Janet Reno's chief of staff at the Justice Department. In addition, a bevy of behind-the-scenes advisers helped guide the campaign, such as Skip Rutherford, head of the Clinton Foundation, and Representative Rahm Emanuel, Clinton's former 1992 finance director. Literally dozens more ex-Clinton aides filled Clark's campaign staff from top to bottom.

"None of those top people went to work for Clark without getting a big thumbs-up from Clinton," said one top Democratic strategist in the campaign. "Clark is a total creature of the Clintons," added an operative for another Democratic candidate. "They're puffing him up to keep everyone off-balance."[29]

Pundits conjectured that Clark had been urged by Clinton into the campaign to be a stalking horse for Hillary. According to this scenario, once Clark dimmed Dean's luster and turned the primaries into a wide-open horse race Hillary would step in to save the Democrats from anarchy. Both Clintons realized that they had to silence these stalking-horse whisperers with emphatic denials. At a *Christian Science Monitor* breakfast with journalists, Senator Clinton called the idea that the Clintons were supporting a Clark candidacy "an absurd feat of imagination." On top of that, she added, she and her husband were "not supporting or endorsing any candidate."[30] For good measure, Bill called at least three of the candidates or their campaign staffs—Dean, Kerry and Lieberman—and personally reassured them once again that he was not going to endorse anyone during the primaries.

Hillary's disclaimer was important because she aimed to be nothing less than the brightest star among the Democrats' national elected officials. Recognition that she was, at least, a great draw came with an invitation to give the keynote speech at Iowa's most important annual fundraiser, the Jefferson-Jackson Day dinner gala, an emcee post she could not accept if she had endorsed one of the candidates. Hillary's popularity with the Democratic rank and file was such that ticket sales set records for swiftness of sales and for the amount raised, $300,000. On the way into the event at Des Moines Veterans Memorial Auditorium on the evening of November 15, it was hard to see a blade of grass or a tree trunk for all the candidate signs covering the lawn and trees. Inside it was pandemonium for the 7,500 Democrats, six presidential candidates, and hundreds of reporters gathered. The scene was more suggestive of a college football game than politics. Five half-naked men had the letters K-E-R-R-Y spelled out on their chests; Edwards had a not-so-well-practiced flip card section. Beside the signs and constant cheerleader chants ("Here we go, Edwards, here we go"), there were the radio-controlled blimps of the Kerry and Edwards campaigns buzzing overhead.

The candidates—not including Clark, who was skipping the Iowa caucuses to concentrate on the New Hampshire primary—rolled out their routine rants as well as new catchphrases. Howard Dean, who got a deafening reception, managed to shout a dozen times while pointing at the crowd: "You've got the power!" Edwards, in a direct put-down of Dean, yelled above the din: "Anger won't change America; action will." And Kerry tried out a new Bush-challenge line, "Bring it on," to resounding cheers. But the Democratic faithful saved their most unrestrained ovation for the keynote speaker, incessantly chanting HILL-A-RY as she came out to the sound of U2's "Beautiful Day." Harkin introduced her as the Democratic Party's "rock star," and it was a while before she could begin her speech. Just above the bedlam, she promised during her eighteen-minute oration that one of the Democrats would soon be in the White House: "It begins in Iowa; it ends at Pennsylvania Avenue." She urged alliteratively: "Never forget; never forget. Pundits and polls don't pick presidents. People pick presidents." Hillary later remarked that the enthusiastic reception she got was overwhelming: "I couldn't tell if I was at a revival or a World Wrestling event. But it was a great night." To some observers, the evening ended with the incongruous sight of Howard Dean and Hillary Clinton dancing together amid the confetti and mosh-pit-like frenzy of the partying ticket holders.[31]

The next day, a *Des Moines Register* headline reflected a majority feeling among the Democrats at the Jefferson-Jackson dinner: "Many Say Clinton Would Get Their Votes." That was what Kristin Scurderi, an Iowa Republican Party official, remembered hearing most after the event. "I thought it just went to show what a weak field of candidates they had. Everybody was saying, 'Hillary should run.'"[32]

A couple of weeks later, Senator Clinton left for an announced Thanksgiving tour of military operations in Afghanistan and Iraq. No one doubted that the New York senator, who had campaigned for a position on the Senate Armed Services Committee despite her antimilitary record in previous years, was burnishing national security credentials for a White House run in 2008 or 2012. All did not go well. Word leaked that there were soldiers who refused to dine or even meet with her. One was photographed making a hand gesture known to the military as a distress signal. Finally, her carefully staged public relations stunt was overwhelmed by the sudden unannounced Thanksgiving visit from the commander-in-chief, President George W. Bush. He had planned the trip for weeks but, for security reasons, had not even informed his own parents until after Air Force One lifted off from the Baghdad airport for its return journey. "I was just looking for a warm meal somewhere," he joked with the surprised troops. "Thank you for inviting me to dinner."

Meanwhile, Hillary's husband went beyond advising Democratic presidential primary candidates only. He took a dive into active politics, campaigning in two California races. The results once again adumbrated the Clinton Curse. It even befalls those for whom the former Boy President campaigns.

For Bill Clinton, California—with an economy the size of France's and a population of 35 million—should be friendly country, an easy mark for Hollywood's favorite president. Registered Democrats outnumbered registered Republicans by ten points. *Every* statewide office was held by a Democrat, as were both seats in the United States Senate. The majority of both houses of the state legislature and a majority in the congressional delegation were Democratic. But by late summer, Governor Gray Davis was on the ropes. In the late 1990s, he had led state government on a free-spending trend that was fueled by the state's high-tech sector. The bubble burst in 2000 when technology stocks plummeted. In 2001, the state had an energy crisis. Davis responded slowly and inadequately. The only way the dour and dull man won reelection in 2002 was by first unleashing vicious attack ads during the *Republican* primary against the front-runner, former Los Angeles Mayor Richard Riordan. Then he did the same against the man who beat Riordan in the Republican primary, Bill Simon, Jr. Even then, and even with the dominance of the Democratic vote, Davis won reelection only narrowly, 47 to 42 percent.

A few weeks after his reelection, Governor Davis revealed that the projected budget deficit was going to be a whopping $38 billion, requiring tax hikes and deep cuts in social service expenditures. Many of those who had voted for him felt he had cynically tricked them. His approval rating quickly dropped to 20 percent. The time was ripe for a recall initiative, the first one in the state's history that would prove successful. At first, Davis thought it was a joke promoted by kooks and cranks. But then the recall drive was funded to the tune of more than $1 million by conservative Republican representative Darrell Issa, who had made a fortune in the car-alarm business. By late July, the angry and fully funded recall rebels had nearly a million signatures—more than enough to force a recall election.

Davis, shaken and fearing for his political life, called his political guru, Bill Clinton, and asked for his best advice on how the highly unpopular governor could win a no-recall vote on October 7. Seeing Davis's recall as similar to his impeachment and amenable to the same defense, Clinton rattled off his tried and true three-step approach to political resurrection. First, apologize for any mistakes. Second, blame it on a Republican conspiracy to steal the election. Third, say that the whole thing is not about Gray Davis but about the bigger issue of whether the Democrats are going to let those dratted right-wing Republicans get away with it.

Davis faithfully followed the Clinton script, and used it as the basis for an August 19 television address. "I know that many of you feel that I was slow to act during the energy crisis," he said with implausible humility. "I got your message and I accept that criticism." Check off the apology. Then he warned that the recall was a "right-wing power grab" that was "part of an ongoing national effort by Republicans to steal elections they cannot win." As examples, he cited Clinton's 1998 impeachment and the dispute over Florida votes in the 2000 presidential election. Check off the exploitation of Democratic paranoia. Davis was not now arguing for his personal political future, he went on. This struggle was for the good of the Democratic Party, the well-being of California, the hope of a better world free of Republican hellishness. Check off item three: the "bigger-than-me" appeal.

When Clinton went out to campaign by Davis's side, he stayed "on message" with what he had already scripted for Davis. To a black congregation at a large Los Angeles church, he intoned with evangelical fervor: "Gray Davis and I have been friends for a long time, and I don't want this happening to him. But this is way bigger than him. It's you I'm worried about. It's California I worry about. I don't want you to become a laughing stock or the beginning of a circus in America where we throw people out for making tough decisions." Pause, pause. "Don't do this!" Pause. "Don't do this!"[33]

The sensible voters of California did it anyway. Clinton had it all wrong. Some 1.3 million voters had signed the recall petition, and many were Democrats. In the largest voter turnout of recent decades, 55.4 percent voted to recall Gray Davis, and of the nearly five million who voted against Clinton's candidate, a large number were from his party. Only fifteen of the state's fifty-eight counties voted against the recall, and every one of those fifteen was in or near the San Francisco Bay area, long a left-liberal world unto itself.

Next was the election of a new governor. The ballot ran to eight pages and included 135 candidates for governor. The leading Republican candidate, Arnold Schwarzenegger won with 48.6 percent of the vote. Again many Democrats spurned Clinton and cast their vote for the actor-turned candidate. The nearest competitor, Lieutenant Governor Cruz Bustamante, a Democrat, was seventeen points behind.[34]

Clinton had little to say after the huge campaign failure in which he had invested much of his own effort and energy. Apparently, however, he decided that, contrary to his prediction, the state that rejected Governor Davis had yet to become a "laughing stock" or "the beginning of a circus." By December, the former president was once again back in California, stumping for another candidate. Clinton feared that the Democrats might lose the mayor's mansion in San Francisco, not to a Republican but to the local Green Party. Gavin Newsom, the Democratic candidate tapped to succeed the venerable Mayor Willie Brown, was making heavy weather of it against the Green Party's Matt Gonzalez, who was even more liberal than Newsom. Newsom was the typical Limousine Liberal. The conservatively dressed son of a judge had made millions in the restaurant business and lived in a $3 million mansion with his wife, a glamorous prosecutor and self-described "former lingerie model." Gonzalez was a bohemian bachelor, a sort of retooled beatnik who chose poets and artists for company, and slept on a futon in an apartment he shared with three roommates. But evidence of the threat he posed was apparent. Only two of the eleven-member Board of Supervisors, on which he and Newsom sat, supported Newsom.

It was going to be a close race, so Clinton was called in for a last-minute rescue. His election-day appearance, mostly a twenty-minute pep talk at Newsom's campaign headquarters to motivate one last push from his troops, may well have assisted Newsom toward his five-point victory. The libidinous former Boy President may have been particularly influential with a special San Francisco constituency that Newsom lumped under the ungainly acronym, LGBTQI, standing for "Lesbians, Gays, Bisexuals, Transgendered, Questioners, and Intersex." On the other hand, Clinton's sexual tastes may have merely bemused the stalwarts of LGBTQI as being too, too tedious. Whatever the case, Gonzalez had garnered an amazing 47 percent of the vote, though outspent by Newsom by ten-to-one and bereft of the famous Democrats who came to Newsom's support.

An irony of this race is that Clinton had helped install a mayor whose subsequent antics might have tipped the nation towards President Bush in 2004. It was Mayor Newsom who, only two months after his election, exceeded his authority by issuing marriage licenses to same-sex couples. Some 4,000 gay and lesbian couples got married in the feverish aftermath of Newsom's grand gesture. Then the liberal California Supreme Court unanimously ruled that the mayor had no authority to circumvent a state law against same-sex marriages. The marriage licenses were nullified, but the damage was done. The nationally televised spectacle of these San Francisco weddings incensed many voters, creating a national issue in the 2004 presidential race that should not have existed and that the Democrats could not win.

Whether Clinton paused to take stock of his political achievements at the end of 2003, one can only speculate. By the Iowa steak fry he had returned as the Democratic Party's political master. No longer was he looked to merely for the fundraising miracles he had achieved for his pal Terry McAuliffe. Now he was sought after by all the active presidential candidates for his advice and his blessing. He would even have a horse in the 2004 race, General Clark. Yet his political record when he ventured outside the party was not very good, either in 2002 or 2003. Did it make him wonder what the future might bring? We have seen that his aspirations for high office remained, perhaps as mayor of New York or United

Nations secretary-general. In chapter eight we shall see that he even developed a scheme to return himself to the presidency. Did he wonder why the mastery he showed over Democrats was not duplicated with voters when he ventured beyond the party?

An explanation might have been provided to him on the evening of December 14, 2003. That Sunday evening he could have tuned the *E!* channel to watch its weekly *True Hollywood Story*. It is a show that often specializes in featuring the lurid tale of how a "star" descends from fame to shame. On this Sunday evening the show featured Bill Clinton. It was the first time the *True Hollywood Story* moved from its absorption with disgraced Hollywood figures to a prominent, living politician. Included in the two-hour show were ample interviews of past Clinton paramours (Gennifer Flowers and Paula Jones were included and Monica was featured), lurid details of his trysts, and even five close-ups of Lewinsky's blue dress, along with shots of both Bill and his half-brother Roger in tears.

A week after that came the results of the annual Gallup Poll of most-admired Americans. For more than a half-century, respondents have been asked to name off the top of their heads a living man and woman they most admired. The Reverend Billy Graham was named for the forty-sixth time on the top-ten list. Pope John Paul, II appeared for his twenty-sixth time. (Ronald Reagan made the list thirty times.) But at the top of this list this year was President George W. Bush, named by 29 percent of those surveyed. Next was Secretary of State Colin Powell, then the Pope. Bill made the number four slot but with a paltry two percent of the vote.[35] This was the man whose coattails so many of the Democratic presidential contenders were trying to grab for a lift up?

There was some more inauspicious news in late 2003. Presidential scholars Lori Cox Han and Matthew J. Krov wrote in the *Presidential Studies Quarterly* that "During the first year after a president has left office, the tone and topic of news media coverage can influence a legacy greatly." They found that Clinton was in the news far more frequently in his first year out of office than either Ronald Reagan or George Bush. Unfortunately, the news was far more negative than that of his predecessors. Scandals might have consequences after all—at least outside the Democratic Party, now a party in decline.[36]

SEVEN

FEELING BLUE SEEING RED

It was late in 2003, and Howard Dean—his momentum building—had acquired a secret. Even his campaign manager, Joe Trippi, was not privy to it. Of course, the irrepressible Dr. Dean is not very good at controlling his emotions. So Trippi almost immediately sensed that something was in the air. He buttonholed the campaign's scheduler and inquired as to why a campaign stop in Cedar Rapids, Iowa, had suddenly appeared on the schedule for December 9. The subordinate was equally in the dark but surmised that it might have something "to do with the governor asking me to find a sixteen-seat Gulfstream for New York for the same day, and he told me not to tell anyone about it." Trippi reached Dean on his cell phone and accidentally set off another spontaneous combustion in the volatile country doctor. "I can't tell you what it's about," Dean shouted. Upset by the scheduler's revelation, he would only tell his campaign manager that he was getting a "big endorsement." The endorsement would take place in Harlem, whereupon they would fly to Cedar Rapids.

"Harlem," Trippi mused, feeling a bit queasy. "My first thought was that Bill Clinton's office was in Harlem. But Clinton's centrist wing of the Democratic Party seemed dead set against a Dean candidacy." He remembered wondering, "There was no way it could be Clinton, could it?" Later Trippi wrote: "I found out the same day as everyone else that it was Al Gore."[1]

The endorsement infuriated the other candidates, who presumed the former vice president would follow Clinton's example and abstain from endorsing anyone during the primaries. Gore's support was arguably the most stupendous boost any candidate could receive short of an endorsement from the newly resurrected Bill Clinton.

Some of the primary competitors took it personally. In 2000, Richard Gephardt had sat out the presidential race in favor of Gore and then provided pivotal campaign support for him in the Iowa campaign after ex-senator Bill Bradley of New Jersey entered the race. John Kerry considered Gore a personal friend and political ally. He also had sat out the 2000 race in deference to Gore, and then rushed to New Hampshire to shore up Gore's candidacy when his struggle against Bradley became dicey. Shortly before Gore's benediction of Dean, Kerry read in the *New York Times* that it might happen, so he put in a call to Gore's cell phone. "This is John Kerry," he said when Gore answered. Gore hung up on him. Kerry tried to call a few more times but never got through. He was hurt.[2] Politicians, once campaign season heats up, are often not very reliable friends or even very civilized.

Of course, no one deserved a heads-up and explanation of the upcoming endorsement more than Gore's running mate in the 2000 election, Joe Lieberman. After all, during that campaign Gore had repeatedly described Lieberman as the most qualified politician in all America to command the Oval Office after the Gore administration. If anyone deserved Gore's endorsement, it was Lieberman. Surely, the Connecticut senator deserved at least a warning call. Yet, as James Carville, gripped by Cajun eloquence, was to observe, Gore had gone for "secrecy over decency."[3]

On the morning of Gore's endorsement, Lieberman sputtered to reporters, questioning Gore's disloyalty: "I'm not going to talk about Al Gore's sense of loyalty this morning," he said.[4] "I have no regrets about the loyalty that I had to him when I waited until he decided whether he would run to make my decision, because that was the right thing to do."[5] Lieberman was referring to his own earlier pledge only to run in 2004 if Gore chose not to run. Lieberman had not announced his candidacy until Gore's December 2002 retirement from the race.

Throughout 2002 Gore had been a sponge for derision. At some point even he took note of the quips and guffaws and recognized that 2004 was not to be his year. He quit the presidential field, leaving it wide open for everyone from the veteran Lieberman to the upstart Dean.

As the day progressed Lieberman collected his thoughts. Finally, he related to reporters a less personal, more substantive reason for his shock over Gore's endorsement. Ticking off the former Vermont governor's positions on defense, taxes, trade, and values, Lieberman observed: "Al Gore is endorsing somebody who has taken positions in this campaign that are diametrically opposite to what Al himself has said he believed in over the years." More generally, he added, "Al is supporting a candidate who is so fundamentally opposed to the basic transformation that Bill Clinton brought to the Democratic Party in 1992."[6]

Here Lieberman had arrived at the heart of the matter. In the weeks leading up to Gore's endorsement, Dean had assumed a starkly anti-Clinton position on almost everything the forty-second president had claimed to stand for. To be sure, Dean had never denigrated Clinton personally, but he was clearly running to Clinton's left. For instance, he believed that Clinton had erred in declaring that "the era of big government is over." Though Dean would not actually evangelize for "big government," he declaimed that it was time for "fairer government," which, of course, meant bigger government than what Clinton espoused. "I believe we must enter a new era for the Democratic Party—not one where we join Republicans and aim simply to limit the damage they inflict on working families," Dean pontificated. The translation was obvious: Clinton's trumpeted "middle way" between liberalism and conservatism, which Europeans, mimicking Clinton, called "the third way," was to be abandoned.[7]

The Clintons got the message. Dean's hordes were threatening their Clintonized Democratic Party. Clinton responded with a not-so-subtle swipe at Dean during an interview with the *American Prospect* magazine: "We can't win if people think we're too liberal. I don't believe that either side should be saying, 'I'm a real Democrat and the other one's not.'"[8] That, of course, was precisely what Dean was doing. To the cheers of his audiences, Dean routinely introduced himself with: "I'm Howard Dean and I represent *the Democratic wing of the Democratic Party.*" (Emphasis added.) The only conclusion the Clintons could draw from this was that in Dean's mind Bill Clinton was a Democrat by registration only, not by political position. The coming struggle between Dean and the Clintons was fast approaching.

The struggle could not have been anticipated back when the Clintons were in the White House. In those days I frequently sat across from Governor Dean on a weekly PBS talk show taped in Montreal (*The Editors*). On every show, he defended the embattled Clinton with what appeared to be the latest White House talking points. It was as though he had received his marching orders that very morning directly from a Clinton war room. Dean was a Democratic regular then and a Clinton loyalist. But he was also very ambitious. My fellow panelists got a jolt in 2000 when we found out that our colleague from rural Vermont had his sights set that year on the presidential nomination, Vice President Gore's candidacy notwithstanding. By 2004, the hungry campaigner had spotted a useful new constituency, one that came to be called the Angry Left. He latched onto it, though it meant contradicting his eight-year defense of Clinton. Such quick-witted opportunism soon made him the frontrunner for the 2004 nomination. Unfortunately, it also made him the Clintons' mortal enemy, which probably ensured his doom.

Precisely why Clinton's running mate from the 1990s gravitated to Dean, who served as a wrecking ball for the Clinton-Gore legacy, remains subject to speculation. Was it revenge against the Playboy President who made Gore's strategic choices so difficult in 2000? Was it a fallen-away liberal seeking to redeem himself with his party's resurgent left? Whatever the reason, Gore not only endorsed Dean but deliberately picked up Dean's gauntlet and hurled it down in front of Clinton. During his speech endorsing Dean Gore declared, "We need to *remake the Democratic Party*."[9] (Emphasis added.) Not very subtle, that, but as we have seen Gore's last years with Clinton were mortifying. Recall his appearance on the White House lawn with all the other Democratic eminentoes the day of Clinton's impeachment. There he solemnized that The Groper was "one of our greatest presidents."

"This endorsement is about the Clinton-Gore divorce," wrote the *Philadelphia Inquirer*'s Dick Polman. Gore was not only repudiating Clinton's centrist positions, but he was also "thumbing his nose" at the kind of consultant-driven, Washington, D.C.-based politics the Clintons practiced. "He's standing on their lawn, threatening to burn their house down," Polman wrote.[10] Gore had chosen to do it in Clinton's backyard near his Harlem office—an intentional insult added to injury. Some pundits saw it more strategically, as a move by Gore to capture the left wing of the Democratic Party in the event that George W. Bush was reelected in 2004. One friend said it was simpler: "Al saw something in Dean that he wished he had been—a little more feisty, down there on the street with a two-by-four." But most knew it had a lot to do with animosity towards the Clintons themselves and what they represented. "Dean was the outsider Gore felt he had become," explained Chuck Todd, the editor of the *National Journal's Hotline*. "Gore felt very betrayed by the Washington establishment Democratic crowd epitomized by the Clintonites. Make no mistake about it: this guy was pissing in the eyes of Clinton."[11]

In the wake of the Gore endorsement, both Clintons chose silence as the better part of wisdom; though Senator Clinton's newfound cool was sorely tried. Asked by a *New York Daily News* reporter if she agreed with Gore that the Democratic Party needed to be remade, she hissed, "No," and sped off. Bill tried to be upbeat. Intent on congratulating Dean on his new supporter, the former President reached him on his cell phone just as the happy candidate and Gore were disembarking from their plane at Cedar Rapids for the day's second press conference. Dean was cavalier about the olive branch, which must have been difficult for Clinton to extend. As if he were too busy to be bothered, the increasingly arrogant frontrunner cut their conversation short, handing his phone to one of the many Iowa supporters on hand to cheer Dean's arrival. "Say hello to Bill Clinton," Dean said with a smile to fifty-two-year-old Dick Stater, owner of a custom woodworking business in Lisbon. "It was a major surprise," Stater said. Remembering the call, Stater noted that Clinton had said "nothing that could be interpreted as an endorsement of Dean." The former president was sticking to his game plan.[12]

Through it all, Dean's campaign chief, Trippi, was appalled. He probably would have advised against accepting the Gore endorsement. "It was clear to me the second the announcement was made that we had a huge target on our back," Trippi recalled. "Everybody was going to mobilize against us, and especially the Clintons. I remember thinking, 'If he wasn't already awake, this is going to wake up a sleeping giant: Bill Clinton.'"[13]

Joe Trippi was right. The Gore endorsement of Dean was the beginning of the end to the muddle of the Democratic presidential primary season. Coming a month before the Iowa caucuses, it gave Dean's opponents plenty of time to finish him off. Behind the scenes no one was more active in doing precisely that than Bill Clinton. Nor was Clinton particularly reticent about his opposition to Dean. Former Speaker of the House Newt Gingrich recalls a chat he had with Clinton before the Iowa caucuses. At the time most political observers saw Dean as an unstoppable freight train rumbling through the primaries and on to glory at the summer's Democratic National Convention. Clinton surprised Gingrich with his skepticism. When asked about the Vermonter's prospects, Clinton mused ominously that the Democratic National Convention was still a long way off.[4]

The primary source for the spate of anti-Dean stories that began appearing was Clinton's favorite dirty trickster, Chris Lehane. Self-described as a "master of disaster," Lehane is one of the foremost opposition research experts in the business. In an early primary season shakeup, Lehane had resigned from the John Kerry campaign and shortly thereafter, at Clinton's behest, joined the Clark campaign. His instructions from Chappaqua were to take Dean out and clear the way for Clark. The *Atlantic Monthly* later revealed that within a day or two of the endorsement, Lehane, with Clark's research director, Ben Holzer, made "a series of visits to the major television networks, newspapers, and newsmagazines. They toted a three-ring binder that contributed as much as anything else to Dean's rapid demise. The Clark campaign had classified the stories in it as singles, doubles, triples, or home runs, based on the damage they were expected to inflict. Holzer and Lehane offered producers and reporters exclusives on many of these stories with the proviso that if they were not used quickly, they would be handed to a rival. In the competitive world of political journalism this pretty much guaranteed swift airing or publication."[55]

Clark had called Clinton the day of the Gore endorsement just to check in. Clinton asked him how he felt about the news. "I don't pay any attention to endorsements unless they're for me," Clark laughed. "That's exactly right," Clinton reportedly responded.[16] Clinton made it clear to Clark that he would redouble his behind-the-scenes assistance to Clark. He wanted Dean gone, and he would help Clark eliminate Dean.

The next six weeks—from mid-December to late January 2004—marked the most intense and personal involvement by Clinton in the entire 2004 presidential election. Not counting his more-frequent phone consultations with Clark and Clark's ex-Clinton campaign officials, the former president was on the telephone almost daily with Eli Segal. Sometimes, after having softened up a wealthy Democratic donor with high praise for Clark, he would tell Segal to call the individual immediately and nail down a contribution. For example, after Texas fundraiser and former DNC finance chairman Jess Hay held a $300,000 fundraising event for Clark, Hay explained his support for the retired general. He had been talking with Clinton when, out of the blue, "he encouraged me to take a look at Clark and to discuss the possibility with Eli Segal of getting involved in the campaign." Even without Clinton's behind-the-scenes calls to donors, his "two stars" remark about Hillary and Clark at the Chappaqua dinner party the previous September was enough of a boost for Clark to raise substantial money from Hollywood stars and other top Democratic donors. In the last quarter of 2003, the Clark campaign pulled in $10 million. His Internet operation, assisted by the largesse of Clinton's financial supporters, was putting him in a position to do serious damage to Dean, who himself had a last quarter harvest of $15 million. No other Democrat came close.

Soon another well-known Clinton supporter, filmmaker Linda Bloodworth-Thomason, was assisting the retired Arkansas general. The producer of TV shows such as *Designing Women* and *Evening Shade*, Bloodworth had relatives in Arkansas. Her husband, director Harry Thomason, is an Arkansas native. As we have seen, the Thomasons—though uninvited—accompanied the Clintons to visit the Bushes at Bill's first inaugural and Harry was a constant sidekick to the retiring president during his last hours at the White House. During the 1990s, few people were closer to Clinton. On behalf of their old friend, the Thomasons had produced *The Man from Hope*, the affecting biopic of Clinton's rise shown at the 1992 Democratic Convention, and excerpted in subsequent ads. Now they agreed to do the same for Clark. The result was *American Son*, seventeen minutes of melodrama on Clark's Arkansas upbringing and decorated military career released December 18, a week after Gore's endorsement of Dean. The film was used at hundreds of fundraising "house parties" across the country on that date. Television stations were encouraged to use portions of it in their political coverage.

Eleven days after *American Son* appeared, Clark pulled an excerpt of it for inclusion in his first TV ad, shown December 29. It stirred Democrats everywhere. The centerpiece of the 30-second ad was color footage showing President Bill Clinton crossing a stage at the White House and hanging a medal around General Clark's neck. "What if we could have a president who in his lifetime has seen ordinary people do extraordinary things, because he believed in them, who was decorated for valor and service to our country?" intoned the voice-over. "Who helped negotiate a peace and has dedicated his life to protecting our country? Because like you, he believes America is ready to do great things. A new American leader. Wesley Clark." Shown applauding in the background during the voice-over was First Lady Hillary Rodham Clinton. The fact that the Clintons never protested the use of their implied endorsement in the ad, which aired in key primary states, was still more evidence of their strong desire to see Clark succeed.

The Clinton-backed Clark campaign succeeded in knocking Dean and his revolution out of the presidential campaign with a little help from NBC, which prior to the Iowa caucuses aired a twenty-second snippet of Dean apparently deriding the Iowa caucus system. The footage was from one of our broadcasts of *The Editors* taped sometime in 2000 during the Democratic primaries of that year. NBC's editing job made Dean's remarks appear more caustic than they had been, but now Dean had a terrible time explaining himself to aggrieved Iowans. Then there was the Clark candidacy. By slowing Dean's momentum with his announcement and skipping the Iowa caucuses, Clark (and, indirectly, Clinton) aided the come-from-behind win of John Kerry in the January 19 Iowa caucuses. Kerry won 38 percent of the delegates. John Edwards was a surprise second-place finisher with 32 percent, and Dean, the former frontrunner, was a distant third with 18 percent. On January 27, Kerry decisively won the New Hampshire primary. Despite Clinton's substantial behind-the-scenes backing, Clark's support in the New England state was too shallow, his effort too late to overcome Kerry's momentum. By now Dean's campaign had become a series of comic blunders. The ultimate outcome was obvious. Once again Clinton's support had failed to bring victory for his chosen candidate. Two days after the New Hampshire primary Clinton, at an off-the-record Capitol Hill Democratic strategy session related to the campaign, went out of his way to praise Senator Kerry.

On February 3, Kerry took five of seven states in contention. Edwards had a victory in South Carolina and Clark won Oklahoma. Still, Clark adviser Chris Lehane was chipper with reporters, urging them not to write off Clark yet, and reminding them that in 1992 Clinton lost eleven of his first fourteen primaries. A week later, on February 10, Clark dropped out. By March 3, the day after Super Tuesday, Senator John Kerry was the undisputed Democratic nominee for president.

Bill Clinton's last involvement with the presidential campaign until his opening night speech at the Democratic Convention occurred at the party's March 25 Unity Day dinner. The event was the highlighted end of a ten-day fundraising campaign launched by a Bill Clinton e-mail plea to 2.3 million Democrats on the mailing lists of the Kerry campaign and the DNC; it raised $10 million in short order. The gala dinner, held in the Washington, D.C. National Building Museum, featured the world's most expensive barbecue. The 2,000 attendees had forked over $11 million altogether to eat partisan red meat on paper plates, and hear a series of speeches from losing Democratic primary candidates, former veep Gore, and two former presidents, Jimmy Carter and Clinton.

The choreography for the important end-of-the-night "unity" photo of these top Democrats turned into a free-for-all. Clinton and Gore ended up nowhere near each other, by choice; their falling-out was still apparent. Nor was Clinton next to Kerry at center stage. Instead, John Edwards, who was months away from being selected as Kerry's running mate, somehow slithered in between Clinton and Kerry. Perhaps this was the way Kerry wanted it.

In fact, during the entire presidential campaign, John Kerry and Bill Clinton, never the best of friends, only appeared together at a campaign rally *once*. Whether that distance—which both protested was not deliberate—was Kerry's idea or Clinton's will remain one of the campaign's mysteries. Conspiracy theorists surmised that Clinton was deliberately trying to submarine a Kerry victory, fearing a Kerry administration might delay Hillary's run for the presidency until 2012, when she would have lost her youthful charm. Whatever the reason, Clinton made it clear after the unity dinner that he had better things to do during the next five months than to campaign for Kerry. Clinton's hour as a celebrity author was at hand . . . to the consternation of Democratic Party leaders. Even his friend, DNC chairman Terry McAuliffe, worried about that.

The publication of *My Life* had been on McAuliffe's mind since the late spring. As everyone who knows Clinton is aware, the chronically disorganized political prodigy is never on time. So when he promised his friend McAuliffe that his memoir would be published "well before" the July 26 to 29 Democratic National Convention in Boston, McAuliffe could only cross his fingers. They both knew that with all the anticipated hoopla surrounding the book's release, including a *60 Minutes* interview, Clinton would dominate the news for a week or more. That would rob Democratic presidential candidate Kerry of free media time to get his political message and persona on air and in print.

From 2001 to 2003, Clinton had dawdled over his book, preoccupied, as we have seen, with a hectic speaking schedule that may have made him a multimillionaire but left his autobiographical manuscript a mess. He had insisted on writing it himself and in longhand, no less—remember, klutz that he is, he had yet to master the computer. In the hope of accumulating oral memoranda for the eventual writing of the book, Clinton had asked Pulitzer Prize-winning author Taylor Branch to interview him for an hour or so each month in the White House. The secret sessions netted a cache of eighty hours of tapes on his White House life as it was unfolding. Later at Chappaqua once or twice a month he spent hours taping more oral history. He called these his "book-talking days" and spent them with one of his former speechwriters, Ted Widmer, now teaching American history at Maryland's Washington College. Widmer's duty was to coax useful information out of a moody and distracted former president. As his deadline drew near, the Boy President's publisher was confronted with a mound of his scrawled notes and taped interviews; but those hardly composed a fluent manuscript. Given his long absences, his editors were growing panicky. A writing team was sweating to create a narrative from what had become a junkyard of reminiscences, government documents, and miscellaneous information. Time was running out.

As 2004 dawned, Clinton's editors at the Alfred A. Knopf publishing house were in despair. It was not the vaunted $10 million advance they worried about. As we have seen, they never advanced him a dime. Rather his contract was a guarantee against future royalties, in effect a tax dodge to allow the highly paid speaker to put off declaring his book income until he had his fortune in the bank with only a minimum taxed. Rather than fearing a lost $10 million advance, Knopf's editors feared Clinton's tardiness would cripple their marketing plans. The president had missed deadline after deadline. For such a large, important book, his editors explained to him, they needed at least two months to get the final manuscript in order, printed, and delivered to the bookstores. If he went past April without finishing the manuscript, then it might be published on top of the Democratic Convention—or after it, which was unthinkable. Clinton well knew that if he drew attention to himself, and away from Kerry, between the convention and election, the Kerry people and many other Democrats might feel he was trying to sabotage Kerry's chances and set things up for Hillary to run in 2008.

Finally, the headstrong memoirist took the manuscript that his professional writers had cobbled together and disappeared into the two-story barn that he had converted into a writing studio behind his Chappaqua home. There he perpetrated another of his chaotic endings. Into their text he interpolated more of his self-indulgent personal anecdotes and fanciful charges against his enemies, filling the book with historical errors and bizarre assertions. These were the same vain excesses that he later committed in personally editing the historical displays at his presidential library, as we shall see when we pay a visit to that great edifice in this book's Epilogue.

Clinton's last-minute editing made *My Life* a dreadful presidential memoir, chaotic in shape, abundant with obvious deceits, but forever revealing the delusions of the eternal adolescent who was president during that brief "holiday from history" between the end of the Cold War and the oncoming War on Terror. The index of *My Life* testifies to the chaos of its eleventh-hour editing. Many of Clinton's most egregious emendations never made it into the index. For instance, one will find no index reference to Sir Edmund Hillary, despite repetition of the Clintons' claim that Hillary was named after the New Zealander.

At least he got the memoir done. To the relief of his editors (and of McAuliffe, Kerry, and other Democratic leaders), Clinton finally delivered *My Life* to Knopf in the first week of May. A few days later, on May 11, during an appearance at Harlem's Apollo Theater, he moaned, "I need my life back." By then he was in daily consultation with Knopf's editors over changes. He had been too long in a "writer's jail," he added. "For three months, I have done nothing but try to finish the story of my life that was hard enough to live the first time."[17] Yet by June 3, the day he appeared as the keynote speaker at BookExpo America in Chicago, it was evident the great memoir albatross had been lifted from him. He was ready to coast, and in good humor at that. "A lot of presidential memoirs, they say, are dull and self-serving. I hope mine is interesting and self-serving," he joked.[18]

Actually Clinton need not feel any guilt about abandoning Kerry's campaign. Kerry was doing better without him, approaching Bush in the polls and for a while nudging ahead of the President. This, however, had little to do with any improvement Kerry was showing on the campaign trail. Rather, it was attributable to a damaging series of events breaking against Bush:

1) The National Commission on Terrorist Attacks Upon the United States, more commonly known as the 9/11 Commission, began holding public hearings in March. For a month, the bipartisan panel (five Republicans; five Democrats) grilled every top national security official

with counterterrorism responsibility in the Clinton and Bush administrations. Both Clinton and Gore submitted to the questioning. On April 10, after two years of stalling, Bush finally released a declassified version of the December 4, 1998, President's Daily Brief, titled "Bin Laden Preparing to Hijack U.S. Aircraft and Other Attacks." An additional flap occurred over whether Bush would allow his national security adviser, Condoleezza Rice, to testify publicly; she finally did. Bush and Vice President Cheney themselves submitted to questioning by the panel for more than three hours in the Oval Office. By April word was circulating that the panel's report, due in July, would claim that both administrations had been lackadaisical about terror threats and ignored multiple warnings preceding the 9/11 attack. But Kerry, who had had nothing to do with that White House, could not be hurt by criticism of Clinton's lackluster counterterrorism efforts. Better, he was helped by equally critical conclusions about President Bush and his people, particularly after former Bush counterterrorism coordinator Richard A. Clarke pointed an accusatory finger at George W. both in his March 24 testimony and subsequently in his new book.

2) Bush stumbled badly during an April 13 press conference, only the twelfth he had held since taking office three and a half years earlier. Most memorable was Bush's answer to the suggestion he name one mistake he had made in his first three-plus years. The president was stumped. "I'm sure something will pop into my head here in the midst of this press conference, with all the pressure of trying to come up with an answer, but it hasn't yet." Nonetheless, despite news reports of the administration's mishandling of terror warnings and Bush's bungled press conference, the president remained ahead of Kerry in the polls, 48 to 43 percent. Then his fortune changed.

3) On April 28, CBS *60 Minutes II* first exposed the abuse and torture of prisoners at the Abu Ghraib prison in Iraq, complete with lurid photos. Now the negative stories were beginning to take a toll, and along with them a consensus formed among the nation's leaders that Saddam

did not have weapons of mass destruction when Bush led us to war claiming such weapons as a *casus belli.*

By May 20, Kerry and Bush were dead even, at 46 percent each. Then Michael Moore's anti-Bush documentary, *Fahrenheit 9/11*—though flawed, blatantly biased, and error-filled—won the Cannes Film Festival, putting another smudge on Bush's commander-in-chief image among undecided voters. By June 17, Kerry was ahead in the polls, 48 to 44 percent. He did not then need Clinton, and Clinton was happy not to be needed. In five days his book would be out, launching him on a book tour that would become one of his most narcissistic revels ever.

On June 14, Clinton's ego got a big boost when President Bush graciously hosted an official presidential portrait unveiling, full of kind words for the ex-president. Perhaps Bush's most memorable lines were: "It took hard work and drive and determination and optimism [for Clinton to succeed]. And after all, you've got to be optimistic to give six months of your life running the McGovern campaign in Texas." From laughter Bush brought Clinton to tears with: "I am certain that Virginia Kelley (Clinton's late mother) would be filled with incredible pride this morning." Several hundred Clinton administration officials had been invited to the ceremony which, necessarily, included many ex-Clinton/Clark aides now working for Kerry. Many of them praised Bush for his generosity toward Clinton—quite a feat of grace, as former Clinton spokesperson Dee Dee Myers put it, since, with "the top Kerry brain trust in the room, President Bush [must have] felt like the Trojan horse had been wheeled in under his nose."[19] Tellingly Gore, though he had been invited, was not on hand to honor his former boss.

Clinton's tome, *My Life*, was released on June 22, selling 400,000 copies in the first day. It was an amazing feat, though a more suavely told work of fiction sold five million copies the first day out, *Harry Potter and the Order of the Phoenix.*[20] Eager for the adulation, Clinton took off on an extended book tour that proved both personally gratifying and financially rewarding. The tour proved one other thing: Clinton's coattails remained nonexistent even in the campaign for book sales. Book publishers had hoped that excitement over Clinton's book might boost the sales of other books, but no such trend was detected . . . except that Hillary's year-old book, *Living History*, rose to number two on the Amazon.com list after *My Life* came out. It plummeted to number 450 a week later.[21]

Clinton's book tour meant that during July and August, except for the week of the Democratic Convention, he was unavailable to campaign for Kerry, to the relief of those Democrats who had had enough of him and to the disappointment of those who again beheld in him a messiah. A flap just before the convention spotlighted these conflicting emotions within the Democratic Party. Kerry's managers had denied Hillary a choice speaking role anywhere on the convention program. Their lame explanation was that she was already scheduled to appear with the rest of the Democrats' female senatorial delegation gathered around the prime-time speaker, veteran Senator Barbara Mikulski. This was but the latest provocation in an ongoing spat between the Kennedys and the Clintons. Long before Massachusetts Senator Kerry was the nominee, the state's senior senator, Teddy Kennedy, had sparred with Senator Clinton over the location of the 2004 convention, Teddy urging Boston, Hillary urging New York. Kennedy won the internal party struggle and brought the convention home. Fresh from this victory Kennedy's people overreached. They thought they could deny Hillary any spotlight in Boston whatsoever.

Obviously Bay State Democrats had failed to note that despite the Clintons' scandalous White House departure, the Clintons were back on top. Since becoming a senator, Hillary had raised an estimated $30 million for the national party. She had stumped for scores of Democratic candidates. Her husband, too, had raised vast amounts of money and also campaigned for candidates, if less successfully. Democrats were grateful. Of Hillary, former New York governor Mario Cuomo said, "She was by far the most popular Democratic presidential candidate in all of the polls so it would make no sense to say 'no' to her if she wanted to speak," concluding, "and besides, having Bill and Hillary at the convention *would be like having the sun and the moon to the Democrats.*"[22] (Emphasis added.) Kerry's people relented, and Hillary was given her lunar moment, an eleven-minute introduction of her irrepressible husband, the sun that shone for twenty-five self-absorbed minutes.[23]

John Kerry got a temporary uptick in the polls from the convention, but he began falling behind again in August, and not just because of the pro-Bush headlines from the Republican National Convention in New York City. The Swift Boat Veterans for Truth, who criticized Kerry's erratic military service and medal inflation, began their ad campaign on August 5 to immediate and devastating effect. Kerry's approval ratings sagged. When Kerry was slow to respond, his poll numbers sagged even more, leaving Bush with a double-digit lead. "Leadership" was looming ever larger as the key national issue of Campaign 2004. Kerry's listless response to the Swift Boat ads multiplied the damage done by the substance of the ads themselves.

Kerry blamed his campaign manager, Mary Beth Cahill, for miscalculating the damage that the Swift Boat veterans caused. He held her responsible for the campaign's slow-footed response to the Swift Boat ads and to earlier challenges. Cahill had come to the Kerry campaign in the fall of 2003 from Senator Kennedy's staff, where she had been chief of staff. It was hoped that she could bring order to Kerry's primary campaign after he had fired his first campaign manager, Jim Jordan. Though thankful to her for his primary victories, Kerry lacked confidence that she was equal to the demands of a national campaign. He doubted her strategic sense. Other problems had developed. Kerry had repeatedly hinted to Cahill that she should fire their communications chief, Stephanie Cutter. Reporters had come to him with complaints about Cutter, and his own staff had begun to use her e-mail name—Scutter—as a verb. "To scutter" meant to "f---up." But Cahill had neither demoted nor fired her, much to Kerry's frustration.

Kerry's response, encouraged by Bill Clinton himself, was to bring in a proven team of rapid-response veterans, a team that had been with

Clinton in the good times, the bad times, and the really bad times. In came Clinton's last press secretary, Joe Lockhart, who had won respect from White House correspondents for deftly handling the Lewinsky affair. Kerry also signed on Clinton's former presidential assistant, Joel Johnson, and his former White House political director, Douglas Sosnik. By early September a key fourth man arrived, former Clinton press secretary Mike McCurry. Thus was created the "fabulous four" that would save the day for Kerry. Earlier, Kerry had quietly reinforced his strategy staff and communications team. In the spring he brought aboard Hillary's former chief of staff, Howard Wolfson, and former Clinton political adviser Paul Begala. Unfortunately, the turf-conscious Cahill and Cutter had run them off. The question now, at the end of August, was whether this fresh contingent of Clintonistas brought into the campaign would gain enough power to make a difference.

Meanwhile, suddenly and unexpectedly Clinton heard a bell tolling, and it was tolling for him. He was in big trouble, and this time the trouble demanded not the conjurings of lawyers and public relations consultants but the expertise of the medical corps.

While the 1992 presidential campaign had been a great political victory for Clinton, it had wreaked havoc on his health. On the campaign trail, he would eat as many as seven meals a day, including untold numbers of Big Macs and every fat-filled local specialty offered to him. By inauguration day the six-foot-two president-elect weighed in at 226 lbs. Late night comedians took to calling him "Tubba Bubba"; Jay Leno said he was in desperate need of a "Thighmaster General." While the criticism prompted him to jog three miles a day, five times a week around the capital, he did not shed many pounds because he would not change his eating habits. He still had McClard's, his favorite barbecue joint back in Hot Springs, cater meals aboard *Air Force One* that consisted of fifteen pounds of chopped beef, fifteen pounds of pork ribs, and two gallons each of beans and cole slaw. He later remarked that there is just "one weakness I don't have . . . I never liked chocolate."[24] By the time he left the White

House, Clinton's cholesterol level was a parlous 233. His blood pressure was 136 over 84.

He had tried several diets only to regain more weight than he had lost. One diet—combined with an exercise regimen—finally worked beginning in the summer of 2003. Dr. Arthur Agatston's low-carb low-fat South Beach Diet finally proved to be effective for the post-presidential Clinton. Over the next year, eating healthier and exercising regularly, Clinton shed forty pounds, and everyone who saw him remarked on how trim he had become. At times, he fell off the wagon. The extended book tour, during which his exercise dropped off and he indulged his pre-South Beach Diet's tastes, sent him down a slippery slope. For example, in late August when he traveled to Iceland with Hillary and her senatorial colleague, John McCain, he was spotted wolfing down a hot dog or two at Iceland's most popular hot dog stand. And on September 1, in New Orleans, he had a sweet, greasy breakfast of beignets (fried doughnuts generously covered with powdered sugar), followed by a French Quarter lunch of battered catfish swimming in butter, rich sausage gumbo, and blackeyed peas.

Two days after the New Orleans repast, and just a day after President Bush accepted his party's nomination for president at the New York City convention, Bill Clinton, complaining of chest pains and shortness of breath, sought treatment at the hospital closest to his home, Westchester Medical Center. An angiogram found that "well over 90 percent" of his arteries were blocked; he could have had a fatal heart attack at any time. A simple stent would not save him; a quadruple bypass was necessary—as soon as possible. Though he had generally been healthier in the last year than at any time since he was governor of Arkansas, that was not enough to reverse a family history of genetic heart disease, nor the damage he had done to himself in the previous years. Dr. P. K. Shah put it tersely: "How could it happen? Very simple: you cannot reverse a lifetime of heart-unhealthy habits by getting religion for a year."[25]

As Clinton was transferred the same day, Friday, September 3, to New

York Presbyterian Hospital/Columbia for the surgery, Senator Clinton cut short her annual politicking at the New York State Fair to join him there. Chelsea flew home from England. That evening, in a call to CNN talk host Larry King, who was himself a former heart patient, Clinton confessed that he was "a little scared." But it was probably his own fault that he was in the hospital because "I was too careless about what I ate." Then he quipped: "You know, Republicans aren't the only people who want four more years here."

Between Boggle games with Hillary and Chelsea, and joking with other visitors, Clinton thought about the Kerry campaign, and the resuscitation it needed. The solution Clinton came up with was the addition of still more Clintonistas. The next day, Saturday, James Carville arrived at Kerry campaign headquarters in Washington for a showdown with Mary Beth Cahill. He had his old boss's blessing. Carville asked former Clinton pollster Stan Greenberg to accompany him along with Lockhart, who was already aboard the Kerry campaign. *Newsweek*'s Evan Thomas reconstructed the meeting:

> Carville came right out and said that Cahill had to step aside and let Lockhart, the Clintonista newcomer, run the campaign. "You've got to let him do it!" implored Carville, pounding Lockhart's arm until it was bruised. Carville spoke as if Mary Beth weren't in the room.
>
> "Nobody can gain power without someone losing power. If somebody doesn't lose power, nobody's gained power," he lectured. The "somebody" sitting a few feet away just remained silent. Carville threatened to go on *Meet the Press* the next day "and tell the truth about how bad it is" if Cahill didn't give effective control to Lockhart.
>
> Cahill and all the others later dressed up the truth—it had been her idea, they said, to bring in Lockhart and other old Clinton aides to strengthen the campaign. But, in fact, the campaign had undergone a silent coup. Kerry's hand was hidden, but he had given his silent assent.[26]

Just as significant, though, was Bill Clinton's hidden hand. He had made it clear to Kerry that Carville was acting for him—doing what the former president thought was necessary for Kerry in the final sixty days of the campaign. Clinton and Carville set in motion a one-two-three punch that clinched the not-so-subtle takeover of the campaign by the Clinton team. The oft-disgraced Boy Clinton was back atop the Democratic Party.

The first punch was the Carville-Cahill showdown, at which Cahill ceded power because she knew her boss, Kerry, was behind it as well. The second punch was a prearranged 10:00 p.m. conference call between Clinton, from his hospital bed, and Kerry, on the campaign trail. Aides listened in. Reportedly, it was mostly Clinton lecturing Kerry. Beyond the personnel shakeup, Clinton advised Kerry to forget Vietnam. Clinton, the draft dodger, advised Kerry, the windbag vet, to move on from his Vietnam service. Kerry's war record was a failed gambit. Voters, Clinton advised, needed a positive reason to vote for the Democratic candidate. They needed to know what President John Kerry would do differently than the incumbent. So forget talking about the past unless it is President Bush's past and his mistakes as president. Voters are interested in bread-and-butter issues, counseled Clinton, especially the economy. Clinton reminded Kerry of Reagan's question: Ask the voters if they are better off now under Bush than they were four years ago. They know the deficits are bad, and the economy is stumbling. Your Vietnam service and anti-war protests afterwards are starving the campaign of oxygen, remonstrated Clinton. You need a message of hope for the future. Clinton concluded: "If you're the message in this campaign, you lose. If Bush is the issue in the campaign, you win. Stay in his face."[27]

It was nearly midnight when the call ended. Carville later said that a nurse came in toward the end of the conversation and found Clinton's blood pressure had gone up notably during the animated ninety-minute conversation. Or was it the arrival of the nurse? Conan O'Brien quipped that the call was apparently "the first time Clinton made a phone call from bed that didn't start with, 'What are you wearing?'"[28]—still more evidence of *The Starr Report*'s enduring influence upon an entire generation of American comedians.

The next day one of Clinton's former aides now high in the Kerry campaign leaked a detailed account of the Clinton lecture to the *New York Times*. It was the final punch of the Clinton-Carville one-two-three. To the Clintonistas it mattered not that this leak was bound to discomfit Kerry when it appeared in print. Nor did it matter that the leak made him appear desperate—perhaps even weak—in seeking advice from a man on his sickbed. The point was to put Kerry on public notice that if he failed to follow the boss's advice, they would wash their hands of him. Then Clinton could say that he had tried to help Kerry win, even though a Kerry win would probably put Hillary's presidential race on hold until 2012. He had done his damnedest to help the ungainly Kerry, but the long-faced lamebrain just would not take the advice of a master.

As the Sage of Chappaqua's wise counsel was being trumpeted in print and broadcast nationally, Clinton went under the knife. Three surgeons and a twelve-person medical staff worked on him. The lead surgeon was Dr. Craig Smith, chief of the hospital's cardiothoracic surgery division. A $2,000 contributor to President Bush's reelection campaign, Dr. Smith had been driving to his summer home in the Adirondacks to celebrate his thirty-fourth wedding anniversary when the call came. He turned around, and planned to do his best for the fifty-eight-year-old former president, despite his own party persuasion. Politics stops at the water's edge and the hospital's doors.

In 80 percent of these bypass operations, Dr. Smith explained, it was not necessary to stop the heart. But Clinton was in bad shape. So, at a crucial moment in the four-hour operation, Dr. Smith stopped Clinton's heart and placed him on a heart-lung machine for seventy-three minutes. It was probably at this point that Clinton had the haunting vision he later recalled to ABC's Diane Sawyer: "I saw dark masks crushing, like death masks being crushed in series. And then, I'd see these great circles of light. And then, like, Hillary's picture or Chelsea's face would appear on the light. And then they'd fly off into the—distance. And other people that I knew and cared about. It was amazing. . . . But I think somewhere deep in your subconscious, that you know you're very close to your own mortality when they saw you open and flop your heart out, you know?"[29]

Weak and able only to take very short walks, Clinton emerged from the hospital on September 10, four days after his surgery. His doctors told him to forget campaigning for anyone. He would need at least two months to recuperate from the surgery, which would put his convalescence a week past the November 2 election.

Before his heart stopped him, Clinton had agreed with McAuliffe to make ten appearances for the Kerry-Edwards ticket in September, and double that number in October. He had also agreed to headline eight major fundraisers for the DNC, and the Democratic Congressional and Senatorial campaign committees. Certainly the hyperactive Clinton (who as with FDR and other born politicians is energized by campaigning) longed for the campaign trail. But reports that he was chomping at the bit to campaign, if only Hillary would let him, were public relations poppycock. He slept a lot, and it was early October before he could slowly walk outdoors for even an hour. A quadruple bypass is serious business, and it stops just about anyone cold for a couple of months or more. Around mid-October, the patient candidly expressed the wish to a friend that he had "six weeks more"—through December—to recover fully.[30]

Meanwhile, Kerry, continually prompted by the top Clinton people in his own campaign, was following the tactics Clinton had dictated from his hospital bed. The day after Clinton's surgery, *60 Minutes II* aired a report that put Bush on the defensive about his National Guard service. The report's documentation was soon exposed as bogus. In the attendant controversy, Kerry/Clinton aide Lockhart admitted he had been in contact with Dan Rather's chief source on the story. Obviously Kerry's people were trying to keep Bush off balance. On September 17, Kerry accused the president of secretly planning to send more troops to Iraq. Next Kerry began predicting that Bush might bring the draft back. When the Bush campaign countered with a TV ad showing Kerry windsurfing and suggesting his flakiness, the Clinton veterans on Kerry's rapid-response team counterpunched within a few hours with an ad of their own.

During this time, Clinton was advising Kerry on the telephone at least once a week. More important, he was frequently telephoning the Clintonistas now surrounding Kerry. By late September, Lockhart, McCurry, and longtime Kerry associate John Sasso were running the daily Kerry campaign, having sidelined Cahill. Clinton's primary telephone contact was Carville who, along with Begala, was heavily involved in Kerry strategizing. That they were actively involved in the Kerry campaign while co-hosting CNN's *Crossfire* is but another example of how the *Kultursmog* works and of how brazen liberals are in creating their *smog*. CNN is "not being honest by keeping those two guys on," competitor Bill O'Reilly complained. "If we did it at Fox, we would be ripped up." Republicans argued that never before had major media been so partisanly Democratic, and from CBS to CNN to the *New York Times*, the evidence of their open partisanship was everywhere.

O'Reilly had the perfect put-down. He brought former Clinton aide Dick Morris onto his show, and he reminded viewers that having Carville and Begala as advisers to Kerry might actually benefit Republicans. They might have deserved credit for Clinton's 1992 victory, but they had failed him abysmally during his presidency, allowing him to lunge leftward early in his administration with the gays-in-the-military issue and with Hillary's healthcare fiasco. It was Morris who had been brought in to save the Clinton presidency by pushing the administration back to the center for Clinton's 1996 re-election. Postulating a Clinton conspiracy to cause Kerry's loss, Morris reminded viewers that Carville and Begala were "working for Clinton when he blew it in 1993 and 1994." Clinton "got rid of them, and he wouldn't use them for his own reelection campaign. So why is Clinton recommending them to Kerry? That may be the best evidence yet that Clinton doesn't want Kerry to win."[31]

Kerry, however, continued to do well with the new strategy, and seemed to be closing the gap with Bush, especially after convincing appearances in the presidential debates. (Interestingly, Kerry referred to Ronald Reagan more than to Bill Clinton in those debates.) When Clinton talked with Kerry after the final October 13 debate, the former president finally told Kerry that he thought he might be able to campaign during the final week of the election. After that, there were many delicate negotiations between the campaign and Clinton about how many appearances he could make, how much time he needed to rest in between them, and where he would best be used.

The first outing was an October 25 Philadelphia lovefest. At least it was a lovefest for Clinton. There was the natural drama of the star player coming back after an injury for the last game of the season. There was the rare phenomenon of seeing Clinton next to Kerry, the only time the two shared the podium at a campaign rally during the entire presidential election. There was the sheer history of it. According to one account, this was Clinton's "first campaign appearance [supporting a candidate] since leaving office" in January 2001. Finally, there was the genuine affection that the Philly crowd showed Clinton. It was a noontime crowd of 100,000 standing shoulder-to-shoulder and a quarter-mile deep in downtown Philadelphia, many wanting to see the Comeback Kid make one more historic comeback. Mayor John Street introduced him as "the last duly-elected president of the United States." Accepting the characterization with a smile, Clinton, looking a little shaky and so thin that his wedding ring slipped halfway down his finger, quieted the cheers and began: "If this isn't good for my heart, I don't know what is," as the shouting ("We love you, Bill!") swelled again. His speech was short, on point, and repeatedly interrupted by applause. When Kerry followed, he said that in a discussion with Clinton just before coming on stage, he had asked the former president if he felt he had anything in common with George W. Bush. Clinton thought for a moment and responded, "In eight days and twelve hours, we will both be former presidents."

Pennsylvania had been Clinton's first outing because the usually true-blue (Democratic) state had become a battleground state. It was no longer securely in Kerry's corner. As it happened, Pennsylvania stayed a blue state, but by a very narrow margin, going 51 to 49 percent for Kerry. Whether Clinton's appearance made enough of a difference remains an unknown. It was, however, the one and only state in which Clinton campaigned during the final days that went Democratic.[32]

Clinton flew from Philadelphia to Florida the same day for his next two campaign appearances. Suspecting Florida might not go Kerry's way, Clinton began with a disclaimer while speaking at a Miami rally: "Let me say something. I have never believed that in a presidential race the mere presence of some candidate or some former president could change any votes. My mama used to tell me when she was still alive, she said, 'Bill, you can persuade me on any election except the president. I think I know as much about that as you do.' So let me say, as wonderful as you've been here to me tonight, I don't expect my presence to change any votes."[33] If not, what was he doing there? Anyway, the next morning he was in Boca Raton speaking to more than 1,700 at the B'nai Torah Congregation, hoping his remarks, amplified by the press, would appeal to Florida's 500,000 Jewish voters. He was to be disappointed. Florida went to Bush 52 to 47 percent.

After a few days of rest, Clinton was back at it. This time he was in the battleground state of Nevada. He spoke for twenty minutes on October 29 to a small crowd of 2,500 in Las Vegas. It was a fair gamble since Clinton had won the state himself during both elections. Again he was disappointed. Bush won, 50 to 48 percent.

Partly as a favor to Governor Bill Richardson, his former secretary of energy who had offered career guidance to Monica Lewinsky during "tough times," Clinton appeared the next day in New Mexico. He had won New Mexico in both of his presidential races. But now it was one of those too-close-to-call battleground states. Joined by actor Martin Sheen, the former president spoke to about 11,000 in Santa Fe before heading off with Richardson for a chicken-and-enchilada dinner at the governor's mansion. Bush won in a squeaker, 50 to 49 percent.

Clinton's last appearance was Sunday, October 31, in his home state of Arkansas, which had now become a battleground state. Clinton's rousing Halloween rally with old friends and fans was not particularly helpful. Bush smashed Kerry, 54 to 45 percent.

On Election Day itself, Bill Clinton had a telephone to his ear almost constantly, doing interviews—usually with African-American radio hosts in various states—as one last effort to get out the vote for a Democratic victory. By the end of the night, it was not good news. Not exactly a rout, but this time Bush won both the popular vote (62 million to 59 million) as well as the electoral college (286 to 252). Clinton, as he watched the results spread across the electoral maps of various newscasts, must have been feeling blue seeing red.

Other Democrats, too, were feeling blue seeing red. A good number could attribute their loss to the political genius himself, Bill Clinton.

For Tar Heel Congressman Martin Lancaster his defeat was a clear case of the Clinton Curse. Always described as a genuine "nice guy," Lancaster was raised on his father's 300-acre tobacco farm. He paid for his college education by tending the two acres of tobacco his father had given him. Later, as a lawyer, he served in the state House for eight years before winning a seat as a Democrat in the House of Representatives in 1986. He was reelected four times and doing fine until the Clintons came to Washington. Lancaster knew he would have a tough time getting reelected in 1994 as a Democrat. The unpopularity of the Clinton administration had sunk his approval rating to 30 percent, and it was continuing to drop.

Then Bob Woodward's book, *The Agenda*, came out and revealed how poor Lancaster had been snookered by the Clintons. In 1993, Lancaster let Hillary know that he was aware that she planned to finance her health-care reform with a $2-a-pack tax on tobacco. He would oppose that tax. At least, he said, tax other "sin" products, too, like alcohol. She refused to make any promise, at least until the final day of the close vote on the economic stimulus package. Then, to secure his vote, and that of several other Southern congressmen for whom he spoke,

Hillary pledged that she would not single out tobacco if he and the others would vote for the administration's economic bill. He agreed. Shortly after, Lancaster was pulled off the floor of the House by a call from President Clinton who wanted to assure the Congressman that he personally backed his wife's deal. Being naive enough to believe that when they made a promise the Clintons intended to keep it, Lancaster and the others voted for their bill, which won by only one vote. Within months, both Clintons reneged on the pledge with a health care plan that taxed only one product, tobacco. Neither ever apologized.[34]

While the public revelation of being suckered by the Clintons was embarrassing to Lancaster, the ultimate cause of his defeat was a photograph that was snapped of his jogging with Clinton in Washington. The opposition used it repeatedly in an effective attack ad. The "attack" was simple: as the photo appeared on the TV screen it slowly expanded while a narrator said: "Look who he's running around with. . . . In Washington, they're a team." That was all it took. Lancaster lost his four-term seat by six points.

Clinton's image in the state had not improved. The Lewinsky scandal incensed the born-againers in a state sometimes described as "the buckle of the Bible Belt." After the Lewinsky revelations, Senator Jesse Helms of North Carolina said that if Clinton were to visit North Carolina, Helms could not guarantee Clinton's safety. He suggested Clinton bring extra bodyguards.

Erskine Bowles, Clinton's former White House chief of staff, recognized Clinton's unpopularity in North Carolina, so when he made what would be his second run for the Senate since leaving Washington, he referred as infrequently as possible to his association with Clinton. Nevertheless he became the second Tar Heel to be cut down by the Curse. A man of wealth from his ownership of investment firms, Bowles financed a run for the Senate in 2002. Unfortunately, the White House recruited Elizabeth Dole to run against him and he never came close to her. After spending $6.8 million of his own money, Bowles lost to Dole by nine points. But he had become an incurable politico. "My daddy once said, 'Son, politics is like drinking whiskey—once you get it in your system, it's tough to get it out,'" he explained.[35]

So when Senator John Edwards announced in 2003 that he would abandon the Senate for a presidential run Bowles tried again. For a while his prospects looked good. White House strategist Karl Rove recruited five-term Representative Richard Burr to run against Bowles, but Burr could not make much headway. Bowles raised nearly $10 million and put another $3.8 million of his own money into the race. He produced early ads that touted his record as head of the Small Business Administration and as White House chief of staff, during which he negotiated the country's first balanced budget in a generation. Mindful of Clinton's bad odor after all his White House scandals, Bowles employed cautious ads, never mentioning the president whom he had served while accomplishing these admirable deeds. Bowles remained comfortably ahead in the race. Then Bowles suffered a dreadful scare: his old boss's memoir came out hailing Bowles as a Clinton stalwart. Somehow the threat passed. *My Life* was selling brilliantly, but apparently not even political reporters were reading it, certainly not in North Carolina. No one seemed to care what Clinton said about anyone or anything in his book—more evidence of what a uniquely unserious presidential memoir Clinton had written. Throughout the summer and into September, Bowles continued to enjoy a double-digit lead.

Then an advertising barrage smashed his campaign. Burr began airing a series of attack ads on September 16. Supposedly they were about issues such as a tobacco buyout, international trade, and health care. Yet in each, pictures of Bowles and the president he had served were shown, often using the tagline that Bowles was "just like Clinton." That was enough. Bowles' lead wilted. Bowles tried to do the reverse to Burr, suggesting that he was not an independent North Carolinian but a Bush lackey who had voted with the president more than 95 percent of the time. Burr's response was to embrace the idea, expanding on his connection to the president. Bowles was running away from the president he had served, and Burr was running towards the current one. On Election Day, with nothing left to lose, Bowles asked his old boss to do some radio shows to try to energize African-Americans and other voters for him. Clinton was glad to do it, but it was futile. Bowles lost by five points.[36]

Bowles' was not the only nonpresidential race for which Clinton had campaigned in 2004. I have tracked eight others. Here are the results.

- In February, Clinton headlined a fundraiser that fetched nearly $2 million for Senate Minority Leader Tom Daschle of South Dakota, who was facing a tough reelection race against Representative John R. Thune. As the race progressed, Thune's advisers found that the best way to hobble Daschle was to tie him to the Clintons and to Ted Kennedy. One TV ad used video from remarks Daschle had made to New York voters: "I want to thank you for sending Hillary Clinton to Washington to represent you. No one does it better." That hurt Daschle's standing, and he knew it. The Democratic leader countered with—get this—ads that showed him bear-hugging President Bush after 9/11. When Daschle lost by two points, he became the first Senate leader to be ousted at the polls in fifty-two years.

- Democrats smelled blood when four-term Senator Arlen Specter of Pennsylvania was savaged in the state's Republican primary by conservative three-term Congressman Patrick J. Toomey, who charged that Specter was too moderate a party man. Thus weakened, Democratic Representative Joe Hoeffel figured Specter could be knocked off. The Clintons did, too. Hillary was committed to Hoeffel by her friendship with Hoeffel's older sister, a Wellesley classmate. She headlined a June fundraiser for Hoeffel, and former president Clinton hosted another one in Pittsburgh on August 30, four days before he was hospitalized. Together, they put $620,000 into Hoeffel's coffers—all for naught. Hoeffel stood by Clinton at the October 25 Philadelphia rally as the former president touted him as "Joe Hoeffel, our next United States senator." A week later, Hoeffel was clobbered by Senator Specter, 53 to 42 percent.

- When Senator Bob Graham of Florida resigned from the Senate to pursue the Democratic presidential nomination, the state's senatorial race was thrown wide open. Former University of South Florida president Betty Castor became the Democratic nominee. Once again, the Bush White House handpicked a Republican contender. With control of the Senate in sight, Karl Rove asked Cuban émigré Mel Martinez to resign his post in the Bush cabinet as secretary of housing and urban development to challenge Castor. Martinez agreed. Always a battleground, Florida attracted both parties' big guns. Both Clintons personally campaigned for Castor in the state. Clinton did it as part of his October 25 and 26 appearances, in which he boomed both Kerry and Castor. At a Miami rally, Clinton said: "I am pulling for Betty Castor in that debate tonight, because we need her in the United States Senate. I have known her since I was a governor, and she was carrying the education banner here in Florida with then Governor Graham."[37] The race was *very close*, but Martinez pulled it out by one point, 49 to 48. Clinton's only consolation was that he got a write-in vote for Hillsborough County Sheriff . . . along with Jesse James, convicted murderer Scott Peterson, Fidel Castro and Satan.

- Of Clinton's five other candidates, four lost. Running for Senate in Louisiana, Representative Chris John was defeated by Representative David Vitter, 51-29. (A third candidate, a Democrat, received 15 percent, with other candidates receiving another 5 percent. Even if those votes were added to John's, the latter would still have lost.) Clinton stumped for two

> Pennsylvanians, Lois Murphy and Joe Driscoll, in House races. Murphy lost to Jim Gerlach, 51 to 49, and Driscoll was slaughtered by Charlie Dent, 59 to 39. Clinton recorded telephone messages urging support for Representative Martin Frost in Texas where he was running for a redistricted House seat and did the same for incumbent Delaware governor Ruth Ann Minner. Frost lost badly, 54 to 44, while Minner won handily, 51 to 46.

Four years into his retirement, Clinton was beginning to be presented in the *Kultursmog* as a Political Genius. By 2005, journalists were describing him and his wife—as the *Washington Post*'s John F. Harris did,—"the two most important political figures of their generation."[38] Yet these political geniuses had presided over the long decline of a party that had dominated American politics since the 1930s. As for the former president, in campaigning for others he has been pretty much a failure. In the 2004 election cycle, for example, twelve of his fourteen candidates lost—including Gray Davis, Wesley Clark, John Edwards, John Kerry, and the unfortunate eight candidates just noted. Clinton's only two successful candidates were the current San Francisco mayor (who ran without a Republican opponent) and the governor of Delaware.

In 2006 Clinton campaigned for veteran Democratic Senator Joe Lieberman's renomination in the Connecticut Democratic primary, and Lieberman lost to a political neophyte. In the autumn off-year elections, the majority of candidates for whom Clilnton campaigned won, but then it was a Democratic year. The majority of Democrats running won. In none of the races where Clinton campaigned was his presence deemed critical. Asked by Dale Van Atta if Clinton influenced any of the 2006 races, Chuck Todd, the perceptive editor of the *National Journal*'s online political report, "The Hotline," responded, "No. I really don't think Clinton had much of an influence. . . . He was never a determining factor. What's odd is that a lot of the Democrats that won are not Clintonian.

Particularly the Senate guys. They are sort of the opposite of what Bill Clinton was. . . . They're actually anti-trade, and all sorts of differences."[39]

In retirement Clinton has raised millions, mostly for failed candidates—at least before 2006. Until the Democrats' off-year victory in 2006—a victory that is the norm for the opposition in a two-term president's sixth year—the Democratic Party continued to shrivel in Clinton's presence. Nonetheless, his personal stature as Political Genius increased. How is a rational observer of politics to explain it?

EIGHT

BILL AND HILLARY BEYOND THE BLUE

Bill Clinton's restoration from disgrace to the lofty estate of Political Genius, despite the defeat of most of the candidates for whom he has campaigned, is the *Kultursmog*'s first Wonder of the twenty-first century. And what is one to make of Hillary's equally implausible political restoration? Surely, it is the *Kultursmog*'s second Wonder of the young century. Her incessant jitterbug between repute and disrepute has paralleled Bill's. So we can perhaps understand why, within the *Kultursmog*, she too is now described as a "rock star." But there is more. Within the *smog* she is also described as "charismatic," much as most Kennedys are described as "charismatic" and Fidel Castro and the occasional good-looking, well-spoken serial killer. How can a dowdy, middle-aged woman of matronly proportions with bags under her eyes after a day in the Senate and a laugh that is a chilling cackle be described as charismatic? Maybe it is precisely her intimations of authoritarian ruthlessness that inspire the compliment. After all, in the 1920s, admiring Western liberals described Benito Mussolini as charismatic; and *Il Duce* was completely bald. Today even Hillary's critics have to admit that she has a nice head of hair.

When Hillary left the White House in 2001 she left under the same hail of spitballs then pelting her husband. A month later her approval rating was down to 38 percent; and, as we have seen, Democrats all over the country were condemning her, even many New Yorkers. The Clintons' Episodic Apologists had reached the end of their patience. Recall, if you will, that the *New York Observer* editorialized: "we [New Yorkers] have made a terrible mistake, for Hillary Rodham Clinton is unfit for elective office. Had she any shame, she would resign."[1] The venerable *Times* was not much more hospitable. As you might recall from chapter two, the paper called for congressional investigations. Yet by August of 2002, the now familiar cycle was coming round again. As if the year 2001 had been deleted from the record book, the *Washington Post* found itself favorably reporting on Senator Clinton's "potential campaign to become the first woman president." The story made no reference to the Clintons' popularity crash of a year before.[2]

Actually, Hillary's emergence as Political Genius was even more improbable than her husband's recovery from the spitballs. As we have seen, when it came to the actual practice of politics, she had always been a bungler. One remembers her contributions to the Boy Governor's humiliation in 1980. True, she helped in his 1982 return to the governor's mansion, but through the rest of the decade, every time she clasped the levers of power, every member of the governor's staff reached for a crash helmet. Her best remembered botch was a massive statewide education reform to rescue Arkansas from its lowly national rating. Her ministrations alarmed and offended practically every Arkansan involved in the school system and did nothing whatsoever to lift Arkansas from the education swales. In its enormity, Hillary's education reform neatly prefigured the monstrosity she attempted to bring down on American health care as First Lady. Here again is an instance of the Clintons' Arkansas mischief serving as a preview of their White House follies. Arkansas being a one-party oligarchy, the education reform's political damage could be absorbed. Her health care reform, however, gave Republicans at the national level the break they needed in the 1994 off-year elections, and they gave the Democratic Party its worst congressional defeat of the twentieth century. The president's party lost control of both houses. After but two years of the Clintons, "the Republicans scored," writes historian James T. Patterson, "the most impressive off-year comeback in modern times."[3] Much of the blame lay with Hillary's shoving her husband to the left.

Through her husband's governorship and his presidency, the only reliable service Hillary provided was as a cover for his many dalliances. Hillary stood by her man, as Bill adjusted his trousers. Her practiced skill in this undignified wifely task made Mrs. Clinton the indispensable wife. Her meatloaf might be mediocre, and her temper tantrums could cause collateral damage; but she stood by her man like no other First Lady. When she covered for him during the Lewinsky episode, a miracle occurred, and she used it to effect one of the most dramatic career changes on record. She moved from political bungler to junior senator from New York. Shortly thereafter she became the Democratic Party's leading presidential contender. Once again history demonstrates that political science is not a science.

The role Hillary played at Bill's side was essential for saving him from his scandals, but it did not make her very likable. She was never popular in Arkansas, and her unpopularity was to continue in Washington. In fact, once in the White House, Hillary served as the most unpopular First Lady of modern times. Arguably the dour wife of President Warren G. Harding, our Boy President's nearest presidential likeness, was equally unpopular. Gruesome photographs record the forbidding countenance of "the Duchess," as she was known, but the popularity of first ladies was not tested in the Hardings' day and would not be for another three decades. By 1996, Hillary became the first presidential spouse in four decades of polling to have a majority of the American people give her thumbs-down. It was a hefty majority. In January 1996, after the notoriety from her health care project, Whitewater, and a disturbing appearance before a grand jury investigating the firings at the White House Travel Office, only 43 percent approved of her.[4] A CNN/*Time* poll showed that 52 percent of respondents thought she was lying about Whitewater and the Travel Office. Twenty-one percent were *unsure*.[5] Sixty-eight percent believed she probably did something "illegal" or "unethical" in her Whitewater dealings.[6] For most of the remainder of her days in the White House she bumped along in the polls, recovering only when Monica Lewinsky got into the act.

The Lewinsky scandal occasioned Hillary's miracle, the Miracle of the Deceived Wife. As she played the role of the deceived wife her favorable ratings soared. Truth be known, she was never deceived. She knew about Lewinsky from the start. Her agent, Deputy Chief of Staff Evelyn Lieberman, had been monitoring the perfume in the Oval Office from the forty-second president's first clutch. Yet most Americans thought Hillary had been in the dark, and they were sympathetic. As impeachment neared, the deceived wife rose in public esteem as did her disgraced husband—still more evidence of politics' debt to abnormal psychology. Though neither was trusted, they were somehow applauded. Very cunningly, Hillary exploited this new esteem and made a victorious run for the Senate in 2000.

Even in that race she showed signs of her old political ineptitude. Yet the Fates smiled on her. The opponent who most certainly would have beaten her, Mayor Rudy Giuliani, hampered by health problems and a distracting divorce, retired from the field. Her eventual opponent, Rick Lazio, a four-term congressman, was not capable of exploiting her mistakes; and she captured retiring Senator Daniel Patrick Moynihan's seat, a seat once been held by another out-of-stater with presidential ambitions, Robert F. Kennedy.*

*Ironically, in Hillary's days as a college radical, Professor Moynihan's moderate positions on public policy—at the time called neoconservative—were a special target for her vituperation. Moynihan did not forget. Even as a senator he disliked the Clintons. Early in the Lewinsky scandal he asserted that were President Clinton to lie under oath he would be impeachable. Indicative of the toll politics takes on principle, when it came to voting on the articles of impeachment, among which was perjury, Moynihan voted to acquit.

Then came Pardongate and news reports that Hillary was covering up for her brothers' commerce in pardons. Simultaneously came the reports that she had made off with White House property and that her staff had booby trapped the White House. Senator-elect Clinton collapsed in the polls. She was furious, but what could she do, aside from throwing a shoe at her woebegone husband? What followed was an as yet unexplained metamorphosis.

Without benefit of a personality transplant or any anger management therapy known to the public, Senator Clinton suddenly became a competent, peaceful, law-abiding senator, servicing her constituents willingly and efficaciously. Time and again as the wife of a governor and then of a president she had been caught by the press seething over some commonplace event of public service: a flag flying at the wrong time over the governor's mansion, a Secret Service agent refusing to carry her luggage, an importunate autograph seeker, perhaps one with a runny nose. Yet now she was Hillary With A Smile On Her Face. Even more surprising, once in the Senate she did not insist on hogging the limelight—at least not often. Being the center of attention has been the major theme of her life. In those early Senate days, however, she put herself to the humble task of learning the rules and mores of the institution. She courted senators on both sides of the aisles, particularly the senior senators, most notably West Virginia's Robert Byrd. She began gathering power like no other Senate freshman since Lyndon Johnson in the 1940s.

There would be backsliding, to be sure. Hillary's 1960s narcissism could not be completely subdued. During 9/11 and its aftermath she—and her husband too—were in a state of peculiar agitation. He actually fretted that he was no longer president and could not partake of George W. Bush's glory. As for his wife, she could not resist grandstanding on *Dateline NBC* with another of those gratuitous lies that often turn out so badly for the Clintons. Hillary suggested to her interviewer, Jane Pauley, that Chelsea almost perished at the World Trade Center. According to Hillary, her daughter had "gone on what she thought would be a great jog. . . . She was going to go around the [Trade Center] towers. She went to get a cup of coffee and—that's when the plane hit."[7] Once again Hillary's stalkers, the Fact Checkers, were not far away. They laid hands on an article in *Talk* magazine where Chelsea wrote in her own hand that she "was alone at a friend's Union Square apartment in Manhattan that morning."[8] A little later Hillary was at her worst when President George W. Bush addressed a joint session of Congress on the events of September 11. Viewers watching the broadcast saw Hillary in another of her pouting-schoolgirl moments: rolling her eyes, sighing theatrically, squirming at each statement of the president's that displeased her. When the members of Congress applauded she did so as though pained by a fellow classmate's sophomoric antics.

Finally we have this stupefying lapse into self-absorption and self-pity. Asked by journalist Nicholas Lemann how she thought Americans "would react to knowing that they were on the receiving end of a mindless rage," the originator of the phrase "Vast Right-Wing Conspiracy" responded: "Oh, I am well aware that it is out there. One of the most difficult experiences that I personally had in the White House was during the health-care debate, being the object of extraordinary rage. I remember being in Seattle. I was there to make a speech about healthcare. This was probably August of 1994. Radio talk-show hosts had urged their listeners to come out and yell and scream and carry on and prevent people from hearing me speak. There were threats that were coming in, and certain people didn't want me to speak, and they started taking weapons off people, and arresting people. I've had first-hand looks at this unreasoning anger and hatred that is focused on an individual you don't know, a cause that you despise—whatever motivates people."[9] "They started taking weapons" from people? Is she saying that opponents of her healthcare reform had armed themselves? Is this another of Hillary's artless fibs?

As long as Hillary is in public life there will be such relapses, which is why one would expect Americans to be reluctant to make her president of the United States. Her last residency in the White House saw her abusing power (Filegate, Travelgate, and as many as a dozen IRS probes of her political opponents), obstructing justice (her aides' illegal entry into the deceased Vince Foster's White House office, her subpoenaed billing records that disappeared for two years before being found in the White House family quarters), and giving what independent counsel Robert Ray called her "factually inaccurate" testimony under oath. The unsavory figures slithering round her Bruno persona—for instance, Filegate's Craig Livingstone and Anthony Marceca, and her private investigators, Jack Paladino and Anthony Pellicano—have had encores even in Hillary's strait-laced Senate years.

Hillary's 2000 senatorial campaign was caught using a thrice-convicted felon, Peter Paul, to raise money, which he donated in violation of campaign finance laws, causing her finance director, David F. Rosen, to be prosecuted. Rosen was acquitted, though in the course of the trial taped conversations between him and Raymond Reggie, Senator Ted Kennedy's brother-in-law, made clear that Rosen was aware that the Clinton campaign knowingly violated federal law. In fact, Rosen was heard on tape calling himself a "guinea pig" and "good soldier" for Senator Clinton's lawyers.[10] Rosen's meaning is unclear, but his debasing descriptions of himself bring to mind poor Webb Hubbell's taped conversation from prison during which he told his wife, presumably in reference to the Clintons: "So I need to roll over one more time."[11] Poor Rosen—the Clinton Curse claims yet another.

Not that the Clinton Senate campaign got off scot-free. Early in 2006 it was reported that the Federal Election Commission fined the campaign, "New York Senate 2000," $35,000 for neglecting to report $721,895 expended on the Paul-Rosen fundraising event. Moreover, Paul's lawsuit against the Clintons got the media attention he obviously coveted. In it he claimed that the former president broke an agreement to work with Paul on a private venture in exchange for his donations to Hillary.[12]

Notwithstanding her run-ins with the law, from sometime in 2002 Senator Clinton has been the Democrats' choice for the presidency. As we have seen, her husband has been promoting her presidential prospects assiduously. Had he his way she would have sought the 2004 nomination and probably lost—yet another casualty of Clinton's parlous political counsel. Publicly, she usually demurs when her presidential potential is mentioned. There was, however, this admission to a German magazine late in 2003 when she was asked why she had not entered the presidential field: "Well, perhaps I'll do it next time around." Asked about her relationship with her roving husband, she replied: "It is actually a kind of job rotation. First, Bill focused on his career, now it's my turn. Bill supports me and gives me tips. He's my best adviser, as I tried to be for him when he was fulfilling political office."[13]

Bill and Hillary moved from their 2001 troubles to her emergence a year later as the Democrats' presidential frontrunner by once again demonstrating their mastery of mob psychology. As we shall see, they know their mob well. It is a mob that needs fantasies and enemies or at least the delusion of enemies. Playing on his supporters' need for enemies is how the Boy President survived Monicagate and impeachment: "OK, so I had an 'inappropriate' relationship but you don't want to side with Starr," the old mesmerizer seemed to be saying. "All right, so I, as I said myself, 'misled people, including even my wife,' but you're not on the side of the House Republicans are you?" Such was the gist of his counter-offensive after the revelations of Miss Lewinsky's stained dress. Even Richard Posner, author of the most intelligent study of the Clinton impeachment, was vulnerable. After concluding that Clinton's misbehavior was indeed grounds for impeachment, Posner opposed the proceedings as unseemly.

As for satisfying their supporters' need for fantasy, what could be more fantastical than the idea of Hillary, a five-foot, four-inch 150-pound career woman, as a rock star? Now it is always possible that the conception of Hillary as a rock star was not the Clintons' idea. Most likely it was the fantasy of sympathetic journalists, who idolize rock stars; but the Clintons surely encouraged it. Saturated as the sympathetic journalists are in pop culture, they believe that to compare a politician to a rock star is the highest compliment. An educated person might compare an admired politician to a philosopher or to a great political figure of the past. An intellectually vacant Clintonista pumping fumes into the *Kultursmog* mindlessly compares the Clintons to rock stars. Elvis Presley is usually the referent in the case of Bill. Who the referent for dowdy Hillary might be is always left unsaid. There are limits even to a Clintonista's capacity to fantasize. In truth, Hillary is precisely what she appears to be, a very ambitious middle-aged female lawyer; and no amount of fanfare or Botox* has warmed her up since her schoolgirl days when classmates called her "Sister Frigidaire." Yet the fantasy works with her supporters, possibly because they, despite middle age and mediocrity, imagine themselves to be potential rock stars, too.

By 2004, the fantasy of Hillary the rock star had become so popular in the media that it was almost a cliché. By the Democratic Convention, frenzy was setting in. The morning after Hillary introduced her husband to the convention for his twenty-five-minute speech, ABC's Charles Gibson reported excitedly, "People were juiced like I don't think I've seen at a convention ever before." By "juiced" he did not mean inebriated. On MSNBC that morning, Chris Jansing turned her attention to Hillary: "Like a pop star, she's known just by her first name: 'Hillary.'" (Actually a similar observation can be made of a sports figure—Lance Armstrong is called "Lance"; or a fashion figure—Martha Stewart is Martha; or a convicted murderer—Scott Peterson was "Scott," at least before his sentencing.) On CBS, Hannah Storm said of Senator Clinton's arrival at the convention, "It was as if she was a rock star coming in here."[14] By 2005 even some light-headed Republicans were making the rock star comparison. When Senator Clinton appeared in Madison, Wisconsin, to address

*Her cosmetic surgery has been widely noted. Not so widely noted is her experimentation with the color of her eyes. A Clinton insider told Matt Drudge "She started experimenting with different blazing blue colors at the White House. She even tried turquoise contact lenses once, but it was not a great look for her," Drudge Report, June 25, 2003.

the nonpartisan Wisconsin Women in Government dinner, Brandon Scholz, formerly director of the Wisconsin Republican Party, observed, "She's star-studded material." Democratic Governor Jim Doyle merely noted the "rock star atmosphere."[15]

Those in the Clintons' mob who are susceptible to the rock star fantasy are equally susceptible to the fantastical claim that Sister Frigidaire has charisma. Brief years, perhaps months, after the disgrace of her larcenous White House exit, whenever she would bustle into a room with her bodyguards, her lawyers, hangers-on, camera crews, and reporters, susceptible journalists would marvel at her "charisma." The fantasy has persisted, notwithstanding its preposterosity—again, doubtless with the Clintons' encouragement. Nonetheless it is hooey as surely as the rock-star fantasy is hooey.

To have charisma a politician needs style, eloquence, a sense of theater, and a gullible following. Hillary has only the last. Liberals were right when they described John F. Kennedy as charismatic, and though they waited until Ronald Reagan died they have been right to acknowledge his charisma. When these men entered a room they had a presence about them. They attracted cameras, lights, and attention because of their physical gifts and verbal skills. Hillary, too, attracts attention but not because of her physical or verbal assets. Often, even in the Senate, she has displayed a tin ear for rhetoric and a propensity to scowl. Hillary attracts attention because of the commotion caused by her entourage and by the sympathetic journalists around her with their cameras and microphones. If the presence of commotion, cameras, and journalists were evidence of charisma, a multicar pileup on Interstate 95 would be charismatic. As I shall relate, Hillary has acquired power in the Senate paralleling the power acquired by the young Senator Lyndon Johnson in the 1940s, but no one ever called Johnson charismatic.

Perhaps even more important than the Clintons' artistry with mob psychology in advancing Hillary's career is the composition of the mob itself. Within it are some very gifted dramatists, all of whom contribute prodigiously to the *Kultursmog*. Hillary is as famous as she is because these talented people *want* her to be very famous and with all her past misbehavior forgotten. This is not a conspiracy. It is a matter of culture, a consequence of her generation's evolution.

Hillary is about the last major Democrat from the left wing of her generation available to take on the generation's right wing. In 2008 it will be those opportunistic 1960s student protesters known as the Coat and Tie Radicals campaigning against the young conservatives dismissed as negligible in the 1960s who a decade later manned the Reagan Revolution. Though the generation that fought World War II is called the "Greatest Generation," the 1960s generation is the most momentous *political* generation of the twentieth century. Now its left and right are squaring off for one last battle to claim title to their generation. Whoever triumphs, it will be as memorable a victory as Franklin Roosevelt's defeat of President Herbert Hoover or as Reagan's victory over President Jimmy Carter. What will make it even more momentous is that Hillary now represents the political heritage of liberalism that Roosevelt began. Though in the Clintons' hands that liberalism has been disfigured, Hillary embodies an Old Order that is desperate for victory. The looming battle between the two wings of the 1960s generation—one championing the Roosevelt heritage, the Old Order, the other championing the Reagan heritage, a New Order—explains much of the bitterness of contemporary politics.

The *Washington Post's* David Broder is the only major political commentator to take note of this intragenerational contest. Observing from a vantage point a generation older than the 1960s generation, Broder wrote that the 2004 dispute over John Kerry's Vietnam record "confirms my fears that my generation may never [live to] see the day when the baby boomers who came of age in that troubled decade are reconciled sufficiently with each other to lead a united country." He even adduced an example of this bitterness, citing the outburst of a 1960s conservative against the 1960s leftists. Broder quotes Vice President Dan Quayle's wife Marilyn (Purdue University '71) at the 1992 Republican National

Convention declaiming: "Dan and I are members of the baby boom generation, too. We are all shaped by the times in which we live. I came of age in a time of turbulent social change. . . . Remember, not everyone joined in the counterculture. Not everyone demonstrated, dropped out, took drugs, joined in the sexual revolution or dodged the draft. Not everyone concluded that American society was so bad that it had to be radically remade by social revolution. . . . The majority of my generation lived by the credo our parents taught us. We believed in God, in hard work and personal discipline, in our nation's essential goodness, and in the opportunity it promised those willing to work for it. . . . Though we knew some changes needed to be made, we did not believe in destroying America to save it."[16]

Those who want Hillary to be famous are for the most part the members of her 1960s generation who shared her Coat and Tie Radicalism and were the targets of Mrs. Quayle's comprehensive ire. They are leftists of various degrees, though years ago they lost sight of Marx or for that matter of any other systematic thinker on the left. In their twenties they went into politics, social work, the media, and the corporate world. They donned bourgeois attire when appropriate or, when advantageous, they affected leftist fashions. That is why, since college days, we on the right have called them Coat and Tie Radicals. In the 1980s, they were driven to the peripheries of politics by the surging forces of Goldwater conservatism then led by Reagan. Hillary's husband returned them to power in 1992. Having through the 1970s been billed as the true voices of the 1960s generation, they now felt vindicated. In the *Kultursmog,* once again, they were presented as the true representative voices of the 1960s, an idealistic and progressive generation that rendered conventional America passé.*

*The media stories of the Baby Boomers entering retirement that began appearing in 2005 usually repeat the same false claim that the Boomers have been overwhelmingly left wing. The fact is that they were always fairly conservative, their conservative voice being heard later in life but heard nonetheless. Even when young, the majority of Boomers was conservative. In 1972 their vote went to Richard Nixon.

Then tragedy struck these left-wingers, and it was worse than the tragedy of Reagan's 1980 victory. In the election of 2000 the other side of their generation rose to a prominence that the media could not ignore. That is to say, the side of the 1960s generation that had not protested and stupefied itself in what was called "flower power" defeated its old rival. A frat boy, George W. Bush (Delta Kappa Epsilon '64), beat Al Gore, a veteran of every 1960s New Age enthusiasm, flower power included. In characteristic 1960s petulance Gore's people claimed that they won the 2000 election but were denied their victory because of skullduggery in the Florida vote count. Then Bush beat them handily in the 2002 off-year elections, elections in which an incumbent president usually suffers congressional losses. Bush actually increased his margins on Capitol Hill. Then in 2004 Bush beat another of the Coat and Tie Radicals' prodigies, Kerry, the anti-Vietnam War Vietnam War hero. To be sure, in the 2006 off-year elections Bush suffered losses; but they were basically only the normal losses that a two-term president can expect to suffer in his second off-year election, and many of the newly-elected Democrats were spouting conservative lines: pro-life, anti-gun control, no new taxes. The election set the stage for a colossal intragenerational matchup in 2008.

For the past three decades, with only the respites of Boy Clinton's 1992 and 1996 victories, the left-wing *wunderkinds* of the 1960s have been suffering decline among the American electorate. Among the elites who shape the political culture, however, they have remained preponderant, for instance, in the media. Now, gearing up behind Hillary, they are readying themselves for one final shot at the White House. It will be the last battle between the Coat and Tie Radicals of the 1960s and their hated rivals, the conservatives who took a pass on student protests for leisure time spent by the beer keg and the barbecue pit. Precisely who the Republicans will run in 2008 is unclear, but most likely the candidate will be surrounded by middle-aged conservative policy wonks who owe their ideas to the small band of free-market economists and Cold War hawks who taught them in the late 1960s and early 1970s when Hillary's Coat and Tie Radicals dominated campus headlines. The conservatives' positions have remained pretty much the same. They advocate free markets, strong national security, and, to varying degrees, conservative social values. Hillary's positions have changed markedly, from being anti-military, anti-authority leftist, to being something more elusive. Today she is a rock star approaching sixty and propounding seemly sentiments and noble goals. Hers will be a campaign of faith and fantasy. Increasingly, Hillary's supporters are like the religious pietists who saw on the face of an old cheese sandwich an image of the Virgin Mary. One paid $28,000 for the thing.[17]

The Clintons are the two most exaggerated figures in modern American political history, more overblown by their supporters than Reagan and Franklin Roosevelt were by theirs. Of course, the Clintons got some minor legislation through in the 1990s. That is the modest assessment of a widening number of professional historians, most of whom note that the Clintons' main preoccupations were to batten down scandals and hold off various independent counsels while important initiatives were delayed—for instance, Social Security reform and the war against terrorism.[18] The Boy President got himself elected and reelected while the Democratic Party's dominance in the country shrank. Hillary got herself elected to the Senate; but she has no legislation to show for it, only presidential preference polls, some of which show that nearly half of the American electorate would "definitely not vote for her."[18] As politicians, the Clintons' main achievement has been raw survival, at a cost that has been enormous in terms of destructive legal precedents, eroded ethics, and infringements on the rule of law.

Though the historians are filing increasingly restrained evaluations of the Clintons' political achievements, the Episodic Apologists continue to inflate the Clintons' importance. A particularly egregious example of this inflation came in the first years of Clinton's retirement when the *Washington Post*'s national correspondent, John F. Harris, published his reassessment of the Clinton presidency, *The Survivor: Bill Clinton in the White House.* Though he is younger than the Clintons, Harris's appraisal of them puts him on their side in the 1960s intragenerational rivalry. Perhaps he will be remembered as one of flower power's fellow travelers.

Writing in the aftermath of Pardongate and the other scandals attending the Clintons' White House departure, and despite growing evidence of Clinton's lax terror policies, Harris appraises the Clintons as "the two most important political figures of their generation."[20] He renders that judgment despite their contemporary, Newt Gingrich's "Contract with America," used by Gingrich in 1994 to end four decades of Democratic control of the House of Representatives. Nor is Harris apparently impressed by another of the Clintons' cogenerationists, George W. Bush, who won the presidency twice and commenced America's War on Terror. Harris's insularity is now characteristic of liberal journalists. One sees it even on the jacket of his book, where another *Washington Post* writer, the early Clinton biographer David Maraniss, claims that Harris "is the most lucid writer in American political journalism . . . especially when he writes about Bill Clinton." Beyond producing stupid observations, this insularity produces delightful moments of comedy, for instance, the selection of photographs Harris includes in his book. One shows Clinton conferring in a public lavatory. There is no hint of irony.

The Clinton-Gore team made its debut in 1992 with these two lovable narcissists jogging through Washington, D.C. in what appeared to be their undershorts. Many adults thought that bizarre, but Harris innocently displays many other bizarre interludes from the Clinton years in his book's photographs, oblivious to what they reveal about his hero. There are pictures of a soused Boris Yeltsin, a contrite and blubbering Webb Hubbell, a self-satisfied Monica Lewinsky, and then there is the Lavatory Scene: Clinton, Gore, and White House aide Harold Ickes (described in the caption as "tough-minded") conferring in a *men's lavatory.* Gore has his hand on the sink, Bill and Ickes their backs to the stalls. Is it even imaginable that their cogenerationist from the right, George W. Bush, would allow himself to be photographed in a lavatory? Possibly, if Hillary wins in 2008, this pioneering picture will be hung in the White House waiting room. So far as I have been able to establish, it is the first picture ever published of a president conferring in a men's room—though possibly it is a women's room. Only stalls, no urinals, are visible.

In truth, neither of the Clintons is the Political Genius that the *Kultursmog* beholds. They are an epiphenomenon of their generation. No political duo caught lying, cheating, and breaking the law so many times would remain politically aloft if there were not support for their publicly exposed misbehavior within the culture. That support comes from the Coat and Tie Radicals whose standards are much different from those of their rivals on the right and from those of the American majority, if recent political trends mean anything. Yet if the Clintons are not Political Geniuses they are political automatons, ceaselessly politicking back and forth, back and forth across America. This sempiternal politicking is another innovation of the Coat and Tie Radical. Bill and Hillary have been doing politics all their lives. George W. Bush, though raised in a political dynasty, has spent more of his life in business than in politics. That is typical of conservatives from his generation. On the other hand, the Clintons have had no life beyond politics. They are political creatures to the utmost, as are Gore and Kerry and most of the Coat and Tie Radicals. Gingrich is the rare conservative whose life has been wholly devoted to politics, but then in his college days he was at least a mild Coat and Tie Radical.

Precisely when the Clintons decided Hillary would enter politics once Bill's career had run its course might never be known. In their long, politically besotted marriage the understanding doubtless simply grew. We do know that at some point in the last years of the Boy President's tumultuous presidency, probably in gratitude for Hillary's services during the Lewinsky hullabaloo and his impeachment, he promised her his political assistance. Further, as we have seen, Hillary set her sights on Moynihan's Senate seat much earlier than she admits in her memoir. As reported in chapter three, the First Lady had her eye on the seat prior to February 12, 1999, when the Senate acquitted her husband. As the Senate deliberated

Bill's fate, Hillary was conferring with Harold Ickes in the White House. With her aides bringing in the latest reports on the impeachment vote, the First Lady questioned her old political adviser on her prospects for a New York senatorial campaign.[21]

Yet, whereas Bill was a natural pol, Hillary had to acquire at least the social skills of politics much as had another charmless, calculating, and relentless political creature, Richard Nixon. Here is where her huckster from Hot Springs was doubtless invaluable. Day in and day out through the decades she could watch his moves and, though she was ungainly at hers, he was always supportive. He may have been unfaithful, but rarely has Hillary's husband failed to be a booster of Hillary. In the social skills of politics—the one area she surely lacked confidence—Bill served as both exemplar and coach.

With her husband's support, she began publicly campaigning for the Senate in July 1999, announcing from Moynihan's upstate farm her plan to travel the state on a "listening tour." As the campaign got underway she had her bad moments. Educated middle-class women were wary of her, as were observant Jews, two constituencies she counted on. She was wooden in public and came across as untrustworthy. In an interview with *Talk* magazine, wherein she attempted to explicate the mysteries of her marriage and Bill's sex life, she trotted out such derisible 1960s psychobabble about his upbringing that commentators all over the state were hooting. An attempt to ingratiate herself to New York's Jewish community blew up after she attended a speech by Yasser Arafat's wife, Suha. Suha accused Israel of poisoning Palestinian women and children. Unaccountably, Hillary applauded and then was photographed kissing Mrs. Arafat. Her effort to silence the uproar elicited still more hoots. She claimed to have discovered a long-lost Jewish stepgrandfather. Her husband's attempt to capture the Puerto Rican vote for her by pardoning seventeen Puerto Rican terrorists backfired, causing her to heave up another of her implausible lies and adding to her reputation for dishonesty. As 1999 expired her campaign was in trouble.

Then came the turnaround. For one thing, Bill took a personal interest and proved to be helpful. For another she had a team of competent, seasoned political advisers led by Ickes. Finally a lot of money was being lined up—she would spend $40 million before the last vote came in. Her husband hit upon an explanation she might use to win over skeptics, particularly women who wondered about the rationale for her marriage and for her sudden candidacy. At a meeting with her and her aides he erupted, "You're a sticker! That's what people need to know—you are a sticker. You stick at the things you care about."[22]

At the same time, Ickes and his team began making effective use of focus groups and of pollsters. They developed clever responses to her opponents' attacks, claiming that only insecure men were alarmed by this ambitious woman, and portraying it a low blow to bring up past scandals. After a September debate with her Republican opponent, Congressman Lazio, in which he and moderator Tim Russert brought up her past, polls turned hugely in her favor—not an auspicious sign for opponents who in 2008 might want to make an issue of the record of the most scandal-tarnished woman in American politics.

Months before that, in the spring of 2000, the first signs appeared of the distance that was going to widen between the Clintons during Bill's retirement. His daily calls to the candidate and to her staff—often his own former staffers—began to go unanswered. They were becoming a nuisance. Her staff was beginning to perceive them as increasingly irrelevant and him as a potential embarrassment. Hillary was campaigning throughout New York. He was wrapping things up in the White House, fretting over his legacy. As her staff rebuffed him, Bill, the amiable weakling that he has so often shown himself to be, especially when his personal gain was not involved, backed off. The separation would become almost total by 2005, save for the occasional fundraising appearances and family holidays with Chelsea.

Yet from her years of acrimonious cohabitation with Bill she has taken with her two great lessons: Raise enormous sums of money regardless of its provenance, and adhere to policies that are centrist left—the press will report them as centrist. How far to the left Hillary might be in her heart of hearts is unknown. As a candidate and as a senator she has been, as she herself has said, "a New Democrat," working with the moderate liberal organization that her husband worked with from the 1980s, the Democratic Leadership Council (DLC). As the 2008 presidential race beckons, she has taken prominent positions in the DLC; announcing in the summer of 2005 that she would travel the country, engaging it in a "national conversation," an effort that, perhaps, brings to mind her New York "listening tour."

Senator Clinton's first two years in the Senate were years of quiet industriousness that reminded political observers of LBJ's early Senate years. She put in such long hours that in 2002 she became one of only six Democrats to earn a Golden Gavel award for presiding over the Senate for more than one hundred hours, admittedly mostly to empty seats. She cultivated senators on both sides of the aisle, particularly senior senators such as the West Virginia Democrat Robert Byrd and the Arizona Republican John McCain, but also such conservatives as then House Majority Leader Tom DeLay, with whom she worked on foster care legislation. Following the Johnson model, she landed choice committee seats including a seat on the Senate Armed Services Committee that in time of war might protect her from her antimilitary past. She also is on the Democrats' powerful Steering and Coordination Committee, thus giving her influence in setting the Democrats' agenda. By 2004 no senator since Johnson had amassed so much power so fast. Hillary has been collegial, but as we saw in chapter six she can also be brutal. Senators still recall her insulting remarks about Senator John Edwards looking "pretty." On another occasion at a closed-door meeting with fellow Democrats she assailed her colleague Senator Russ Feingold for the mischief his campaign finance reform bill had caused her fundraising. "She tore into Feingold," a Senate aide says. "Other people at the caucus were not happy about it. The other senators resent her. But they're so weak. Their weakness permits her to grow."[23]

Perhaps it is with an eye to the schizoid nature of her party, divided as it is between its Angry Left and its Establishment, that she has devised an ambiguous approach: in policy she is centrist; in rhetoric she is caustic—especially toward President Bush, whom the Angry Left detests. The centrism is catnip for the Establishment. The sarcastic rhetoric is raw meat for the Angry Left.

In her Senate floor speech before voting for Bush's option to go to war with Saddam Hussein, she employed her ambiguous approach relentlessly. She criticized the United Nations for limiting inspection sites. She warned of Saddam's ambitions for weapons of mass destruction: "It is clear, however, that if left unchecked, Saddam Hussein will continue to increase his capacity to wage biological and chemical warfare, and will keep trying to develop nuclear weapons." She also worried that an unchecked Saddam could endanger the entire Middle East. On the other hand, she fretted that a "unilateral" attack on Saddam would prompt Russia to attack Chechen rebels in Georgia, China to attack Taiwan, and India to attack Pakistan. Her vote was to enable the president to go to war, but her conclusion was that doing so "on the present facts is not a good option."[24]

So effective has she been in repositioning herself that in 2005, the *Observer*, one of Britain's most prestigious left-wing newspapers, noted, "Her list of conservative credentials is growing." It reported her "espousing homespun values and with a fondness for prayer." She sympathized with a faith-based charity led by a clergyman opposed to homosexual marriage and appeared with "ultra-conservative" Senator Rick Santorum to introduce legislation to probe sexual and violent images in media.[25] As a senator she favors the death penalty and more money for firefighters and other first responders. Despite her vaunted feminism, she has sympathized with opponents of abortion. From the Armed Services Committee she has supported increased veterans benefits and—unlike Senator Kerry—she voted for the $87 billion legislation to fight the Iraq war. But on international relations and economics she is witheringly critical of the Bush administration. She is also a reliable opponent of tax cuts, insisting that they are a scheme to enrich the wealthy and take money from government's assistance to the needy.

With an eye on the growing strength of the Angry Left in her party, she inveighs against the president, particularly on economics and questions of his competence—this, despite Bush's strong economy and the historic disorderliness of the Clinton presidency. Upon depicting the president in July 2005 at the Aspen Ideas Festival as the cartoon figure, Alfred E. Neuman (whose motto in *MAD* magazine was "What, me worry?"), she explained her joke with a thunderous salvo. It encapsulated much of her five-year critique of the president who, she insisted, has been "undermining the national economy with deficit spending and huge tax cuts for the wealthy; endangering U.S. soldiers by not giving them proper equipment to fight the war in Iraq; and harming the nation's historic role as a leader in scientific research and technological innovation by slashing funding for such efforts."[26] Though the Bush economy had been expanding for almost four years and with low inflation, Hillary BS-ed the assembled festival goers, "There has not yet been one net job created in the last four years." (Actually, 240,000 jobs had been added to employers' payrolls in the same month that she made that assertion.[27]) A year later, with the economy still chugging along, she was making the same false charges, notifying the annual meeting of the Democratic Leadership Council: "They're bankrupting our country and failing to address the problems."[28] The problems, she claimed, were economic, though the economy had grown 5.6 percent in the first quarter and created 5.4 million jobs over the past three years.

Presumably this kind of oratory will fetch the Angry Left, but it brings to mind the spuriousness of the Clinton economic myth, which congratulates itself for the growth of the 1990s while deriding the supply-side economics championed by Republicans. The myth is easily exposed. The Clintons claimed that the tax increases in their budget would lead to a decline in deficits and to a drop in interest rates. Actually interest rates on ten-year Treasury bonds went up from 1991 to November 1994. Not until the election of a Republican Congress did they begin to fall, and not until the Republican Congress put pressure on Clinton to cut the capital gains tax and reform welfare did interest rates drop substantially. Clearly tax cuts, not tax increases, have goaded growth, and it is now a matter of record that tax cuts led to increased federal revenues. After the cut in capital gains taxes in 1997 federal revenues surged, rising 12.4% in both 1997 and 1998. Astute as Hillary has been in divining the value of conservative social policy, she remains in the dark as to the economy. Her jeering at tax cuts may win her the Democratic nomination with the Angry Left, but surely it will not win her the presidency with the electorate at large. Tax increases, class warfare, and the gloom she sees in the world have not been winning messages with American voters.

Her prodigious powers as a fundraiser will also help her with the Angry Left, as well as with the Establishment. This is where her husband comes back into the picture. The two are a colossal source of funds for an otherwise financially strapped party, thanks to their friendship with the very rich, comprised mostly of the Hollywood rich and of other shady figures. We have already read, in chapter two, Democratic Party Chairman Terry McAuliffe's testimonials to the disgraced ex-president's fundraising ability, even in the shadow of Pardongate. He steadily got better. In one twenty-four-hour period during the 2002 election cycle he raised $5 million.[29] In early July of 2004 he raised $1 million for Kerry in a day in Chicago,[30] and for Florida Senate candidate Debbie Wasserman Schultz later in the month, $650,000.[31] He even mastered the Internet despite his clumsiness with technology. In an e-mail solicitation for Kerry in the spring of 2004 he raised $2 million in one day.[32] Working with Hillary he raised $10 million for Kerry in ten days in March of 2004.[33]

As for Hillary, from the beginning of her life as a candidate through 2002, more than $31 million was raised in her name.[34] In her first two years in the Senate she gave more than $1,400,000 to Democratic candidates—"tops among party leaders," the *Washington Post* reported.[35] In keeping with her efforts to gain power on Capitol Hill, more than one hundred members of Congress were recipients of her munificence; though she spread it around the country usually to candidates who were sure winners. Her record for supporting winning candidates has been much better than her husband's.

So are the Clintons about to come together, unite their party, and lead the youthful idealists of the late 1960s in a return to the White House and a vindication of their claim to being the true representative voice of their generation? Or is another child of Goldwater conservatism going to sweep past them, reminding the world that Ronald Reagan's 1980s and the administrations of Bush '41 and Bush '43 were not flukes? Republicans are fearful of a Clinton victory. They know the power of the *Kultursmog* can overcome the Clintons' scandalous past and engaud their paltry record. Who knows; maybe these Republicans, too, think Hillary a rock star. Democrats, at least Democrats with their antennae to Middle America, fear she is a sure loser. They fear that her past will not be forgotten. They fear the power of the Republican "smear machine" as deeply as Republicans fear the power of the *Kultursmog*.

Hillary has a tremendous challenge ahead. By 2005 a news story had crept into the media, remaining long enough to take on the character of Truth, to wit, that her party is fragmented and without direction. This became a Truth even in the *Kultursmog*. The fragmentation within the party might have become too bitter even for such masters of mob psychology as the Clintons. On July 25, when Hillary agreed to the DLC's offer to set off on her "national conversation" as part of its "American Dream Initiative," she let the Republicans have it: "After four years of Republican control, our country has not only gone off track, it has reversed course." But she also said something that got her into dreadful trouble hours after she uttered it. She said, "It's high time for a ceasefire. It's time for all Democrats to work together," and "Let's start by uniting against the hard-right ideology."[36]

Kaboom! "Clinton Angers Left with Call for Unity," read the headline in the next day's *Washington Post*. "Long a revered figure by many in the party's liberal wing, Clinton (D-NY) unexpectedly found herself under attack after calling Monday for a cease-fire among the party's quarreling factions and for agreeing to assume the leadership of a DLC-sponsored initiative aimed at developing a more positive policy agenda for the party," went the story whose import echoed in most of the nation's major media. The left-wing blogs such as Daily Kos were gravely disappointed. Spokespersons for the Angry Left's new organizations, such as the Campaign for America's Future and MoveOn.org were also antagonistic. "There has been an activist resurgence in the Democratic Party in recent years," the *Post* noted, "and Hillary risks ensuring that there's a candidate to her left appealing to those activists who don't much like the DLC."[37]

For three decades, the 1960s Coat and Tie Radicals have been the dominant influence in the *Kultursmog* and an influence in the Democratic Party disproportionate to their numbers. Now there are signs that a rising generation might be ready to replace this influence. If so, the intragenerational war between the 1960s left and right might not have its anticipated last battle. Political historians will tell you that, though Hillary has been the frontrunner for the Democratic nomination since her first year in the Senate, no modern-day Democrat who has been a frontrunner so steadily in the years before the election has won the nomination, with the lone exception of Walter Mondale.

Perhaps Hillary's husband will help her career once again. He is abundant with advice, but, as we have seen, his candidates do not fare very well. Further, as we have seen in this chapter, Hillary's aides keep him at a distance. His *liaisons dangereuses* could be an embarrassment at any time, and the dynamics of the Clinton marriage have changed. A source working in the Clintons' Washington house reports seeing him in the spring of 2006 glumly packing personal effects, taking pictures from the walls and preparing to send them to Chappaqua. "Where would you put this stuff?" he asked my informant. My source reports that there is no bedroom specifically for Bill in the house, though Hillary's mother has pleasant quarters.[38] Finally, after all the years his *Ghost Ship* has spent traveling the globe, dropping anchor in Hong Kong ($250K), lumbering on to Tokyo ($500K), stopping off for convivialities on Manhattan's Upper East Side, the Boy President is depleted. After one of his 2005 visits to the White House a member of the White House staff reported that he appeared not just fatigued but actually "shrunken."[39] My observations of the retired president in 2006 as he celebrated his sixtieth birthday in Toronto corroborate this finding, as I note in this book's Prologue.

Yes, in public he seems to have energy. He still jabbers on into the night at table with whoever will listen. He remains the Secret Service's nightmare. A journalist traveling with him in 2005 reported his going "to bed very, very late (on this trip, he never retires before four in the morning). His schedule, which borders on lunacy, is quasi-presidential: he and Hillary have basically given up on connecting each weekend. . . ."[40]

The above reporter has dubbed Clinton's retirement years the "internationalist phase of his life." I prefer to call it his *Ghost Ship* phase. By mid-2005 he had dropped anchor in sixty-seven foreign countries. In one trip to Africa he visited six countries in seven days! Always, there are the lucrative lectures. Increasingly, there are the good causes, most notably AIDS relief. The Clinton Foundation has successfully arranged to deliver AIDS medications at cut-rate prices throughout the Third World. But here again we see his trademark M.O.—disorderliness, the same disorderliness that marked his presidency.

The Clinton Foundation, which oversees his AIDs work, is undermanned and overprogrammed. With an annual budget of just under $7 million, exclusive of its AIDS work, the Foundation also promises assistance to such good causes as inner-city commerce, citizen service, childhood obesity, and global warming. Says Jennifer Senior, the journalist who observed his abovementioned sleepless nights: "Clinton's post-presidency has yet to become synonymous with anything."[41] Though, as always with Clinton's disorderliness, there come the usual ethical lapses. In the fall of 2005, the *New York Sun* reported that the Clinton Foundation had "failed to meet at least six of 19 accountability standards established by the Better

Business Bureau. . . . In addition, the Bureau's charity evaluation service, called the Wise Giving Alliance, said it could not establish whether the foundation was observing five other good-governance practices regarding board meetings, conflict-of-interest policies, budget issues, and donor privacy."[42]

Increasingly in retirement, the white-haired and shrunken Clinton is a forlorn figure, irritable, melancholy, and anxious to be remembered well and to be heard again. He pops up in the press during the sixtieth anniversary of the United Nations with a typical 1960s talkathon, the Clinton Global Initiative. In press interviews he startles reporters with unprovoked denunciations of his impeachment and denials of any wrongdoing, despite the penalties he has paid, the suspended law license, and the admission of guilt that he signed with independent counsel Robert Ray. In public appearances he makes cheeky pronouncements, as he did at the 2005 Texas Book Festival where he chided journalists for letting public officials "get away with lying."[43] What did this famous liar have on his mind when he made that remark?

Clinton in retirement is a tortured man. Desperate to remain a player, he must not upstage Hillary, whose political career is heading for a great denouement. Nonetheless, he and his aides have planted stories adumbrating a grand political future. Early in retirement it was a prospective run for mayor of New York. Later, during his "internationalist phase," the line has been that he is a welcomed candidate to be secretary-general of the United Nations. The claims made for him as a UN leader have the same vapors of fantasy that swirl about his Foundation's claims or the claims made for the Clinton Global Initiative. "Around the world," writes a young sycophant in *Harper's* magazine, "Clinton is viewed as a peacemaker and someone so great that he has outgrown the United States."[44] Meanwhile Hillary has repeatedly spread the word that he is damaged goods. She settled on this explanation for his scortatory appetites sometime after the Lewinsky scandal, and asserted it most vividly when she told *Talk* magazine that her husband suffered "childhood abuse" when he was "barely four" and caught in a "terrible conflict between his mother and grandmother."[45] In private her elaborations on this remark are too cruel to repeat.[46]

Finally, there is this last example of the desperate fantasy in which the only elected president ever to be impeached dwells. During the 2004 campaign political observers presumed that the retired president was toying with the press when he mused about revoking the twenty-second amendment, barring a presidential third term.[47] Now there is evidence that he was not merely grabbing a headline with a provocation. Early in 2005, when Governor Arnold Schwarzenegger was riding high in the polls, Clinton sent an emissary to the foreign-born governor's consultants telling them that Clinton would support them in a constitutional amendment allowing foreign-born Americans to run for the presidency if they would back the repeal of the twenty-second amendment. Before this Grand Alliance could be consummated, Schwarzenegger's polls soured and the discussion fell silent.[48]

It has often been said by those familiar with the patient that he believes he has done nothing wrong. Obviously, the former Boy President lives with other fantasies, too, but his life is increasingly barren.

EPILOGUE

FROM THE CLINTON LIBRARY TO THE HARDING TOMB

Having allowed a prudent period to elapse after the star-studded opening of the Clinton Library on November 18, 2004, I flew into Little Rock—wilds I had frequented so often in the 1990s—for my own reconnaissance of the fabled Library and its historic environs. In the 1990s, I was nailing down stories from the Clinton bodyguards who served him as pimps and whose police credit cards he used freely. I was also investigating reports of real estate deals that were actually land flips and of shady bank transactions—in sum, a systematic abuse of power. Such happenstances composed the rise of the greatest huckster ever to reside at 1600 Pennsylvania Avenue, ably supported by wife Hillary (a.k.a. Bruno), who was almost as fabulous.

My first stop in Little Rock was the Clinton Library, where I hoped to check out a good book. I, in my innocence, presumed the Clinton Library to be a lender's library. How wrong I was! True to the Clintons' lifework, the Library is a taker's library; and they took my attaché case and camera—at least temporarily, for security purposes the attendants said. This vast rectangle of glass and concrete cantilevered toward the banks of the Arkansas River is the monument that some 113,000 donors created for the former Boy President, who doubtless still shimmers in their eyes as "one of our greatest presidents." When Al Gore, R.I.P., rendered that assessment, perhaps he had fixed in his mind such former presidents as James Buchanan, Millard Fillmore, and Warren Harding, the last of whom I too frequently catalogue with Clinton. Now this building, in all its bogus splendor, is the responsibility of the National Archives. Its archivists are going to be kept busy expunging the falsehoods in every exhibit.

Encamped in Little Rock for the next few days, I investigated the archivists' dilemma, and also how the locals had held up over the past decade since their native son's presidential election, his presidential scandals, his impeachment, and the post-presidential whitening of his hair. Throughout the state of Arkansas, I found the same old division that existed during Clinton's governorship and presidency: 1) a cabal of adoring fans and hangers-on, and 2) a smaller, cheerless cabal that wants to introduce visiting journalists to rumors and to police records of the former governor's nefarious pastimes, many of which can actually be categorized as felonies. Between trips to the Library, where I tried to chronicle its many preposterous deceits, I had meetings with members of this second group, listening patiently to their stories of Clinton's 1980s sexual revels, cocaine recreations, and financial irregularities. For now I merely tucked them into my files. You will doubtless be hearing of them from historians in due course.

Arkansas is a pleasant state filled with hearty can-do Americans. Yet it remains perhaps the strangest state in the Union. Along with the ordinary Arkansans reside shadowy figures, just a step or two beyond the reach of the law. Then, too, there is the peculiar condition of the Arkansas polity. The state is an oligarchy. As recollected by I. C. Smith, Special Agent for the FBI in Arkansas from 1995 to 1998, who has been heard from earlier in this book, "not more than 1000 people count in Arkansas, and in that number only 100 or so really count."[1] This oligarchic political structure explains many of the obstructions of justice and abuses of power that brought the Clinton presidency into its historic disesteem.

Two hotels in downtown Little Rock have been famous loci during the Clinton Saga: the Capital Hotel, where national and international journalists have long mixed with Arkansas politicos to swap stories of the Boy Governor, later Boy President; and the Excelsior (now named the Peabody) where, as the *American Spectator* reported, an Arkansas state trooper arranged a private meeting between the soon-to-be forty-second president and a female state employee. By accident the magazine left her first name in the text of the story, but only her first name, Paula. That ostensibly harmless editing error incited the woman to initiate a sexual harassment lawsuit in February of 1994, making our error arguably the most momentous editing mistake in American history. In her lawsuit Paula claimed that the man, who was by then president, had exposed himself to her and asked that she "kiss it." As her lawsuit worked its way towards resolution, an independent counsel got into the act, a grand jury was convened, the Supreme Court was activated, and eventually the United States Congress played a role; for Clinton lied under oath, and he became the first elected president in American history to be impeached. Richard Nixon almost surely would have been impeached, but out of regard for the national interest he resigned. Clinton, though he had intentionally lied and obstructed justice, did not. Instead he fought the proceedings, and on the walls of the Clinton Library it is clear he is still fighting—that is the archivists' dilemma.

After a night's sleep at the Capital Hotel, I freshened up, stepped out of the hotel, and turned right, to see on a hill several blocks before me the Library, whose official name is the William J. Clinton Presidential Center & Park. Yes, "Park." Perhaps someday they will erect a Ferris wheel there and a roller coaster. It is reported that eventually Clinton will be buried in the Park, Arlington National Cemetery being out of the question owing to peculiarities surrounding his draft records. The Park will not need to add a freak show. The array of Clinton's personal effects already on display in the Library—a statue of his deceased dog, his sunglasses worn while playing the saxophone, in fact, several of his saxophones—already achieves the gruesome effect. Walking up the street under a radiant blue sky I passed several art stores filled with locally created kitsch and many entertainment spots: Club Coconuts ("Caribbean Sports Bar"); the Flying Fish, one of the former president's two favorite Little Rock restaurants, which has cleverly hung five old outboard motors along its outside wall about twenty feet above ground; and Sticky Fingerz, some sort of night spot—the message on what passed for its marquee, "Love Live Music," did not invite a second glance.

Then there is the Clinton Museum Store. It is worth reconnoitering. It features some of the same Clinton memorabilia to be found in the Library, but for a price: more sunglasses, replicas of his famous saxophones, clothing with the Clinton Library logo, golf paraphernalia with the same logo, and several incongruously placed books. There is a tome by Maya Angelou, *I Know Why the Caged Bird Sings*; *The Collected Poems of W. B. Yeats*; Thomas Wolfe's *You Can't Go Home Again*; and Thomas à Kempis's *The Imitation of Christ.* The books are on sale, I am informed, because they are among Clinton's favorites. That last book especially caught my eye. Which aspects of Christ's life has Bill been imitating, the miracle of the loaves and fishes? Along this street, newly named "President Clinton Avenue," there are hints of Christian piety in the art stores and on bumper stickers (though not the one reading "Hillary 2008" on the derrière of a pickup truck). Deriding superficial Christian piety, the British iconoclast Malcolm Muggeridge used to snicker, "Christianity without tears." The tiresome Christianity of the ethically challenged Clintons is more like Christianity with several of the Ten Commandments deleted.

Standing a few hundred yards in front of the modern box that is the William J. Clinton Presidential Center & Park, one sees to the right an old red stone railway station that is the great man's office. Usually he is not there. To the left and spanning the slow-moving sludge of the Arkansas River is a huge rusting iron bridge once used by the old Rock Island Railway. It goes no place, having been long ago abandoned.

Historic preservationists saved it from demolition. Perhaps these antiquarians were part of the "Vast Right-Wing Conspiracy," for their handiwork is bound to remind visitors of Clinton's much ballyhooed "Bridge to the Twenty-First Century." Like his presidency, this old bridge goes nowhere. It mocks the boastful edifice that the Clintons have tried to create.

Within, the cavernous ground floor lobby encased in steel, glass, and cheerless gray stone is almost empty, save for a ticket desk and the presidential limousine used on foreign travels. The real action begins up the escalator on the second floor. There after one's first steps, pandemonium breaks out. The Clintons, mostly Bill but occasionally Hillary, are heard orating from every wall, from all of the fifteen exhibits, from ceiling, from floor, everywhere. Endlessly Bill repeats: "longest period of economic recovery," "campaign for the future," "take America back for ordinary Americans," "We want to change America," "I am the light that shines in the darkness"—well, maybe I imagined that last line. But on and on he declaims, all day, probably all night. We all have seen JFK's Eternal Flame. This is the Eternal Bill.

It is also Interactive Bill. This is the most interactive of all the presidential libraries. Touch a screen and Bill intones his message. There is a screen from which he will tell you about all the rooms of the White House, even the Lincoln Bedroom, where one gets Bill discoursing on just about everything save those campaign contributors who spent the night. In the life-size replica of the Cabinet Room there are screens that, with digital stimulation, will summon up legislative information. In the replica of the Oval Office on the Library's third floor, there are screens that summon Bill explaining his days in the Oval. There is, however, no replica of that historic bathroom adjacent to the Oval Office where the president ministered to the needs of at least one intern—as I have reported earlier, others also served. According to my calculations, the Oval Office is just below a fourth-floor complex of private rooms, maintained for the former Boy President when he is in town, which is not as often as the press seems to believe. Library staffers are careful to correct you if you refer to it as the "penthouse." It is, they admonish, "the *executive* suite."

The Library staff is now composed for the most part of serious archivists from the federal government, and they are going to be doing a lot of editing in the years ahead. As is characteristic of the Clintons, they have deposited a lot of discrepancies on the public record. Some are petty: "On the first day the Clintons lived in the White House, they invited more than 3,000 people to the White House and shook hands with every single one"—come, come! Or consider this: the Clintons converted the butler's pantry into a family kitchen. "It was not uncommon," reads the exhibit, "to find the First Family enjoying dinner together, Chelsea and her friends raiding the refrigerator, the president watching a football game with the butlers or Buddy and Socks looking for leftovers." Perhaps it depends on the meaning of "uncommon" or of "family." My reports are that the butlers lived in terror of you-know-who, as did Bill.

Of the fifteen exhibits, my guess is that every one will have to be rewritten. Certainly the exhibit on the economy is distorted, suggesting that Bush handed Clinton an economy in depression rather than an economy recovering from a mild recession. And there are exhibits that ought to be created: for instance, exhibits remembering Travelgate, Filegate, and at least references to the last-minute pardons that brought the Clintons once again into disrepute. Surely the trashing of the White House by Hillary's outgoing staff and the stolen White House furnishings have a place in any library devoted to the Clinton Saga. Yet the most extensive rewrite will have to be of the exhibit now titled "The Fight for Power." It is here that the Clintons treat the president's impeachment with no reference to lying under oath and lying to the American people, no mention of charges of obstruction of justice, no soiled blue dress, or reiteration by the president of his most famous line, "I did not have sexual relations with that woman—Miss Lewinsky."

Clinton treats his impeachment and disgrace as but an accidental episode in an unbroken eight-year struggle by Republicans to remove him from office. One wonders why the Republicans never undertook similar struggles against earlier Democratic presidents, say Johnson, Carter, Kennedy, or Truman. According to the exhibit, "In the 1990s, it became common right-wing practice not just to attack Democrats' ideas, but also to question their motives, morals, and patriotism. The 'politics of personal destruction' was central to the Republican strategy . . . seeking to steer America sharply to the right. . . ." Now wait a minute! America had already gone "sharply to the right," starting with the presidency of Ronald Reagan, proceeding through that of George H. W. Bush, and on through the ineffectual presidency of his unavoidably centrist successor, Bill Clinton. As for questioning "morals," it was difficult to avoid Clinton's morals. He misbehaved very publicly and lied quite ostentatiously—all this after some of us had warned in the public prints that this was precisely what he had done quite flagrantly as governor.

Then there is this concatenation of bosh: Richard Mellon Scaife "funneled about $2,000,000 to private investigators in a *covert effort to discredit the President* [emphasis added by the exhibit with yellow highlighter]. Though the Arkansas Project failed to unearth any credible information, it generated numerous allegations that were published widely in the press and, in some cases, investigated by Congress or the Independent Counsel."

The American Spectator's "Arkansas Project" (which, incidentally, was never a "project" but rather a term of amusement around the magazine's office) is also referred to in this exhibit as "a secret slush fund." Yet there was nothing "covert" or "secret" about this so-called "Arkansas Project." Here is another Clinton falsehood that has made it into the first draft of history. The falsehood is easily exposed. The Arkansas Project's funding was reported quite publicly in Scaife's yearly reports of his charitable giving, much of it under the clear classification "Support for Expanded Editorial and Reporting." This, the Clinton Library exhibit calls a "slush fund," but a slush fund is, as *The American Heritage Dictionary* designates, "a fund for undesignated purposes . . . especially for corrupt purposes such as bribery or graft." The Clintons want Library visitors to believe that the investigative journalism of an opinion magazine was a felony. They failed to make that case years ago, in 1998. At the behest of their Justice Department, they had an Arkansas grand jury investigate the *American Spectator* for a year. No wrongdoing was found. Clinton originally made these discredited charges in his memoir, *My Life*, and now again they appear at this exhibit, which Library spokesmen and friends, such as his confidant, Bruce Lindsey, admit he took care to "edit" and, in some cases, to write.

Also false is the claim that *The American Spectator*'s "Arkansas Project" "failed to unearth any credible information." Nothing the *Spectator* reported has ever been disproved. Some of the magazine's stories inspired fruitful congressional investigations into Clinton; for instance, the magazine's early reports on Travelgate. What is more, the *Spectator*'s reporting was helpful to other journalists. As William Safire wrote in a May 17, 2001 *New York Times* column, "I found early *Spectator* material useful in writing columns that helped trigger a reluctant investigation and ultimate conviction of both felons."[2] He was referring to fundraising jugglers John Huang and James Riady.

Perhaps the most insolent deceit made in the exhibit is the whopper that, after several separate investigations costing over "$100 million," "none of these efforts yielded a conviction for public misconduct." There were at least fourteen convictions in the Whitewater investigation. As for the Boy President's public misconduct, as reported earlier in this book, he agreed on his last full day in office to pay a $25,000 fine and accept a five-year suspension of his Arkansas law license to avoid criminal prosecution. Also he agreed that he had given false testimony about Monica Lewinsky. That false testimony had further repercussions. Judge Susan Webber Wright, upon reviewing Clinton's false testimony given by him in front of her, concluded: "The record demonstrates by clear and convincing evidence that the president responded to the plaintiff's questions by giving false, misleading and evasive answers that were designed to obstruct the judicial process." For this obstruction of justice, she fined him $90,000. No mention of this is to be found in the Clinton Library.

There have been stories that the Clintonistas are exaggerating the turnout at the Library. Clinton critics believe that paying visitors are scarcer than the Library's figures show. There have also been stories that the funders of the $165 million Library are unsavory figures, the money coming from Arab sheiks or from beneficiaries of Clinton's last-minute pardons. There is probably truth to these stories, but the real problem is the Library itself. This, the most expensive presidential library in the presidential system, is devoted to proving that the most low-grade lout ever elected president is a great man. The lies that have been fashioned to achieve this result, many by the lout himself, are so numerous and extravagant that the sorely pressed archivists of the federal government are going to be rewriting the exhibits for years to come. When they finish, it will no longer be the Clinton Library. By then, however, only a handful will remember the Clinton presidency. The Library will be like the old Rock Island Bridge next to it, an artifact that goes nowhere.

Or it might one day take its place with another presidential monument, one referred to on its Web page as "one of the most beautiful presidential memorials outside Washington, D.C." The edifice's simple Doric columns of white Georgia marble stand on ten immaculately landscaped acres in Marion, Ohio. They convey the appearance of a circular Greek temple and they surround the mortal remains of Warren Gamaliel Harding and his wife, Fussbudget. Admission is free. Attendants at the Harding Tomb awakened by me for an interview testify that between 5,000 and 7,000 visitors drop by annually.

APPENDIX I

CLINTON ITINERARY

Keeping tabs on the many post-presidential adventures of Bill Clinton would tax the skills, patience, and expense account of the most talented gumshoe. With that in mind, herewith a modest attempt at hounding the hound dog around the globe, complete with dates, destinations, and dollars accrued:

Date	**Place/Event**	**Amount Earned**
02/05/01	New York, NY, Morgan Stanley Dean Witter & Co	$125,000
02/10/01	Aventura, FL, Aventura-Turnberry Jewish Center	$150,000
02/19/01	Redwood Shores, CA, Oracle Corporation	$125,000
02/27/01	New York, NY, Credit Suisse First Boston	$125,000
03/03/01	Universal City, CA, 32nd Annual NAACP Image Awards, Clinton present with Award	
03/08/01	Atlanta, GA, Asian American Hotel Owners Association	$125,000
03/09/01	Vancouver, British Columbia Canada, Jim Pattison Group	$150,000
03/12/01	Maastricht, The Netherlands, Decision Makers InterAction	$150,000
03/13/01	Baden Baden, Hausanschrift, Germany, Media Control GmbH on behalf of Media Peace Prize Committee	$250,000
03/14/01	Copenhagen, Denmark, Borsen Executive Club	$150,000
03/26/01	Salem, MA, Salem State College Foundation	$125,000
04/20/01	East Greenwich, RI, Reception—100 people, home of Mark Weiner, R.I. State Democratic Fund Raiser—$1K plate—both Bill and Hillary attend	

Date	Place/Event	Amount Earned
04/22/01	Abington, PA, Old York Road Temple Beth Am	$125,000
05/02/01	Oakville, Ontario Canada, Morgan Firestone Foundation	$125,000
05/10/01	New York, NY, Fortune Magazine Forum	$250,000
	Hong Kong, PRC, CLSA Ltd.	$250,000
05/14/01	Lysaker, Norway, Dinamo Norge	$150,000
05/15/01	Stockholm, Sweden, The Talar Forum	$183,333
05/16/01	Vienna, Austria, Wirtschafts Blatt	$183,333
05/17/01	Warsaw, Poland, Puls Biznesu, Bonnier Business (Polano)	$183,333
05/18/01	Madrid, Spain, Fundacion Rafael Del Pino	$250,000
05/21/01	Dublin, Ireland, Independent News & Media	$150,000
05/26/01	Hay-on-Wye, England, The Sunday Times Hay Festival	$150,000
06/05/01	Paris, France, Paris Golf & Country Club	$150,000
06/08/01	Leeds, Yorkshire, England, Yorkshire International Business Convention	$200,000
	North Yorkshire, England, Clinton in Europe—preparing to play golf at Rudding Park in Narrogate, he makes an impromptu visit to a wedding ceremony at the club and poses with guests for pictures and movies	
06/12/01	Tampa, FL, Success Events International, Inc.	$125,000
06/15/01	Los Angeles, CA, Radio & Records	$125,000
06/19/01	Tampa, FL, Success Events International, Inc.	$125,000
06/25/01	Toronto, Ontario Canada, Canadian Society for Yad Vashem	$125,000
07/02/01	New York City, Clintons attend hockey game at Madison Square Garden	
07/07/01	London, England, The McCarthy Group	$200,000
07/10/01	Madrid, Spain, The Varsavsky Foundation	$175,000
07/11/01	Sao Paolo, Brazil, Valor Economico S.A.	$150,000
07/27/01	Omaha, NE, infoUSA, Inc.	$200,000
07/30/01	New York City, Clinton moves into Harlem office—very controversial—cheers, boos and no mayor Giuliani	
08/19/01	Aurora, Ontario, Canada, Speech at Magna International headquarters—80 people each paid $2,500—Clinton flew from Washington in Magna corporate jet with Belinda Stronach—CEO of Magna and daughter of founder	
08/20/01	Aurora, Ontario, Canada, SFX Sports Group on behalf of Magna International	$125,000
08/21/01	Tokyo, Japan, MIKI Corporation	$150,000
08/22/01	Tokyo, Japan, MIKI Corporation	$150,000

Date	Place/Event	Amount Earned
08/23/01	Tokyo, Japan, MIKI Corporation	$150,000
08/27/01	Sao Paulo, Brazil, Fundacao Armando Alvares Penteado	$250,000
09/08/01	Sydney, Australia, Markson Sparks! on behalf of the Children's Hospital at Westmead	$150,000
09/09/01	Sydney, Australia, Markson Sparks! on behalf of Labor Council of New South Wales	$150,000
09/10/01	Melbourne, Australia, J.T. Campbell & Co. Pty. Limited	$150,000
10/01/01	Minneapolis, MN, VNU Business Media on behalf of Online Learning 2001 Conf. and Exposition	$125,000
10/03/01	El Paso, TX, El Paso Holocaust Museum & Study Center	$125,000
10/09/01	Washington, DC, Greater Washington Society of Association Executives	$125,000
10/11/01	St. Joseph, MI, Economic Club of Southwestern Michigan	$125,000
10/17/01	Florham Park, NJ, Kushner Companies	$125,000
10/22/01	Trinidad, Tobago, West Indies, Colonial Life Ins. Co (Trinidad) Ltd.	$125,000
10/25/01	Milano, Italy, Comitato per il Congresso Nazionale della Pubblicita	$350,000
10/29/01	Barcelona, Spain, Seeliger Y Conde	$200,000
11/08/01	Calgary, Alberta, Canada, Renaisssance Calgary, Alberta Canada	$125,000
11/09/01	Richmond, British Columbia, Canada, Pinpoint Knowledge Management, The Portables	$125,000
11/11/01	Chicago, IL, America Israel Chamber of Commerce	$125,000
11/14/01	Paris, France, Galeries Lafayette—Monoprix	$250,000
12/02/01	West Hartford, CT, Hebrew Home and Hospital, Inc.	$125,000
12/08/01	Buffalo Grove, IL, International Profit Associates, Inc.	$125,000
12/10/01	Glasgow, Scotland, Jewish National Fund	$133,334
12/11/01	Manchester, England, Jewish National Fund	$133,333
12/12/01	London, England, Jewish National Fund	$133,333
12/13/01	London, England, the London School of Economics and Political Science	$28,100
12/14/01	London, England, British Broadcasting Corporation	$75,000
12/16/01	Freising, Germany, Scherer Consulting Group and Jorg Lohr Training	$150,000
late Dec.	Acupulco, Mexico, Clintons vacation in Aculpulco—Budd killed in Chappaqua	
	Book Royalties, New York, NY, Random House, Inc	Over $1,000

Date	Place/Event	Amount Earned
	Book Royalties, Parsippany, NJ, Simon & Schuster, Inc.—literary work	$2,845,190
	Book Royalties, Parsippany, NY, Simon & Schuster, Inc.—*It Takes a Village*—(No royalties due and owing at 12/31/01. Future value not ascertainable. Senator Clinton donates the royalties from this book to charity.	$6,847
01/14/02	Universal City, CA, University of Judaism	$125,000
01/17/02	Dubai, United Arab Emirates, The Dabbagh Group on behalf of STARS	$300,000
01/18/02	Cairo, Egypt, Future Generation Foundation	$175,000
01/20/02	Jeddah, Saudi Arabia, The Dabbagh Group on behalf of the Jeddah Economic Forum	$300,000
	Dubai, United Arab Emirates, Speech to Dabbagh Group on behalf of Jeddah Economic Forum,	$300,000
01/21/02	Tel Aviv, Israel, Ness Technologies, Inc.	$150,000
01/29/02	Palo Alto, CA, Stree—Global Investments in Women	$125,000
01/31/02	Santa Barbara, CA, Educational Institute The AHLA	$125,000
January	London, England, Clinton in London—Groucho Club—ran up tab of $14,000	
02/07/02	Miami Beach, FL, WIZO	$125,000
02/11/02	Sundance, UT, Group Vivendi Universal	$150,000
02/15/02	Woodbury, NY, Long Island Association, Inc.	$125,000
02/18/02	Montreal, Quebec Canada, ORT Montreal	$125,000
02/22/02	Sydney, Australia, Australian Council for the Promotion of Peaceful Reunification of China	$300,000
02/23/02	Perth, Australia, Markson Sparks on behalf of Princess Margaret Children's Hospital, Perth	$125,000
02/25/02	Adelaide, Australia, Markson Sparks on behalf of The Women and Children's Hospital, Adelaide	$125,000
02/26/02	Adelaide, Australia, Australian Information Industry Association	$250,000
02/27/02	Melbourne, Australia, Markson Sparks on behalf of The Microsurgery Foundation, Melbourne	$125,000
03/01/02	Brisbane, Australia, Markson Sparks on behalf of The Royal Children's Hospital Foundation, Brisbane	$125,000
03/02/02	Sydney, Australia, Markson Sparks on behalf of The Prince of Wales Medical Research Institute, Sydney	$125,000
03/13/02	Medford, MA, Tufts University	$125,000

Date	Place/Event	Amount Earned
03/14/02	New York, NY, One Family—Israel Emergency Solidarity Fund	$125,000
03/16/02	Guayaquil, Equador, Maruri Communications Group	$200,000
03/18/02	LaRomana, Dominican Republic, Listin Diario	$250,000
late March	New York City, NY, Lunch with Willie Mays in Harlem/ also lunch with Robin Williams and Billy Crystal in midtown	
03/31/02	Dominican Republic, Clintons vacation at Oscar de la Renta home	
04/05/02	Montreal, Quebec Canada, Personal Dynamics on behalf of Provente.com	$125,000
04/13/02	Ischgl, Austria, EPC International on behalf of Workshop Ischgl-Club of the Alps	$245,000
04/15/02	New York, NY, Warburg Pincus	$125,000
05/01/02	New York, NY, Clinton meets with CBS regarding talk show	
05/06/02	New York, NY, Hunter College Foundation	$35,000
05/10/02	Dana Point, CA, Compuware Corporation	$125,000
05/15/02	New York, NY, Gruner & Jahr Publishing USA on behalf of The American Jewish Committee	$125,000
05/21/02	Tokyo, Japan, Global Artists on behalf of Nihon University	$200,000
05/22/02	Hong Kong, PRC, CLSA Ltd.	$250,000
05/23/02	Shenzhen, PRC, dnmStrategies on behalf of JingJi Real Estate Development Group	$200,000
05/24/02	Singapore, Success Resources Pte Ltd.	$250,000
05/27/02	Auckland, New Zealand, BMW Group of New Zealand	$137,500
06/06/02	Dublin, Ireland, Protocol Resource and Operation Services	$200,000
06/10/02	Tallin, Estonia, Aripaeva Kirjastus	$150,000
06/11/02	Dubai, UAE, American University in Dubai Dubai,	$150,000
	United Arab Emirates, The American University of Dubai	$150,000
07/06/02	Stockholm, Sweden, Nordstrom International APS on behalf of World Celebrity Golf	$300,000
07/29/02	Toronto, Ontario, Canada, Toronto Hadassah—WIZO	$125,000
08/29/02	New Orleans, LA, PeopleSoft, Inc.	$125,000
09/11/02	New York, NY, Clinton on David Letterman Show	
09/12/02	New York, NY, New York Chapter of Diabetes—Man of the Year Award—Waldorf Astoria	

Date	Place/Event	Amount Earned
09/22–29/02		
	Africa, Clinton in Africa—AIDS work—Visits Ghana, Nigeria, Rwanda, Mozambique, South Africa	
10/04/02	Munich, Germany, The German Union of Small and Medium-Sized Companies	$100,000
10/05/02	Baden Baden, Germany, Media Control GmbH	$100,000
10/19/02	Little Rock, AR, Arkansas Black Hall of Fame—Clinton receives honorary award	
10/27/02	New York, NY, American Friends of the Rabin Medical Center	$125,000
11/04/02	Mississauga, Ontario, Canada, London Drugs	$125,000
11/06/02	New York, NY, The Abraham Fund	$125,000
11/11/02	San Jose, CA, Celebrity Forum II	$100,000
11/12/02	Oakland, CA, MPSF, Inc.	$100,000
11/13/02	San Mateo, CA, MPSF, Inc.	$100,000
11/14/02	San Rafael, CA, MPSF, Inc.	$100,000
11/15/02	Cupertino, CA, Celebrity Forum II	$100,000
11/17/02	Davis, CA, University of California—Davis	$100,000
11/19/02	Mito City, Japan, Mito City Political Research Group	$400,000
11/21/02	Tokyo, Japan, Global Artists	$100,000
12/02/02	New York, NY, Clinton attends business luncheon and makes comments to CNN.com afterwards accusing Republicans of suppressing black vote	
12/02/02	Monterrey, Mexico, Value Grupo Financiero	$175,000
12/07/02	Lancashire, England, National Society for the Prevention of Cruelty to Children	$100,000
12/09/02	Newton, MA, Temple Beth Avodah	$125,000
12/13/02	Rotterdam, The Netherlands, GBD Group	$125,000
12/14/02	Geneva, Switzerland, United Israel Appeal of Geneva	$150,000
12/15/02	Rotterdam, The Netherlands, RDM Group	$125,000
12/18/02	New York, NY, European Travel Commission	$125,000
	Nonemployee Compensation, Omaha, NE, Info USA, Inc.	Over $1,000
	Book Royalties, Parsippany, NJ, Simon & Schuster, Inc.—literary work	$1,149,621
	Book Royalties, Parsippany, NJ, Simon & Schuster, Inc—*It Takes a Village*	$1,237
01/12/03	Scottsdale, AZ, Hearst Magazines	$125,000
01/18/03	St. Lucia, Financial Innovations, Inc.	$100,000

Date	Place/Event	Amount Earned
01/24/03	London, England, St. James Places	$175,000
01/29/03	Hollywood, FL, Aventis	$125,000
01/29/03	Hollywood, CA, Westin Diplomat Resort & Spa Pharma Co.	$125,000
02/06/03	Los Angeles, CA, Rolling Stones free concert—Clinton makes appearance at Staples Center	
02/23/03	New York, NY, Clinton praises U2 rock star Bono at New York reception	
03/26/03	Iowa City, IA, Iowa State University (Clinton said he was donating the money to UI's F. Wendall Miller Fund for AIDS research)	$50,000
04/05/03	Isla Verde, PR, Caribbean Council for Global Studies	$125,000
04/13/03	St. Louis Park, MN, Beth El Synagogue	$125,000
05/03/03	Atlanta, GA, EchoStar Satellite Corporation	$100,000
05/18/03	Trenton, NJ, Greenwood House	$125,000
05/30/03	Boston, MA, JFK Library—gave a speech suggesting a third term for U.S. presidents unknown	
07/02/03	London, England, Westminster Hall—Parliament—Dinner to celebrate the Rhodes Trust with Tony Blair and Nelson Mandela—Clinton did not speak	
07/11/03	Dublin, Ireland, Purchased apartment at K Club in County Kildare, Apt. cost was $1.2 million euros, met with Bertie Ahern, Irish Prime Minister	
08/05/03	Chicago, IL, Clinton meets with California Governor Gray Davis at AFL-CIO meeting	
09/13/03	Indianola, IA, Iowa Senator Harkins fundraiser for Democrats—Clinton spoke	
09/16/03	Seattle, WA, Fool Proof	$125,000
10/09/03	Mexico City, Mexico, Banco de Mexico	$150,000
10/13/03	Veracruz, Mexico, Verinvest S.C. on behalf of Mexico Business Summit	$150,000
10/14/03	Greenbrier, WV, Council of Insurance Agents and Brokers	$125,000
	New York, NY, A&E Television Networks	$125,000
10/20/03	Barcelona, Spain, American Chamber of Commerce in Spain	$250,000
10/21/03	Lisbon, Portugal, Diario de Noticias	$250,000
10/27/03	Washington, DC, Greater Washington Society of Associate Executives	$125,000
11/03/03	Antwerp, Belgium, Antwerp Diamond High Council (Spouse)—Clinton presented with 4.5 carat diamond—	$200,000

Date	Place/Event	Amount Earned
	gift not declared in Senator Hillary Rodham Clinton's U.S. Senate Financial Disclosure Report	
11/06/03	Hong Kong, PRC, dnmStrategies on behalf of Business Week's 7th Annual CEO Forum	$200,000
11/09/03	Mianzhun, Sichuan, China, Jiannanchun Group Co., LTD	$250,000
11/14/03	Seoul, Korea, Seoul Broadcasting System	$250,000
11/17/03	Tokyo, Japan, Sakura Capital Management Company, Ltd. (speech was canceled, proceeds donated to the William J. Clinton Presidential Library Foundation on a tax neutral basis)	$500,000
11/19/03	Nisshin City, Japan, Dentsu Inc. Chubu on behalf of Aichi Gakuin University	$250,000
11/19/03	Kyoto, Japan, Global Artists on behalf of Yamakawa Ryutsu System Co., Ltd.	$140,000
11/20/03	Fukuota, Japan, Global Artists on behalf of Arita Co., Ltd	$140,000
12/09/03	Winnipeg, Manitoba, Canada, MDM Investments Ltd. on behalf of Maz Concerts	$125,000
	Book Royalties, Parsippany, NJ, Simon & Schuster, Inc.—*Living History* (book advanced and royalties)	$2,287,521
	Book Royalties, Parsippany, NJ, Simon & Schuster, Inc.—*It Takes a Village* (Senator Clinton donates the royalties from this book to charity)	$1,238
	Nonemployee Compensation, Omaha, NE, Info USA, Inc.	over $1,000
	Guaranteed payments to partner, Los Angeles, CA, Yucaipa Global Opportunities Fund, LLC	over $1,000
01/25/04	Sunrise, FL, Fantasma	$125,000
02/08/04	Los Angeles, CA, Clinton honored with Grammy Award for word-album for children of *Peter and the Wolf*	
03/12/04	Paris, France, Citigroup	$250,000
05/05/04	Wallace, Nova Scotia, Hon. Frank McKenna's Annual Business Networking Event	$125,000
11/05/04	New York, NY, Urban Land Institute	$125,000
11/10/04	Cherry Hill, NJ, The Star Forum	$125,000
12/03/04	New York, NY, Goldman Sachs	$125,000
	Book Royalties, Parsippany, NJ, Simon & Schuster, Inc.—*Living History*	$2,376,716
	Book Royalties, Parsippany, NJ, Simon & Schuster, Inc.—*It Takes A Village* (Senator Clinton donates the royalties from this book to charity)	$10,012

Date	Place/Event	Amount Earned
	Book Royalties, New York, NY, Random House	over $1,000
	Nonemployee Compensation, Omaha, NE, Info USA over	$1,000
	Guaranteed payments to partner, Los Angeles, CA, Yucaipa Global Opportunities Fund, LLC	over $1,000
02/03/05	Paradise Island, The Bahamas, Serono International	$150,000
02/16/05	Los Angeles, CA, Jewish Federation Council of Greater L.A.	$125,000
02/22/05	Hong Kong, PRC, CLSA	$100,000
03/02/05	Los Angeles, CA, Savage/Rothenberg Productions	$125,000
03/03/05	Los Angeles, CA, Savage/Rothenberg Productions	$125,000
03/04/05	Los Angeles, CA, Association of Southern California Defense Counsel	$125,000
04/20/05	Kiawah Island, SC, Goldman Sachs	$125,000
04/26/05	New York, NY, Global Strategic Ventures	$150,000
05/04/05	Baltimore, MD, Deutsche Bank	$150,000
	Lancaster, PA, Lancaster Chamber of Commerce	$150,000
05/10/05	New York, NY, National Multi-Housing Council	$150,000
05/17/05	Copenhagen, Denmark, KMD	$250,000
05/18/05	Berne, Switzerland, Griwa Consulting GMBH	$250,000
06/01/05	New York, NY, American Academy of Achievement	$150,000
06/06/05	Paris, France, Goldman Sachs	$250,000
06/08/05	Indianapolis, IN, Congregation Beth-El Zedeck	$150,000
06/10/05	Las Vegas, NV, America's Health Insurance Plans	$150,000
06/13/05	Greensboro, GA, Goldman Sachs	$150,000
06/21/05	Mexico City, Mexico, Gold Service International	$200,000
06/22/05	Bogota, Colombia, Gold Service International	$200,000
06/23/05	Sao Paulo, Brazil, Gold Service International	$200,000
06/24/05	Sao Paulo, Brazil, Gold Service International	$200,000
07/24/05	Canary Islands, Spain, Blex S.L.	$350,000
08/11/05	Portsmouth, RI, Carnegie Abbey Club	$150,000
	New York, NY, Deutsche Bank	$150,000
09/20/05	Video Conference from New York, HSM Italia	$125,000
	New York, NY, Young President's Organization	$150,000
10/03/05	Copenhagen, Denmark, Leading Minds	$125,000
10/12/05	Moscow, Russia, Adam Smith Conferences	$125,000
10/17/05	London, Ontario Canada, tinePublic, Inc.	$125,000
10/18/05	Video Conference from Toronto, Canada, International Centre for Business Information	$125,000
	Toronto, Canada, The Power Within	$350,000
10/19/05	Calgary, Canada, The Power Within	$300,000

Date	Place/Event	Amount Earned
10/27/05	Sydney, Australia, Leading Minds	$125,000
11/07/05	Chicago, IL, Jewish Federation of Metropolitan Chicago	$150,000
	Chicago, IL, YPO Windy City Chapter	$100,000
11/08/05	Chicago, IL, Jewish Federation of Metropolitan Chicago	$150,000
11/09/05	New York, NY, Golden Tree Asset Management	$150,000
11/10/05	New York, NY, Macklowe Properties on behalf of State of Israel Bonds Development Corporation	$250,000
11/15/05	Abu Dhabi, Global Business Enterprises	$300,000
11/28/05	Dubai, UAE, Leading Minds	$125,000
12/01/05	Munich, Germany, Hubert Burda Media GmbH	$300,000
12/13/05	Munich, Germany, Leading Minds	$125,000
	Book Royalties, Parsippany, NJ, Simon & Schuster, Inc.—*Living History*	$872,891
	Book Royalties, Parsippany, NJ, Simon & Schuster, Inc.—*It Takes a Village* (Senator Clinton donates the royalties from this book to charity)	$4,465
	Nonemployee Compensation, Omaha, NE, Info USA	over $1,000
	Guaranteed payments to partner, Los Angeles, CA, Yucaipa Global Opportunities Fund LLC	over $1,000

APPENDIX II

PARDONS AND COMMUTATIONS

Had the weather been unseasonably warm as the Clintons' lease closed on the White House, one could have likely cooled himself by standing near one of the nation's many correctional facilities, where the doors were swinging like a wild array of Japanese fans. What follows is an accounting of the many pardons and commutations signed by the boy president in the mania of his final days.

PARDONS

NAME Home Town	Offenses
ALLEN, Verla Jean, Everton, Arkansas	False statements to agency of United States
ALTIERE, Nicholas M. Las Vegas, Nevada	Importation of cocaine
ALTSCHUL, Bernice Ruth Sherman Village, California	Conspiracy to commit money laundering
ANDERSON, Joe, Jr. Grove Hill, Alabama	Income tax evasion

ANDERSON, William Sterling Spartanburg, South Carolina	Conspiracy to defraud a federally insured financial institution, false statements to a federally insured financial institution, wire fraud
AZIZKHANI, Mansour T. Huntsville, Alabama	Conspiracy and making false statements in bank loan applications
BABIN, Cleveland Victor, Jr. Oklahoma City, Oklahoma	Conspiracy to commit offense against the United States by utilizing the U.S. mail in furtherance of a scheme to defraud
BAGLEY, Chris Harmon Harrah, Oklahoma	Conspiracy to possess with intent to distribute cocaine
BANE, Scott Lynn Mahomet, Illinois	Unlawful distribution of marijuana
BARBER, Thomas Cleveland, Hampton, Florida	Issuing worthless checks
BARGON, Peggy Ann Monticello, Illinois	Violation of the Lacey Act, violation of the Bald Eagle Protection Act
BHATKA, Tansukhlal	Income tax evasion
BLAMPIED, David Roscoe Ketchum, Idaho	Conspiracy to distribute cocaine
BORDERS, William Arthur, Jr. Washington, D.C.	Conspiracy to corruptly solicit and accept money in return for influencing the official acts of a federal district court judge (Alcee L. Hastings), and to defraud the United States in connection with the performance of lawful government functions; corruptly influencing, obstructing, impeding and endeavoring to influence, obstruct and impede the due administration of justice, and aiding and abetting therein; traveling interstate with intent to commit bribery

BOREL, Arthur David Little Rock, Arkansas	Odometer rollback
BOREL, Douglas Charles Conway, Arkansas	Odometer rollback
BRABHAM, George Thomas Austin, Texas	Making a false statement or report to a federally insured bank
BRASWELL, Almon Glenn Doravilla, Georgia	Conspiracy to defraud government with respect to claims; perjury
BROWDER, Leonard Aiken, South Carolina	Illegal dispensing of controlled substance and Medicaid fraud
BROWN, David Steven New York, New York	Securities fraud and mail fraud
BURLESON, Delores Caroylene, a.k.a. Delores Cox Burleson Hanna, Oklahoma	Possession of marijuana
BUSTAMANTE, John H. Cleveland, Ohio	Wire fraud
CAMPBELL, Mary Louise Ruleville, Mississippi	Aiding and abetting the unauthorized use and transfer of food stamps
CANDELARIA, Eloida	False information in registering to vote
CAPILI, Dennis Sobrevinas Glendale, California	Filing false statements in alien registration
CHAMBERS, Donna Denise Memphis, Tennessee	Conspiracy to possess with intent to distribute and to distribute cocaine, possession with intent to distribute cocaine, use of a telephone to facilitate cocaine conspiracy
CHAPMAN, Douglas Eugene Scott, Arkansas	Bank fraud
CHAPMAN, Ronald Keith Scott, Arkansas	Bank fraud

CHAVEZ, Francisco Larios Santa Ana, California	Aiding and abetting illegal entry of aliens
CISNEROS, Henry G.	Information not available
CLINTON, Roger	Information not available
COHN, Stuart Harris New Haven, Connecticut	1. Illegal sale of gold options 2. Illegal sale of silver options
COOPER, David Marc Wapakoneta, Ohio	Conspiracy to defraud the government
COX, Ernest Harley, Jr. Pine Bluff, Arkansas	Conspiracy to defraud a federally insured savings and loan, misapplication of bank funds, false statements
CROSS, John F., Jr. Little Rock, Arkansas	Embezzlement by a bank employee
CUNNINGHAM, Rickey Lee Amarillo, Texas	Possession with intent to distribute marijuana
DE LABIO, Richard Anthony Baltimore, Maryland	Mail fraud, aiding and abetting
DEUTCH, John	Described in January 19, 2001 information
DOUGLAS, Richard	False statements
DOWNE, Edward Reynolds	Conspiracy to commit wire fraud and tax evasion; securities fraud
DUDLEY, Marvin Dean Omaha, Nebraska	False statements
DUNCAN, Larry Lee Branson, Missouri	Altering an automobile odometer
FAIN, Robert Clinton	Aiding and assisting in the preparation of a false corporate tax return

FERNANDEZ, Marcos Arcenio Miami, Florida	Conspiracy to possess with intent to distribute marijuana
FERROUILLET, Alvarez	Interstate transport of stolen property, money laundering, false statements
FUGAZY, William Denis Harrison, New York	Perjury in a bankruptcy proceeding
GEORGE, Lloyd Reid	Mail fraud
GOLDSTEIN, Louis Las Vegas, Nevada	Possession of goods stolen from interstate shipment
GORDON, Rubye Lee Tampa, Florida	Forgery of U.S. Treasury checks
GREEN, Pincus Switzerland	Information not available
HAMNER, Robert Ivey Searcy, Arkansas	Conspiracy to distribute marijuana, possession of marijuana with intent to distribute
HANDLEY, Samuel Price Hodgenville, Kentucky	Conspiracy to steal government property
HANDLEY, Woodie Randolph Hodgenville, Kentucky	Conspiracy to steal government property
HARMON, Jay Houston Jonesboro, Arkansas	1. Conspiracy to import marijuana, conspiracy to possess marijuana with intent to distribute, importation of marijuana, possession of marijuana with intent to distribute 2. Conspiracy to import cocaine
HEMMINGSON, John	Interstate transport of stolen property, money laundering
HERDLINGER, David S. St. Simons Island, Georgia	Mail fraud

HUCKLEBERRY, Debi Rae Ogden, Utah	Distribution of methamphetamine
JAMES, Donald Ray Fairfield Bay, Arkansas	Mail fraud, wire fraud, and false statement to a bank to influence credit approval
JOBE, Stanley Pruet El Paso, Texas	Conspiracy to commit bank fraud, and bank fraud
JOHNSON, Ruben H. Austin, Texas	Theft and misapplication of bank funds by a bank officer or director
JONES, Linda	Conspiracy to commit bank fraud and other offenses against the United States
LAKE, James Howard	Illegal corporate campaign contributions, wire fraud
LEWIS, June Louise Lowellville, Ohio	Embezzlement by a bank employee
LEWIS, Salim Bonnor Short Hills, New Jersey	Securities fraud, record keeping violations, margin violations
LODWICK, John Leighton Excelsior Springs, Missouri	Income tax evasion
LOPEZ, Hildebrando San Isidro, Texas	Distribution of cocaine
LUACES, Jose Julio Ft. Lauderdale, Florida	Possession of an unregistered firearm
MANESS, James Timothy	Conspiracy to distribute a controlled substance
MANNING, James Lowell Little Rock, Arkansas	Aiding and assisting in the preparation of a false corporate tax return
MARTIN, John Robert Gulf Breeze, Florida	Income tax evasion

MARTINEZ, Frank Ayala Elgin, Texas	Conspiracy to supply false documents to the Immigration and Naturalization Service
MARTINEZ, Silvia Leticia Beltran Elgin, Texas	Conspiracy to supply false documents to the Immigration and Naturalization Service
McCORMICK, John Francis Dedham, Massachusetts	Racketeering conspiracy, racketeering, and violation of the Hobbs Act
McDOUGAL, Susan H.	
MECHANIC, Howard Lawrence	1. Violating the Civil Disobedience Act of 1968 2. Failure to appear 3. Making false statement in acquiring a passport
MITCHELL, Brook K., Sr.	Conspiracy to illegally obtain USDA subsidy payments, false statements to USDA, and false entries on USDA forms
MORGAN, Charles Wilfred, III Little Rock, Arkansas	Conspiracy to distribute cocaine
MORISON, Samuel Loring Crofton, Maryland	Willful transmission of defense information, unauthorized possession and retention of defense information, theft of government property
NAZZARO, Richard Anthony Winchester, Massachusetts	Perjury and conspiracy to commit mail fraud
NOSENKO, Charlene Ann Phoenix, Arizona	Conspiracy to defraud the United States, and influencing or injuring an officer or juror generally
OBERMEIER, Vernon Raymond Belleville, Illinois	Conspiracy to distribute cocaine, distribution of cocaine, and using a communications facility to facilitate distribution of cocaine
OGALDE, Miguelina Glendale, California	Conspiracy to import cocaine

OWEN, David C. Olathe, Kansas	Filing a false tax return
PALMER, Robert W. Little Rock, Arkansas	Conspiracy to make false statements
PERHOSKY, Kelli Anne Bridgeville, Pennsylvania	Conspiracy to commit mail fraud
PEZZOPANE, Richard H. Palo Heights, Illinois	Conspiracy to commit racketeering, and mail fraud
PHILLIPS, Orville Rex Waco, Texas	Unlawful structure of a financial transaction
POLING, Vinson Stewart, Jr. Baldwin, Maryland	Making a false bank entry, and aiding and abetting
PROUSE, Norman Lyle Conyers, Georgia	Operating or directing the operation of a common carrier while under the influence of alcohol
PRUITT, Willie H. H., Jr. Port Richey, Florida	Absent without official leave
PURSLEY, Danny Martin, Sr. Goodlettsville, Tennessee	Aiding and abetting the conduct of an illegal gambling business, and obstruction of state laws to facilitate illegal gambling
RAVENEL, Charles D. Charleston, South Carolina	Conspiracy to defraud the United States
RAY, William Clyde Altus, Oklahoma	Fraud using a telephone
REGALADO, Alfredo Luna Pharr, Texas	Failure to report the transportation of currency in excess of $10,000 into the United States
RICAFORT, Ildefonso Reynes Houston, Texas	Submission of false claims to Veterans Administration

RICH, Marc Switzerland	Information not available
RIDDLE, Howard Winfield Mt. Crested Butte, Colorado	Violation of the Lacey Act (receipt of illegally imported animal skins)
RILEY, Richard Wilson, Jr.	Possession of cocaine with intent to distribute
ROBBINS, Samuel Lee Cedar Park, Texas	Misprision of a felony
RODRIGUEZ, Joel Gonzales Houston, Texas	Theft of mail by a postal employee
ROGERS, Michael James McAllen, Texas	Conspiracy to possess with intent to distribute marijuana
ROSS, Anna Louise Lubbock, Texas	Distribution of cocaine
RUST, Gerald Glen Avery, Texas	False declarations before grand jury
RUST, Jerri Ann Avery, Texas	False declarations before grand jury
RUTHERFORD, Bettye June Albuquerque, New Mexico	Possession of marijuana with intent to distribute
SANDS, Gregory Lee Sioux Falls, South Dakota	Conspiracy to distribute cocaine
SCHWIMMER, Adolph	Conspiracy to commit an offense against the United States, conspiracy to export arms and ammunition to a foreign country and related charges
SERETTI, Albert A., Jr. McKees Rocks, Pennsylvania	Conspiracy and wire fraud
SHAW, Patricia Campbell Hearst Wilton, Connecticut	Armed bank robbery and using a firearm during a felony

SMITH, Dennis Joseph Redby, Minnesota	1. Unauthorized absence 2. Failure to obey off-limits instructions 3. Unauthorized absence
SMITH, Gerald Owen Florence, Mississippi	Armed bank robbery
SMITH, Stephen A.	Information not available
SPEAKE, Jimmie Lee Breckenridge, Texas	Conspiracy to possess and utter counterfeit $20 Federal Reserve notes
STEWART, Charles Bernard Sparta, Georgia	Illegally destroying U.S. Mail
STEWART-ROLLINS, Marlena Francisca Euclid, Ohio	Conspiracy to distribute cocaine
SYMINGTON, John Fife, III	Information not available
TANNEHILL, Richard Lee Reno, Nevada	Conspiracy and restraint of trade
TENAGLIA, Nicholas C. Lafayette Hill, Pennsylvania	Receipt of illegal payments under the Medicare program
THOMAS, Gary Allen Lancaster, Texas	Theft of mail by postal employee
TODD, Larry Weldon Gardendale, Texas Airborne Hunting Act	Conspiracy to commit an offense against the U.S. in violation of the Lacey Act and the
TREVINO, Olga C. Converse, Texas	Misapplication by a bank employee
VAMVOUKLIS, Ignatious Exeter, New Hampshire	Possession of cocaine
VAN DE WEERD, Patricia A. Tomahawk, Wisconsin	Theft by a U.S. Postal employee

WADE, Christopher V.	Information not available
WARMATH, Bill Wayne Walls, Mississippi	Obstruction of correspondence
WATSON, Jack Kenneth Oakridge, Oregon	Making false statements of material facts to the U.S. Forest Service
WEBB, Donna Lynn Panama City, Florida	False entry in savings and loan record by employee
WELLS, Donald William Phoenix City, Alabama	Possession of an unregistered firearm
WENDT, Robert H. Kirkwood, Missouri	Conspiracy to effectuate the escape of a federal prisoner
WILLIAMS, Jack L.	Making false statements to federal agents
WILLIAMS, Kevin Arthur Omaha, Nebraska	Conspiracy to distribute and possess with intent to distribute crack cocaine
WILLIAMS, Robert Michael Davison, Michigan	Conspiracy to transport in foreign commerce securities obtained by fraud
WILSON, Jimmie Lee Helena, Arkansas	Converting property mortgaged or pledged to a farm credit agency, and converting public money to personal use
WINGATE, Thelma Louise Sale City, Georgia	Mail fraud
WOOD, Mitchell Couey Sherwood, Arkansas	Conspiracy to possess and to distribute cocaine
WOOD, Warren Stannard Las Vegas, Nevada	Conspiracy to defraud the United States by filing a false document with the Securities and Exchange Commission
WORTHEY, Dewey Conway, Arkansas	Medicaid fraud
YALE, Rick Allen Belleville, Illinois	Bank fraud

YASAK, Joseph A. Chicago, Illinois	Knowingly making under oath a false declaration regarding a material fact before a grand jury
YINGLING, William Stanley	Interstate transportation of stolen vehicle
YOUNG, Phillip David Little Rock, Arkansas	Interstate transportation and sale of fish and wildlife

COMMUTATIONS

BENJAMIN BERGER

Offense:	Conspiracy to defraud the United States, 18 U.S.C. § 371; wire fraud, 18 U.S.C. § 1343; false statement, 18 U.S.C. § 1001; money laundering, 18 U.S.C. § 1956(a)(1)(B)(1); filing a false tax return, 26 U.S.C. § 7206(1)
District/Date:	Southern New York; October 18, 1999
Sentence:	30 months' imprisonment; two years' supervised release; $522,977 restitution
Terms of Grant:	Sentence of imprisonment commuted to 24 months' imprisonment

RONALD HENDERSON BLACKLEY

Offense:	False statements; 18 U.S.C. § 1001
District/Date:	District of Columbia; March 18, 1998
Sentence:	27 months' imprisonment; three years' supervised release
Terms of Grant:	Sentence of imprisonment to expire immediately

BERT WAYNE BOLAN

Offense:	Conspiracy to commit mail fraud and illegal remuneration for patient referrals, 18 U.S.C. § 371; mail fraud, 18 U.S.C. § 1341
District/Date:	Northern Texas; April 14, 1995
Sentence:	97 months' imprisonment; three years' supervised release; $375,000 fine
Terms of Grant:	Sentence of imprisonment to expire immediately, unpaid balance of fine in excess of $15,000 remitted

GLORIA LIBIA CAMARGO

Offense:	Conspiracy to possess cocaine with intent to distribute, attempt to possess cocaine with intent to distribute, 21 U.S.C. § 846

District/Date: Southern Florida; February 22, 1990
Sentence: 188 months' imprisonment; five years' supervised release
Terms of Grant: Sentence of imprisonment to expire immediately

CHARLES F. CAMPBELL

Offense: Conspiracy to distribute 50 grams or more of crack cocaine, 21 U.S.C. § 846; distribution of 50 grams or more of crack cocaine, 21 U.S.C. 841(a)(1)
District/Date: District of Columbia; January 25, 1994, as modified on December 17, 1997
Sentence: 240 months' imprisonment; 10 years' supervised release
Terms of Grant: Sentence of imprisonment to expire immediately, on the condition that he serve a five-year period of supervised release with all the conditions set by the court for the period of supervised release previously imposed and a special condition of drug testing, as provided in 18 U.S.C. § 3583(d)

DAVID RONALD CHANDLER

Offense: Capital offense: Murder while engaged in and working in furtherance of a continuing criminal enterprise, 21 U.S.C. § 848(e) Non-capital offenses: Conspiracy to possess with intent to distribute and to distribute over 1,000 kilograms of marijuana and 1,000 marijuana plants, 21 U.S.C. §§ 846 and 841(a)(1); engaging in a continuing criminal enterprise, 21 U.S.C. § 848(a); using or carrying of a firearm in relation to a drug-trafficking crime (two counts), 18 U.S.C. § 924(c); money laundering (four counts), 18 U.S.C. § 1956
District/Date: Northern Alabama; May 14, 1991
Sentence: Death by lethal injection; concurrent life sentence on non-capital counts
Terms of Grant: Death sentence commuted to imprisonment for life without the possibility of parole

LAU CHING CHIN

Offense: Conspiracy to possess heroin with intent to distribute, interstate travel to commit a drug offense, 21 U.S.C. § 846, 18 U.S.C. §§ 1952 and 2
District/Date: Northern Illinois; June 27, 1990
Sentence: 210 months' imprisonment; five years' supervised release
Terms of Grant: Sentence of imprisonment to expire immediately

DONALD R. CLARK

Offense:	Conspiracy to manufacture, distribute, and possess with intent to distribute 1,000 or more marijuana plants, 21 U.S.C. § 846
District/Date:	Middle Florida; November 4, 1994, as modified December 20, 1996
Sentence:	329 months' imprisonment; five years' supervised release
Terms of Grant:	Sentence of imprisonment to expire immediately, on the condition that he be subject to a special condition of drug testing, as provided in 18 U.S.C. § 3583(d), during his period of supervised release

LORETTA DE-ANN COFFMAN

Offense:	Conspiracy, 21 U.S.C. § 846; possession with intent to distribute more than 50 grams of crack cocaine, 21 U.S.C. § 841(a)(1); use of telephone to commit drug offense (five counts), 21 U.S.C. § 843(b); distribution of crack cocaine near school, 21 U.S.C. § 860
District/Date:	Northern Texas; November 12, 1993, as modified June 24, 1996 and February 26, 1998
Sentence:	85 years' imprisonment; five years' supervised release
Terms of Grant:	Sentence of imprisonment to expire immediately, on the condition that she be subject to a special condition of drug testing, as provided in 18 U.S.C. § 3583(d), during her period of supervised release

DERRICK ANTHONY CURRY

Offense:	Conspiracy to distribute and possess with intent to distribute cocaine and cocaine base, aiding and abetting the distribution of cocaine base, and aiding and abetting the possession of cocaine base with intent to distribute, 21 U.S.C. §§ 841(a)(1) and 846, 18 U.S.C. § 2
District/Date:	Maryland; October 1, 1993
Sentence:	235 months' imprisonment; five years' supervised release
Terms of Grant:	Sentence of imprisonment to expire immediately, on the condition that he be subject to a special condition of drug testing, as provided in 18 U.S.C. § 3583(d), during his period of supervised release

VELINDA DESALUS

Offense:	Possession with intent to distribute 50 grams or more of cocaine base, 21 U.S.C. § 841(a)(1) and 18 U.S.C. § 2

District/Date: Middle Florida; December 18, 1992
Sentence: 120 months' imprisonment; five years' supervised release
Terms of Grant: Sentence of imprisonment to expire immediately, on the condition that she be subject to a special condition of drug testing, as provided in 18 U.S.C. § 3583(d), during her period of supervised release

JACOB ELBAUM

Offense: Conspiracy to defraud the United States, 18 U.S.C. § 371; embezzlement from a federally funded program, 18 U.S.C. § 666; wire fraud, 18 U.S.C. § 1343; mail fraud, 18 U.S.C. § 1341; making a false statement, 18 U.S.C. § 1001; filing a false tax return, 26 U.S.C. § 7206; failure to file a tax return, 26 U.S.C. § 7203
District/Date: Southern New York; October 18, 1999
Sentence: 57 months' imprisonment; two years' supervised release; $11,089,721 restitution
Terms of Grant: Sentence of imprisonment commuted to 30 months' imprisonment

LINDA SUE EVANS

Offense:
1. Possession of a firearm by a convicted felon, 18 U.S.C. App. § 1202(a)(1)
2. Harboring a fugitive, 18 U.S.C. § 1071
3. Possession of a firearm by a convicted felon, and false statements in acquiring firearms, 18 U.S.C. §§ 922(h)(1), 922(a)(6), and 924(a)
4. Malicious damage to Government property and conspiracy to damage Government property, 18 U.S.C. §§ 371 and 844(f)

District/Date:
1. Southern New York; November 21, 1985
2. Southern New York; July 10, 1986
3. Eastern Louisiana; May 20, 1987 (modified on December 8, 1988)
4. District of Columbia; December 6, 1990

Sentence:
1. Two years' imprisonment
2. Three years' imprisonment, consecutive to no. 1
3. 30 years' imprisonment (as modified on appeal), consecutive to nos. 1 & 2
4. Five years' imprisonment, consecutive to nos. 1-3

TOTAL SENTENCE: 40 years' imprisonment

Terms of Grant: Sentence of imprisonment commuted to 25 years, eight months, and 11 days, effectuating her immediate release by virtue of having served to her mandatory release date for the aggregate sentence as commuted

LORETTA SHARON FISH

Offense: Conspiracy to manufacture and distribute methamphetamine, 21 U.S.C. § 846

District/Date: Eastern Pennsylvania; December 8, 1994

Sentence: 235 months' imprisonment; five years' supervised release

Terms of Grant: Sentence of imprisonment to expire immediately, on the condition that she be subject to a special condition of drug testing, as provided in 18 U.S.C. § 3583(d), during her period of supervised release

ANTOINETTE M. FRINK

Offense: Conspiracy to aid and abet the possession of cocaine with intent to distribute, aiding and abetting the possession of cocaine with intent to distribute, and counseling others to travel in interstate commerce with the intent of facilitating the possession of cocaine with intent to distribute; 21 U.S.C. §§ 846 and 841(a)(1) and 18 U.S.C. § 1952

District/Date: Middle Georgia; July 11, 1989

Sentence: 188 months' imprisonment; five years' supervised release

Terms of Grant: Sentence of imprisonment to expire immediately, on the condition that she be subject to a special condition of drug testing, as provided in 18 U.S.C. § 3583(d), during her period of supervised release

DAVID GOLDSTEIN

Offense: Conspiracy to defraud the United States, 18 U.S.C. § 371; wire fraud, 18 U.S.C. § 1343; embezzlement from a federally funded program, 18 U.S.C. § 666; mail fraud, 18 U.S.C. § 1341

District/Date: Southern New York; October 18, 1999

Sentence: 70 months' imprisonment; three years' supervised release; $10,118,182 restitution

Terms of Grant: Sentence of imprisonment commuted to 30 months' imprisonment

GERARD ANTHONY GREENFIELD

Offense: Possession of phencyclidine (PCP) with intent to distribute, 21 U.S.C. § 841(a)

District/Date: Utah; September 9, 1993
Sentence: 192 months' imprisonment; five years' supervised release; $25,000 fine
Terms of Grant: Sentence of imprisonment to expire immediately, on the condition that he be subject to a special condition of drug testing, as provided in 18 U.S.C. § 3583(d), during his period of supervised release

JODIE ELLEYN ISRAEL

Offense: Conspiracy to manufacture, possess with intent to distribute and distribute marijuana, 21 U.S.C. §§ 841(a)(1) and 846 and 18 U.S.C. § 2; conducting financial transaction with proceeds from sale of controlled substances (three counts), 18 U.S.C. §§ 1956 and 2; distribution of marijuana (seven counts), 21 U.S.C. § 841 and 18 U.S.C. § 2
District/Date: Montana; February 4, 1994
Sentence: 135 months' imprisonment; five years' supervised release
Terms of Grant: Sentence of imprisonment to expire immediately, on the condition that she be subject to a special condition of drug testing, as provided in 18 U.S.C. § 3583(d), during her period of supervised release

KIMBERLY D. JOHNSON

Offense: Conspiracy to possess with intent to distribute cocaine base, 21 U.S.C. § 846
District/Date: South Carolina; November 14, 1994
Sentence: 188 months' imprisonment; five years' supervised release
Terms of Grant: Sentence of imprisonment to expire immediately, upon the condition that she be subject to a special condition of drug testing, as provided in 18 U.S.C. § 3583(d), during her period of supervised release

BILLY THORNTON LANGSTON, JR.

Offense: Conspiracy to manufacture PCP, 21 U.S.C. § 846; manufacture of PCP, 21 U.S.C. § 841(a)(1)
District/Date: Central California; September 9, 1994 (as modified by 1996 court order)
Sentence: 324 months' imprisonment; five years' supervised release
Terms of Grant: Sentence of imprisonment to expire immediately, on the condition that he be subject to a special condition of drug

testing, as provided in 18 U.S.C. § 3583(d), during his period of supervised release

BELINDA LYNN LUMPKIN

Offense:	Conspiracy to possess with intent to distribute crack cocaine and marijuana, 21 U.S.C. §§ 841(a)(1) and 846
District/Date:	Eastern Michigan; March 24, 1989
Sentence:	300 months' imprisonment; three years' supervised release
Terms of Grant:	Sentence of imprisonment to expire immediately, on the condition that she serve a five-year period of supervised release with all the conditions set by the court for the three-year period of supervised release previously imposed and a special condtion of drug testing, as provided in 18 U.S.C. § 3583(d)

PETER MACDONALD, SR.

Offense:	1. Racketeering, racketeering conspiracy, extortion by an Indian tribal official, mail fraud, wire fraud, and interstate transportation in aid of racketeering, 18 U.S.C. §§ 1962(c), 1962(d), 666(a)(1)(B), 1341, 1343, and 1952 2. Conspiracy to commit kidnapping, third-degree burglary, 18 U.S.C. §§ 1153, 371, and 1201(c), and 18 U.S.C. §§ 1153 and 2 and Arizona Revised Statutes § 13-1506
District/Date:	1. Arizona; November 30, 1992 2. Arizona; February 16, 1993
Sentence:	1. 60 months' imprisonment; 36 months' supervised release; $10,000 fine; $1,500,000 restitution 2. 175 months' imprisonment; 60 months' supervised release (concurrent with no.1); $5,000 fine; $4,431.03 restitution
Terms of Grant:	Sentences of imprisonment to expire immediately

KELLIE ANN MANN

Offense:	Conspiracy to distribute LSD, 21 U.S.C. § 846; possession of LSD with intent to distribute, 21 U.S.C. § 841(a)(1); use of mail to facilitate a drug offense, 21 U.S.C. § 843(b)
District/Date:	Northern Georgia; January 26, 1994
Sentence:	120 months' imprisonment; five years' supervised release
Terms of Grant:	Sentence of imprisonment to expire immediately, on the condition that she be subject to a special condition of drug

testing, as provided in 18 U.S.C. § 3583(d), during her period of supervised release

PETER NINEMIRE

Offense:	1. Manufacturing marijuana, 21 U.S.C. § 841(a)(1) 2. Failure to appear, 18 U.S.C. § 3146(a)(1)
District/Date:	1. Kansas; April 26, 1991 2. Kansas; June 28, 1991
Sentence:	1. 292 months' imprisonment; eight years' supervised release 2. 30 months' imprisonment, consecutive to no. 1; three years' supervised release
Terms of Grant:	Sentences of imprisonment to expire immediately, on the condition that he serve a five-year period of supervised release with all the conditions set by the court for the periods of supervised release previously imposed and a special condition of drug testing, as provided in 18 U.S.C. § 3583(d)

HUGH RICARDO PADMORE

Offense:	Possession with intent to distribute cocaine base, 21 U.S.C. § 841(a)(1) and 18 U.S.C. § 2
District/Date:	Eastern North Carolina; October 31, 1995
Sentence:	135 months' imprisonment; five years' supervised release
Terms of Grant:	Sentence of imprisonment to expire immediately, on the condition that he be subject to a special condition of drug testing, as provided in 18 U.S.C. § 3583(d), during his period of supervised release

ARNOLD PAUL PROSPERI

Offense:	Filing a false tax return and making, uttering, or possessing a counterfeited security with intent to deceive another, 26 U.S.C. § 7206(1) and 18 U.S.C. § 513(a)
District/Date:	Southern Florida; March 27, 1998
Sentence:	36 months' imprisonment; one year's supervised release; $25,000 fine
Terms of Grant:	Any sentence of imprisonment imposed or to be imposed that is in excess of 36 months commuted; any period of confinement imposed to be served in home confinement

MELVIN J. REYNOLDS

Offense:	Bank fraud, 18 U.S.C. § 1344; wire fraud, 18 U.S.C. § 1343; making false statements to a financial institution, 18 U.S.C.

	§1014; conspiracy to defraud the Federal Election Commission, 18 U.S.C. § 371; false statements to a federal official, 18 U.S.C. § 1001
District/Date:	Northern Illinois; July 15, 1997
Sentence:	78 months' imprisonment; five years' supervised release; $20,000 restitution
Terms of Grant:	Unserved portion of sentence of imprisonment commuted to a period of equal length to be served in a community corrections center designated by the Bureau of Prisons, on the condition that he comply with Bureau of Prisons rules and regulations concerning confinement in a community corrections center

PEDRO MIGUEL RIVEIRO

Offense:	Conspiracy to possess with intent to distribute cocaine, 21 U.S.C. § 846
District/Date:	Southern Florida; February 9, 1995
Sentence:	102 months' imprisonment; five years' supervised release
Terms of Grant:	Sentence of imprisonment to expire immediately, on the condition that he be subject to a special condition of drug testing, as provided in 18 U.S.C. § 3583(d), during his period of supervised release

DOROTHY RIVERS

Offense:	Obstruction of a federal audit, 18 U.S.C. § 1516; false statements to a federal agency, 18 U.S.C. § 1001; tax evasion, 26 U.S.C. § 7201; failure to file tax returns, 26 U.S.C. § 7203; wire fraud, 18 U.S.C. § 1343; mail fraud, 18 U.S.C. § 1341; theft from a federally funded organization, 18 U.S.C. § 666
District/Date:	Northern Illinois; November 17, 1997
Sentence:	70 months' imprisonment; three years' supervised release
Terms of Grant:	Sentence of imprisonment commuted to 50 months' imprisonment

SUSAN LISA ROSENBERG

Offense::	Conspiracy to possess unregistered firearm, receive firearms and explosives shipped in interstate commerce while a fugitive, and unlawfully use false identification documents, 18 U.S.C. § 371; possession of unregistered destructive devices, possession of unregistered firearm (two counts), 26 U.S.C. §§ 5861(d)

	and 5871; carrying explosives during commission of a felony, 18 U.S.C. § 844(h)(2); possession with intent to unlawfully use false identification documents, 18 U.S.C. §§ 1028(a)(3), 1028(b)(2)(B), 1028(c)(1) and 1028(c); false representation of Social Security number, possession of counterfeit Social Security cards, 42 U.S.C. § 408(g)(2)
District/Date:	New Jersey; May 20, 1985
Sentence:	58 years' imprisonment
Terms of Grant:	Sentence of imprisonment commuted to an aggregate of 27 years, seven months, and 19 days, effectuating her immediate release by virtue of having served to her mandatory release date for the aggregate sentence as commuted

KALMEN STERN

Offense:	Conspiracy to defraud the United States, 18 U.S.C. § 371; embezzlement from a federally funded program, 18 U.S.C. § 666; wire fraud, 18 U.S.C. §1343; mail fraud, 18 U.S.C. § 1341; filing a false tax return, 26 U.S.C. § 7206(1)
District/Date:	Southern New York; October 18, 1999
Sentence:	78 months' imprisonment; three years' supervised release; $11,179,513 restitution
Terms of Grant:	Sentence of imprisonment commuted to 30 months.

CORY HOLLIS STRINGFELLOW

Offense:	1. Conspiracy to possess with intent to distribute and to distribute LSD, 21 U.S.C. §§ 846 and 841(a)(1), (b)(1)(A) 2. False statements in a passport application, 18 U.S.C. § 1542
District/Date:	1. Colorado; July 21, 1995 2. Utah; November 17, 1995
Sentence:	1. 188 months' imprisonment; four years' supervised release 2. Four months' imprisonment (consecutive to no. 1); four years' supervised release
Terms of Grant:	Sentence of imprisonment of 188 months for conspiracy to possess LSD with intent to distribute to expire immediately, on the condition that he serve a five-year period of supervised release with all the conditions set by the court for the four-year period of supervised release previously imposed and a special condition of drug testing, as provided in 18 U.S.C. § 3583(d),

leaving intact and in effect the consecutive four-month prison sentence imposed upon him for making false statements in a passport application

CARLOS ANIBAL VIGNALI, JR.

Offense:	Conspiracy to distribute cocaine, 21 U.S.C. § 846; using facilities in interstate commerce with intent to promote a business enterprise involving narcotics, 18 U.S.C. § 1952(b); illegal use of communication facility to facilitate commission of controlled substance offense, 21 U.S.C. § 843(b)
District/Date::	Minnesota; July 17, 1995
Sentence:	175 months' imprisonment; five years' supervised release
Terms of Grant:	Sentence of imprisonment to expire immediately, on the condition that he be subject to a special condition of drug testing, as provided in 18 U.S.C. § 3583(d), during his period of supervised release

THOMAS W. WADDELL, III

Offense:	Conducting an illegal gambling business, 18 U.S.C. § 1955; conspiracy to commit money laundering, 18 U.S.C. §§ 1956(a)(1)(B)(1) and (h)
District/Date:	Northern California; January 13, 2000
Sentence:	24 months' imprisonment; three years' supervised release; $7,500 fine; criminal forfeiture
Terms of Grant:	Sentence of imprisonment commuted to 12 months' imprisonment and one year's supervised release, to be served before the three-year period of supervised release already imposed

HARVEY WEINIG

Offense:	Conspiracy to commit money laundering, criminal forfeiture, and misprision of felony, 18 U.S.C. §§ 1956(h), 982(a)(1) and (b)(1)(A), and 4
District/Date:	Southern New York; March 22, 1996
Sentence:	135 months' imprisonment; three years' supervised release
Terms of Grant:	Sentence of imprisonment commuted to five years and 270 days, on the condition that he serve a period of supervised release of three years and 95 days with all the conditions set by the court for his previously imposed three-year period of supervised release

KIM ALLEN WILLIS

Offense:	Conspiracy to distribute cocaine, aiding and abetting the attempt to possess with intent to distribute cocaine, 21 U.S.C. §§ 841(a)(1), 841(b)(1)(A), and 846
District/Date:	Minnesota; April 20, 1990
Sentence:	188 months' imprisonment; five years' supervised release
Terms of Grant:	Sentence of imprisonment to expire immediately, on the condition that he be subject to a special condition of drug testing, as provided in 18 U.S.C. § 3583(d), during his period of supervised release

NOTES

PROLOGUE

1. *The 9/11 Commission Report: Final Report of the National Commission on Terrorist Attacks Upon the United States* (United States Government Printing Office, 2004), 189.
2. Andy Geller, "Bill Turning Into Grumpy Old Man," *New York Post*, August 16, 2006, 15.
3. Patrick Luciani, "Happy Birthday, Mr. President," *Toronto Globe and Mail*, September 4, 2006.
4. Al Kamen, "In the Loop," *Washington Post*, July 19, 1995.
5. David Remnick, "The Wanderer," *New Yorker*, September 18, 2006.
6. Ibid.

CHAPTER ONE: FROM RAGS TO RICHES

1. Gallup Poll: *The Gallup Poll: Public Opinion 1935–71,* 1032.
2. "I Didn't Want to Know," interview with George Stephanopoulos, *Newsweek*, March 15, 1999, 42.
3. Robert K. Murray, *The Harding Era: Warren G. Harding and His Administration* (University of Minnesota Press, 1969), *passim.* My Harding comparison is made with the historians as my guides. Professor Murray's fine book has this observation of Harding by his contemporaries, observers who lived seven decades before anyone ever heard tell of America's "first Black president": ". . . his compulsive need for friends. To Harding, friends were as important as life itself. Later writers variously attributed this to his small-town background, to a defect in his character, to an attempt to compensate for his alleged

Negro blood, to an abnormal craving for recognition and acceptance, to a basic insecurity. . . ." 115–116.

4. David McCullough, *Truman* (Simon & Schuster, 1992), Chapter 17, *passim,* but particularly 863–864, 865–866, 871–872.
5. Ibid., 932
6. Ibid., 928–932.
7. Alonzo L. Hamby, *Man of the People: A Life of Harry S. Truman* (Oxford University Press, Inc., 1995), 467.
8. Interview with Michael Colgan in Dublin at the Shelbourne Hotel, June 1, 2004.
9. Andy Soltis, "Clinton Received Red Flag on Hijackings in '98," *New York Post,* July 23, 2004, 7.
10. Interview by author on August 14, 2004 with Stefan Halper, who studied with Clinton during a stay at Oxford from 1967 to 1971.
11. Danny Hakim, "Hillary, Not as in the Mount Everest Guy," *New York Times,* October 17, 2006, A20.
12. Joe Klein, interview with Bill Clinton, *New York* magazine, January 20, 1992.
13. Meredith L. Oakley, *On the Make: The Rise of Bill Clinton* (Regnery Publishing, Inc., 1994), 30.
14. William Jefferson Clinton, *My Life* (Alfred A. Knopf, 2004), 711.
15. Statement of Special Counsel Michael E. Shaheen, Jr. issued by Office of the Independent Counsel, July 28, 1999.
16. Amy Goldstein and Susan Schmidt, "Clinton's Last-Day Clemency Benefits 176; List Includes Pardons for Cisneros, McDougal. Deutch and Roger Clinton," the *Washington Post,* January 20, 2001, A1.
17. McCullough, 918–919.
18. Vincent Morris, "New Pardon-Probe Target Zips Her Lip—Denise Pal Taking the 5th," *New York Post,* February 27, 2001, 008.
19. Christopher Andersen, *American Evita* (HarperCollins, 2004), 5.
20. Lt. Col. Robert "Buzz" Patterson, USAF (Ret.), *Dereliction of Duty: The Eyewitness Account of How Bill Clinton Compromised America's National Security* (Regnery Publishing, Inc., 2003), 55–58.

CHAPTER TWO: SUNRISE IN CHAPPAQUA

1. John F. Harris, "For the Clintons' Last Act, Reviews Don't Look Good," *Washington Post,* January 27, 2001, A1.

2. Thomas B. Edsall, "Clintons Take Away $190,000 in Gifts," *Washington Post*, January 21, 2001, A18.
3. "Former President Bill Clinton and Senator Hillary Clinton Receive Over $190,000 Worth In Gifts," NBC News, January 24, 2001.
4. Interview with current White House staffer who wishes to remain anonymous, June 2004.
5. Ellen Nakashima, "Panel: Clintons Took $362,000 in Gifts," *Washington Post*, February 13, 2002, A4.
6. "On the Prowl," *American Spectator*, March 2000, 14.
7. Jerry Zeifman, "Hillary's Watergate Scandal," *New York Post*, August 16, 1999.
8. I.C. Smith, *Inside: A Top G-Man Exposes Spies, Lies, and Bureaucratic Bungling in the FBI* (Nelson Current, 2004), 164–165.
9. Interview with Clinton military aide who wishes to remain anonymous, March 2005.
10. Interviews with security personnel and military aides in 2004 and 2005 who also desire anonymity.
11. Nigel Hamilton, *Bill Clinton: An American Journey* (Random House, 2003), 362.
12. Interview with retired FBI agent I.C. Smith, December 2004. Smith served during the Clinton administration as Special Agent for Arkansas and had two sources for this story.
13. Jonathan Alter, "Citizen Clinton Up Close," *Newsweek*, April 8, 2002.
14. Jonathan Alter interviewing Bill Clinton, *Newsweek*, April 8, 2002 [Author's comments].
15. Telephone interview by Jon Ward with Terry McAuliffe, August 5, 2004.
16. Interview in Little Rock, Arkansas, with former Clinton administration aide David Watkins, February 13, 1997.
17. David Brock, "Living With the Clintons," *American Spectator*, January 1994, 23.
18. Ibid., 23.
19. Lisa Schiffren, "Bill and Hillary at the Trough," *American Spectator*, August 1993, 20–21, and Becky Brown, the nanny interviewed by the author, May 19, 1995.
20. R. Emmett Tyrrell, Jr., "Boy Clinton in Prague," *American Spectator*, July 1996, 30.

21. William Jefferson Clinton, *My Life* (Knopf, Borzoi Books, 2004), 22.
22. Interview with former security chief at the Plaza Hotel who wishes to remain anonymous, October 2004.
23. Lisa Schiffren, "Bill and Hillary at the Trough," *American Spectator*, August 1993, 20.
24. Sources within the Secret Service interviewed in summer 2004.
25. Jerry Seper, "Grand Jury Probes Rich-Saddam Link," *Washington Times*, December 17, 2004, A1.
26. "Unpardonable," *Washington Post*, January 23, 2001, A16.
27. "Between Two Eras," *New York Times*, February 11, 2001, A16.
28. "Clinton Corruption Plays Us For Fools—We Won't Forget," *New York Observer*, February 28, 2001.
29. Donald Lambro, "Carter Calls Clinton's Rich Pardon 'Disgraceful,'" *Washington Times*, February 22, 2001, A1.
30. Ibid.
31. Ibid.
32. Tony Blankley "Unpunished Wickedness," *Washington Times*, February 28, 2001, A19.
33. Lambro, "Carter Calls Clinton's Rich Pardon 'Disgraceful.'"
34. Robert B. Reich, "The Democrats Aren't Just Resting," *Washington Post*, March 11, 2001, B7.
35. John F. Harris, "Controversy Casts Shadow On Clinton's Party Role; Democrats Squirm at Damage Done in White House Exit," *Washington Post*, February 14, 2001, A12.
36. Bob Herbert, "Cut Him Loose," *New York Times*, February 26, 2001, 15.
37. Donna Brazile, "What Kind of Party for the Democrats," *New York Times*, February 25, 2001.
38. Editorial, "Clinton Corruption Plays Us for Fools—We Won't Forget," *New York Observer*, March 5, 2001, 1.
39. "Few Want to be Seen with Image of Clinton," *New York Times*, March 18, 2001, National Desk, 15.
40. Associated Press, "Clinton Popularity Sags," *Chattanooga Times Free Press*, March 8, 2001, A4.
41. "Few Want to be Seen with Image of Clinton," *New York Times*, March 18, 2001, National Desk, 15.
42. McAuliffe interview, August 5, 2004.
43. Ibid.

CHAPTER THREE: THE GHOST SHIP

1. Nigel Hamilton, *Bill Clinton: An American Journey* (Random House, 2003), 308.
2. R. Emmett Tyrrell, Jr. *Boy Clinton: The Political Biography* (Regnery Publishing, Inc. 1996) Introduction, xix.
3. Interview with former Arkansas state trooper, L.D. Brown, January 7, 2005.
4. Report from an *American Spectator* investigator who wishes to remain anonymous, June 2005.
5. See Appendix I.
6. George A. Chidi, Jr., "Oracle AppsWorld: Ellison Says Hands Off Our Apps," *InfoWorld Daily News*, February 21, 2001.
7. Joel Siegel, "Backin' Away From Bubba," *New York Daily News*, February 28, 2001, 13.
8. Toby Harnden, "Bankers Drop Invitation to Clinton," *Daily Telegraph*, February 15, 2001, 16.
9. Joyce Milton, *The First Partner: Hillary Rodham Clinton* (William Morrow and Company, 1999), 142.
10. Michael Isikoff, "Clinton Team Works to Deflect Allegations on Nominee's Private Life," *Washington Post*, July 26, 1992, A18.
11. Greg Pierce, "Inside Politics," *Washington Times*, February 7, 2006, A10. Also reported during an interview with an anonymous source March 13, 2005 who was a target of Pellicano's services for the Clintons in the 1990s.
12. Interview with an independent counsel who wishes anonymity, December 1, 2005.
13. Daniel Wattenberg, "Love and Hate in Arkansas," *American Spectator*, April/May 1994, 33. Also see Roger Morris, *Partners in Power* (Henry Holt and Company, Inc., 1996), *passim.* For that matter, the evidence of the affair is to be found in many authoritative accounts of the Clintons' lives. That it is not general knowledge is still more evidence of the *Kultursmog's* pollution of the media.
14. Don Van Natta reported in the *New York Times* on August 29, 1999, that after an outing with former President Gerald Ford and golf legend Jack Nicklaus, Clinton infuriated both by turning in the phony score of 80 for 18 holes, causing Nicklaus to scoff to Ford that Clinton's score was actually "80 with 50 floating mulligans."
15. Frank Wolfe, "Others Don't Recall What Clinton Does," *Arkansas Democrat-Gazette*, June 9, 1996.

16. Doris Kearns Goodwin, *Lyndon Johnson and the American Dream* (St. Martin's Press, 1976), xv.
17. Ibid., xvi–xvii.
18. Jonathan Alter, "Citizen Clinton Up Close," *Newsweek*, April 8, 2002.
19. December 2006 interview with a source who picked up the story from the Florida physician who attended Clinton after his fall.
20. Associated Press, "Clinton Falls Frolicking with Buddy the Dog," January 26, 2001.
21. Interviews with a source seeking anonymity, March 2006.
22. Thomas J. Craughwell, *Stealing Lincoln's Body* (Belknap Press of Harvard University Press, 2007), 105.
23. Interview with I.C. Smith, corroborated during a January 17, 2005 interview with Buzz Patterson, President Bill Clinton's Air Force aide from May 1996 to May 1998. The first report of a trooper being suggested as a carrier of the "football" appeared in Daniel Wattenberg's "Love and Hate in Arkansas," *American Spectator*, April/May 1996, 40.
24. David Brock, "Living With the Clintons," *American Spectator*, January 1994, 24.
25. Interviews with I.C. Smith by the author in July 2005.
26. Brock, 25.
27. Interviews with former Secret Service guards detailed to the Clintons who wish to remain anonymous, autumn 2004.
28. Interview with Buzz Patterson, April 2005.
29. Interview with former White House military aide who requests anonymity, April 2005.
30. Interview with Buzz Patterson, April 2005.
31. Interview with a source who wishes anonymity, January 22, 2005.
32. Martin Kasindorf, "Clinton Explains Cuts of a New Sort," *Newsday*, April 8, 1993, 8.
33. Report from investigator in Septmber 2004 who seeks anonymity.
34. John McCaslin, "Inside the Beltway," *Washington Times*, December 9, 1998, A5.
35. *Referral to the U.S. House of Representatives Pursuant to Title 28, U.S.C §595 (c) Appendix, sub'd by the Office of the Independent Counsel, Sept. 9, 1998* (hereafter "*Appendix to Starr Report*"), 1297.
36. *The Starr Report* (Pocket Books, 1998), 80.
37. Ibid., 414.

38. Interview with a former member of Congress who requests anonymity, June 2005.
39. *Appendix to the Starr Report*, 1299.
40. *The Starr Report*, 161–163.
41. Report from investigator who seeks anonymity, September 2004.
42. *American Spectator* researcher whose name is confidential.
43. Report from anonymous investigator, 5–6.
44. The author's interview with private investigator Gil Macklin, July 15, 2005.
45. *The Starr Report*, 57–58.
46. Ibid., 116–117.
47. Dick Morris, *Rewriting History* (HarperCollins, 2004), 223.
48. David Maraniss, *First in His Class: A Biography of Bill Clinton* (Simon & Schuster, 1995), 440–441.
49. Jack Anderson/Dale Van Atta, "Senator Hillary Rodham Clinton, D-N.Y.?" November 27, 1998, United Features Syndicate.
50. "Washington Prowler," *American Spectator Online*, March 1, 2004.
51. Interviews with Dale Van Atta in the summer of 1999.
52. Disclosed by the officer during a September 2004 interview with anonymous interviewer.
53. Gail Sheehy, "Hillary's Solo Act," *Vanity Fair*, August 2001.
54. Vincent Morris, "Hill's Pals Seeing Red Over Rich," *New York Post*, July 3, 2001, 4.

Chapter Four: Pardongate

1. Interview with Vice President Richard Cheney by Dale Van Atta, February 20, 2001.
2. Jennifer Harper, "Inside Politics," *Washington Times*, June 13, 2002.
3. *New York Post*, "Page Six," June 19, 2003, 6.
4. Conversation with James Blanchard, Montreal, Canada, winter 2003.
5. Doug Struck, "Defection Boosts Canadian Premier Before Crucial Vote," *Washington Post*, May 18, 2005, A13.
6. Report from an investigator who seeks anonymity, September 2004, 4.
7. Linda Massarella, "Bill & Hannibal Are Bikini Cannibals," *New York Post*, August 28, 2001, 05.
8. Richard Miniter, unpublished memorandum drafted in Ghent, Belgium, October, 2001, and submitted to the author.

9. Armey Archard, "Coast to Coast, Prez Has Showbusy Weekend," *Daily Variety*, December 6, 1993.
10. ABC News, *20/20*, April 27, 2001.
11. Kate Perrotta, "How Denise Conquered New York," *New York Post*, September 15, 1998.
12. U.S. House of Representatives, Committee on Government Reform, *Justice Undone: Clemency Decisions in the Clinton White House*, 107th Cong., 2nd sess., 2002, H. Rpt. 107–454, Chapter One, 74.
13. Andrew Demillo, "Presidential Center's Donor Display Remains Offline," *Arkansas Democrat-Gazette*, January 26, 2005.
14. Anonymous former White House lawyer in interview with researcher, August 2004.
15. Associated Press, "Bill Clinton Says He Regrets Rich Pardon, 'It Wasn't Worth the Damage to My Reputation,'" *Washington Post*, April 1, 2002, A4.
16. Anonymous source interviewed by researcher, August 2004.
17. House Government Reform Committee, *Justice Undone*, Chapter One, 78.
18. Alison Leigh Cowan, "Rich Pardon Reportedly Followed Pledge to Charity of Former Wife," *New York Times*, May 1, 2001, A1.
19. Alison Leigh Cowan, "Panel Says Top Justice Department Aide Held Information on Rich's Pardon," *New York Times*, March 13, 2002, A1.
20. "Executive Summary," *Justice Undone: Clemency Decisions in the Clinton White House*, 5.
21. "Between Two Eras," *New York Times*, February 11, 2001, A16.
22. "The Clinton Indulgences" (Editorial), *Washington Post*, February 13, 2001, A20.
23. House Government Reform Committee, *Justice Undone*, Introduction, 13.
24. Jonathan Alter, "Life is Fleeting, Man," *Newsweek*, March 31, 2002.
25. House Government Reform Committee, *Justice Undone*, Introduction, 2.
26. Interviews with sources involved in the Independent Counsel's office, December 2005.
27. House Government Reform Committee, *Justice Undone*, Executive Summary, 7–8.
28. Interview with L.D. Brown, December 2, 2005.
29. Jim McElhatton, "Hillary's Brother Barred from Bank Account," *Washington Times*, July 27, 2006, A1.

30. Liz Trotta, "White is 'Smart and Tough' Lawyers Say of Rich Prober," *Washington Times*, March 6, 2001, A13.
31. *Congressional Record*, Extension of Remarks: Rep. Bob Barr (R-Ga.).
32. Don Van Natta, Jr. and Marc Lacey, "Access Proved Vital In Last-Minute Race for Clinton Pardons," *New York Times*, February 25, 2001, 1.
33. Alter, "Life is Fleeting, Man."
34. Nigel Hamilton, *Bill Clinton: An American Journey* (Random House, 2003), 368.
35. Brian Wilson, NBC interview with former President Bill Clinton, June 1, 2005.
36. Sidney Blumenthal, *The Clinton Wars* (Farrar, Straus and Giroux, 2003), 399.
37. *The NewsHour with Jim Lehrer* (PBS television broadcast), September 23, 1996.
38. House Government Reform Committee, *Justice Undone*, Introduction, 7.
39. Bodyguard interviewed by my researcher, August 2004.

CHAPTER FIVE: THE "CHOP SUEY CONNECTION"

1. Interviews with former American intelligence officers, January 26, 2006.
2. Richard Lawless as quoted in Bill Gertz's "The Chinese Dragon Awakes," *Washington Times*, June 26, 2005, A1.
3. James Ring Adams, "What's Up in Jakarta?" *American Spectator*, September 1995, 30.
4. Edward Walsh, "Senate Panel Finds 1st Direct DNC Link to Foreign Funding," *Washington Post*, July 16, 1997, A1.
5. U.S. Senate, Committee of Governmental Affairs, *Investigation of Illegal or Improper Activities in Connection with the 1996 Federal Election Campaign*, 105th Cong., 2nd sess., 1998, S. Rpt. 105–167, Chapter 20, 2718.
6. I.C. Smith, *Inside: A Top G-Man Exposes Spies, Lies, and Bureaucratic Bungling in the FBI* (Nelson Current, 2004), 214–218.
7. Eric Schmitt, "Rumsfeld Warns of Concern About Expansion of China's Navy," *New York Times*, February 18, 2005.
8. John N. Petrie (ed.), *Essays in Strategy 12* (Diane Publishing, 1996), 15.
9. Kenneth R. Timmerman, "The DNC's Chinese Money Laundry," *American Spectator*, November 1998, 81.
10. Ibid.

11. Edward Timperlake and William C. Triplett, II, *Year of the Rat: How Bill Clinton and Al Gore Compromised U.S. Security for Chinese Cash* (Regnery Publishing Inc., 1998), 27–28.
12. Ibid., 28.
13. Ibid., 43.
14. I.C. Smith, 219.
15. David Willman, Alan C. Miller, and Glenn F. Bunting, "An Investigative Report; What Clinton Knew; How A Push For New Fund-Raising Led To Foreign Access, Bad Money And Questionable Ties," *Los Angeles Times*, December 21, 1997, A1.
16. Jeff Gerth and Stephen Labaton, "A Wider Circle at White House Knew of Efforts to Help Hubbell," *New York Times*, April 10, 1997.
17. Timperlake and Triplett, 37–38.
18. Andy Thibault and Jerry Seper, "Hillary Forced Huang on Reluctant Brown: First Lady's Tie to Foreign-Linked Political Contributions Called 'Common Knowledge,'" *Washington Times* November 8, 1996, A2.
19. Senate Committee of Governmental Affairs, *Investigation of Illegal or Improper Activities in Connection with the 1996 Federal Election Campaign*, Chapter 14, 1181.
20. Timperlake and Triplett, 51.
21. Kenneth R. Timmerman, "Casualties of China Connection," *Washington Times*, February 24, 2000, A16.
22. Jeff Gerth and David E. Sanger, "Aircraft Deal With Chinese is Questioned," *New York Times*, October 30, 1996, A1.
23. Timperlake and Triplett, 139.
24. Ibid., 140.
25. "Transcripts of Clinton-Jiang News Conference," *Washington Post*, October 30, 1997.
26. President Richard M. Nixon and Chairman Mao Zedong, *Joint Communique of the United States and the People's Republic of China*, Shanghai, People's Republic of China, February 28, 1972.
27. Henry Kissinger, *White House Years* (Little, Brown & Co., 1979), 1076.
28. William Burr (ed.) *The Kissinger Transcripts* (The New Press, 1998), 186.
29. Stephen Fidler and James Kynge, "Summit Nuclear Arms Pledges Anger India," *Financial Times*, June 29, 1998, 4.
30. Interview with source on the 9/11 Commission, July 21, 2006.

31. Marcia Kunstel and Joseph Albright, "China in China; Words Are Heard, But Meaning Is Murky," *Atlanta Journal-Constitution*, June 30, 1998, 6A.
32. Jonathan Peterson and Tyler Marshall, "Clinton Backs China on Issue of Free Taiwan," *Los Angeles Times*, June 30, 1998, A1.
33. Richard Halloran, Global Beat Issue Brief No. 40, July 14, 1998. Center for War, Peace and the News Media.
34. Richard Halloran, "U.S. Policy Shift on Taiwan Gives Beijing an Edge," *Washington Times*, July 17, 1998, 14.
35. Charles Hutzler, "Taiwan President's Visit Leaves Sino-U.S. Ties Rocky," Associated Press, June 23, 1995.
36. Dick Morris, *Behind the Oval Office: Getting Reelected Against All Odds* (Renaissance Books, 1999), 33.
37. Ibid, 34.

CHAPTER SIX: THE FIRST COMEBACK OF THE TWENTY-FIRST CENTURY

1. Kathy Kiely, "Campaigns Still Clinton's Strength," *USA Today*, September 12, 2003.
2. Adam Nagourney, "Clinton, In Rare Move, Denounces Bush Record," *New York Times*, September 15, 2003.
3. Telephone interview by Jon Ward with Terry McAuliffe, August 5, 2004.
4. President Bill Clinton conversation with Dale Van Atta, October 24, 2000, as reported by Van Atta.
5. Terence Samuel, "Clinton's Furtive, Final Run: Should Gore Have Let Him Do More to Help?," *U.S. News & World Report*, November 13, 2000.
6. Interview with Bob Mulholland, Communications Director, California Democratic Party, March 9, 2005.
7. William Safire, "Return of the Clintonites," *New York Times*, February 28, 2002, A27.
8. Kathy Kiely, "Campaigns Still Clinton's Strength," *USA Today*, September 12, 2003.
9. P.J. O'Rourke, "The Bill Show," *Atlantic Monthly*, March, 2003.
10. Karen Tumulty, "The Man on the Phone," *Time*, October 14, 2002.
11. Margaret Carlson, "Say Good Night, Bill," *Time*, November, 18, 2002.
12. Scott Shepard, "Democrats Talk Tough for Iowa Union Members," *Atlanta Journal Constitution*, August 15, 2003.
13. Dan Balz and Tania Branigan, "A Fresh Appetite for an Ex-President;

Clinton's Aid Would Be Welcome, Candidates Say," *Washington Post*, September 14, 2003.

14. Mike Glover, "Clinton Rally Delights Iowa Democrats," Associated Press, September 14, 2003.
15. Basu Rekha, "In Iowa Field, Democrats Look Like Democrats Again," *Des Moines Registrar*, September 17, 2003, 11A.
16. John Wagner, "Clinton Dominates Democratic Rally," *Sacramento Bee*, September 14, 2003.
17. Mike Glover, "Former President Clinton's Name Returns to Democratic Campaign in Iowa," Associated Press, September 13, 2003.
18. "Dean Defends Middle East Remarks," CNN.com, September 10, 2003.
19. Interview with Joe Trippi, March 7, 2005.
20. Jim Dwyer, "Senator Clinton Says No to '04, but Playfully Hints at Yes," *New York Times*, September 9, 2003, B1.
21. Walter Shapiro, *One-Car Caravan* (PublicAffairs, 2004), 228–9; Joe Trippi, *The Revolution Will Not Be Televised* (ReganBooks, 2004), 160.
22. "Clinton Holds Fund-Raiser in Iowa," *CNN Saturday Night*, September 13, 2003.
23. Michael Kranish, "Wesley K. Clark, Candidate in the Making," *Boston Globe*, November 17, 2003.
24. Ibid.
25. R. Jeffrey Smith, "Clark Papers Talk Politics And War; General Cites Pressure From Clinton Aides Over Kosovo Conflict," *Washington Post*, February 7, 2004.
26. Peter J. Boyer, "General Clark's Battles," *New Yorker*, November 17, 2003, 70.
27. Chris Matthews interview with General Wesley Clark, "Hardball," MSNBC, December 8, 2003.
28. Trippi, *The Revolution*, Ibid., 160.
29. Thomas M. DeFrank, "Clark Hit for Iraq Flip-Flop, *New York Daily News*, September 20, 2003, 8.
30. David T. Cook, "Hillary Clinton," *Christian Science Monitor*, September 25, 2003, 25.
31. *Anderson Cooper 360 Degrees*, CNN, October 25, 2004.
32. Interview with Kristin Scurderi, Communications Director, Iowa Republican Party, March 10, 2005.
33. Beth Fouhy, "Clinton Rails Against Recall as GOP Strives for Unity,"

The Associated Press State and Local Wire (California), September 14, 2003.

34. Since 1911, when the California constitution first included a provision for recall petitions, there had been 31 unsuccessful (often frivolous) attempts to recall a California governor. The only previously successful recall attempt among the states that allow them was the 1921 ouster of a governor in North Dakota.

    As for the successful Davis recall, among the 135 candidates on the ballot for governor were Congressman Issa, who had funded the recall drive, as well as a former child actor, a sumo wrestler, a porn actress, a retired meatpacker, a watermelon juggler, and the Clintons' Minister of Culture, pornographer Larry Flynt.
35. Jeffrey M. Jones, "George W. Bush, Hillary Rodham Clinton Most Admired in 2003," *Gallup Poll News Service*, December 12, 2003.
36. Lori Cox Han and Matthew J. Krov, "Out of Office and In the News: Early Projections of the Clinton Legacy," *Presidential Studies Quarterly*, December 1, 2003, 925.

CHAPTER SEVEN: FEELING BLUE SEEING RED

1. Joe Trippi, *The Revolution Will Not Be Televised* (ReaganBooks, 2004), 173–5, 178.
2. Evan Thomas, "Fits and Starts," *Newsweek*, November 15, 2004.
3. Appearance on the *Imus In the Morning* show, MSNBC, December 12, 2003.
4. NBC *Today Show* December 9, 2003.
5. Dan Balz and Edward Walsh, "Lieberman Lashes Out at Dean; Senator Says Endorsement Runs Counter to Gore's Views," *Washington Post*, December 10, 2003, A10.
6. Noelle Straub, "Lieberman Blasts Gore's Stealth Dean Endorsement," *Boston Globe*, December 10, 2003.
7. Donald Lambro, "Battle for the Democratic Soul," *Washington Times*, December 15, 2003.
8. Michael Tomasky, "The Clinton Formula," *American Prospect*, November 2003.
9. Donald Lambro, "Battle for the Democratic Soul."
10. Dick Polman, "By Endorsing Dean, Gore is Thumbing His Nose at Bill and Hillary," *Philadelphia Inquirer*, December 14, 2003.
11. Interview with Chuck Todd, Editor-in-chief, *National Journal*'s "Hotline," March 3, 2005.

12. Liz Sidoti, "Clinton surprises Iowans," Associated Press, December 11, 2003.
13. Interview with Trippi, March 7, 2005.
14. Newt Gingrich, speaking to *The American Spectator's* Saturday Evening Club in Washington, D.C., September 9, 2004.
15. Joshua Green, "Playing Dirty," *Atlantic Monthly*, June 2004.
16. "The Buzz," *Kansas City Star*, December 14, 2003.
17. Agence France Press, "Memoirs Tipped to Fit Bill," *Herald Sun* (Melbourne, Australia), May 13, 2004.
18. Josh Gerstein, "Clinton: 'My Life' Doesn't Attempt to Settle Scores," *New York Sun*, June 4, 2004.
19. Emily Goodin, "Hotline Extra," *National Journal*, June 19, 2004.
20. Once historians have assessed *My Life's* cover-to-cover mendacity, it might be reclassified as a work of fiction loosely based on a true story.
21. Charlotte Abbott, "On Clinton's Coattails," *Publishers Weekly*, July 5, 2004.
22. Frederic U. Dicker and Vincent Morris, "Rebel Dems Raise Hill—Rip Convention For Silencing Her," *New York Post*, July 15, 2004, 4.
23. *National Journal's* "Hotline," "Dem Convo: Is Hillary Crashing Kerry's Party?" July 15, 2004.
24. Martha T. Moore, "Clinton Busy Writing Own Job Description," *USA Today*, February 16, 2004.
25. Michael Lemonick and Matthew Cooper, "I've Got A Problem . . ."; Bill Clinton got serious about diet and exercise, but it was too late to save him from major heart surgery, *Time*, September 13, 2004, 71.
26. Evan Thomas, "The Vets Attack," *Newsweek*, November 11, 2004.
27. John F. Dickerson, "Inside the War Rooms," *Time*, November 15, 2004, 88.
28. "Late Show Laughs," *Calgary Sun*, September 12, 2004.
29. Bill Clinton appearance with Diane Sawyer, ABC's *Primetime Live*, October 28, 2004.
30. *National Journal's* "Hotline," "(Sen.) Clinton: Making Sure Bill Takes It Easy," September 16, 2004.
31. *O'Reilly Factor*, Fox News Channel, September 7, 2004.
32. Lara Jakes Jordan, "Little Love For Bush in Street-Packed Kerry Rally With Clinton," *Associated Press*, October 26, 2004.
33. As seen on *Anderson Cooper 360 Degrees*, CNN, October 25, 2004.
34. Bob Woodward, *The Agenda: Inside the Clinton White House* (Simon & Schuster, 1994), 293–4; Cline Ne, "Next Time, Martin Lancaster Will Be

a Lot Less Trusting of His Political Allies," Greensboro (N.C.) *News & Record*, July 10, 1994.

35. Kerra L. Bolton, "Candidates' Differences Wide," *Asheville Citizen-Times*, October 14, 2004, 1C.
36. Interviews with Doug Heye, Communications Director for Sen. Richard Burr, R-N.C., and previously his 2004 campaign spokesman, March 2, 2005; Rob Christensen, veteran political reporter, Raleigh *News & Observer*, March 2, 2005; Dean Myers, state director for Sen. Burr, but his campaign manager in 2004, March 7, 2005.
37. *Anderson Cooper 360 Degrees*, CNN, October 25, 2004.
38. John F. Harris, *The Survivor: Bill Clinton In The White House* (Random House, 2005), 111.
39. Dale Van Atta interview with Chuck Todd for this book, November, 2006.

CHAPTER EIGHT: BILL AND HILLARY BEYOND THE BLUE

1. Editorial, "Clinton Corruption Plays Us for Fools—We Won't Forget," *New York Observer*, March 5, 2001, 1.
2. Ron Fournier, "Sen. Clinton Building National Political Machine for Potential Presidential Race," Associated Press, August 16, 2002.
3. James T. Patterson, *Restless Giant: The United States from Watergate to Bush v. Gore* (Oxford University Press, 2005), 344.
4. "The Highs and Lows of Being Hillary," *Buffalo News*, May 2, 1999, 9M.
5. Angie Cannon, "First Lady Forced to Defend Herself at Every Tour Stop," *Detroit Free Press*, January 17, 1996, 1A.
6. Meredith Oakley, Editorial, *Arkansas Democrat-Gazette*, January 19, 1996, 7B.
7. Interview with Jane Pauley, *Dateline NBC*, September 17, 2001.
8. Chelsea Clinton, *Talk*, December 2001.
9. Nicholas Lemann, "The Hillary Perspective: Government Suddenly Looks Good Again," *New Yorker*, October 8, 2001, 41.
10. Josh Gerstein, "Reggie Sentenced to a Year in Jail After Pleading Guilty to Fraud Charges," *New York Sun*, November 30, 2005, 4.
11. Marie Brenner, "The Price of Loyalty," *Vanity Fair*, June 2001.
12. Associated Press, "Clinton Fundraisers Are Fined $35,000," *Washington Post*, January 6, 2005.
13. Kerstin Jaeckel, "Wenn die Macht eine Frau schoen macht . . . ," *Bunte*, November 27, 2003, 52–55.

14. CyberAlert, the Media Research Center, July 27, 2004 PM Edition.
15. Craig Gilbert and Stacy Forster, "Clinton Brings 'Rock Star Atmosphere' to Madison," *Milwaukee Journal Sentinel*, April 30, 2005.
16. David S. Broder, "Swift Boats and Old Wounds," *Washington Post*, August 24, 2004, A17.
17. BBC News, "'Virgin Mary' Toast Fetches $28,000," November 23, 2004.
18. Patterson, *passim.*
19. CNN.com, Poll: Clinton Gets High 'no' Vote for 2008, June 20, 2006.
20. John F. Harris, *The Survivor: Bill Clinton In The White House* (Random House, 2005), 111.
21. Ibid., 377.
22. Ibid., 379.
23. Mark Davis' interview with a Senate aide who prefers anonymity, August 2003. This interview was in preparation for Davis and Tyrrell's *Madame Hillary: The Dark Road to the White House* (Regnery Publishing Inc., 2004).
24. Congress, Senate, Senator Clinton of New York Speaking for the Joint Resolution to Authorize the Use of United States Armed Forces Against Iraq, S. J. Res. 45, 109th Congress, *Congressional Record* 148 (10 October, 2002): S10289.
25. Paul Harris, "New Moderate Hillary is in for the Long Run," *Observer*, March 13, 2005, 22.
26. John Colson, "Sen. Clinton Off on Iraq, but Not 2008 Ambitions," *Aspen Times*, July 11, 2005.
27. "Employment Up Again in August," *Monthly Labor Review*, Washington, D.C., September 2005.
28. Associated Press, "Hillary Bashes Bush's Record, Pitches 'Dream,'" *Washington Times*, July 25, 2006.
29. Jim VandeHei, "For Ex-President, a Careful Return to Fray," *Washington Post*, October 18, 2002, A14.
30. John McCormick and Monica Eng, "Clinton Draws Chicago Crowds," *Chicago Tribune*, July 2, 2004, 14.
31. Beth Reinhard, "Clinton Raises Funds for Battle Over Senate," *Miami Herald*, July 23, 2004, B6.
32. Julie Hirschfeld Davis, "Kerry Campaign Welcomes Clinton-Fund-Raising," *Baltimore Sun*, March 25, 2004, 3A.

33. Sharon Theimer, "Dems Try to Raise Kerry $10m in 10 Days," Associated Press Online, March 16, 2004.
34. R. Emmett Tyrrell, Jr., *Madame Hillary: The Dark Road to the White House* (Regnery Publishing, Inc., 2004), 24.
35. Jim VandeHei, "Clinton Develops Into a Force in the Senate," *Washington Post,* March 5, 2003, A1.
36. Mike Glover, "Hillary Courts Centrists," *Washington Times,* July 26, 2005, 1.
37. Dan Balz, "Clinton Angers Left With Call for Unity," *Washington Post,* July 27, 2005, A3.
38. Interview with the author, winter 2006.
39. Report from a White House aide who prefers to remain anonymous. Interview took place in December 2005.
40. Jennifer Senior, "Bill Clinton's Plan for World Domination," New York, August 15, 2005.
41. Ibid.
42. Josh Gerstein, "Watchdog Cites Failures at Charity," *New York Sun,* September 28, 2005, 1.
43. Liz Austin, "Democrats Must Address Tough Issues, Clinton Says," *Houston Chronicle,* October 29, 2005.
44. Parag Khanna, "United They Fall, Why Only Bill Clinton Can Save the U.N.," *Harper's,* January 2006.
45. Lucinda Franks, "The Intimate Hillary," *Talk,* September, 1999.
46. Heard in conversation with a Clinton insider but not to be repeated by me. Doubtless it will be reported in time.
47. Robert Sam Anson, "Bill and His Shadow," *Vanity Fair,* June 2004.
48. Confirmed from two sources in 2005 by a nationally prominent journalist who wishes to remain anonymous.

EPILOGUE: FROM THE CLINTON LIBRARY TO THE HARDING TOMB

1. Interview, July 13, 2005.
2. William Safire, "The Senate Plumbers," *New York Times,* May 17, 2001, A25.

INDEX